I love you (ew)

Flashback
Canada

Flashback Canada

by
J. Bradley Cruxton
and
W. Douglas Wilson

TORONTO
Oxford University Press
1978

This is for Karin, Mark, Sarah, and all the other students
who will learn to enjoy Canada's history through the
reading of this book.

Canadian Cataloguing in Publication Data

Cruxton, J. Bradley
 Flashback Canada

Bibliography: p.392
Includes index.
ISBN 0-19-540284-7

1. Canada – History – 1841-1867. 2. Canada –
History – 1867-1914. I. Wilson, W. Douglas.
II. Title.

FC170.C78   971   C78-001401-4
F1026.C78

Designed by Marg Round
Illustrated by Marg Round and Fortunato Aglialoro

ISBN 0-19-540284-7 12345-21098

Printed and bound in Canada by
FRIESEN PRINTERS LTD.
Altona, Manitoba R0G 0B0

Contents

Native People.

English-French Relations.

Government.

Confederation.

Transportation.

Immigration.

Economics.

Women.

Canadian-American Relations.

Rebellion.

Settlement.

Law and Order.

Labour. Industry and Farming.

These symbols are used throughout the book to identify major themes in Canadian history.

WANTED

William Lyon Mackenzie

One Thousand Pounds,

to any one who will apprehend, and deliver up to Justice, WILLIAM LYON MACKENZIE; and FIVE HUNDRED POUNDS to any one who will apprehend, and deliver up to Justice, DAVID GIBSON—or SAMUEL LOUNT—or JESSE LLOYD—or SILAS FLETCHER—and the same reward and a free pardon will be given to any of their accomplices who will render this public service, except he or they shall have committed, in his own person, the crime of Murder or Arson.

And all, but the Leaders above-named, who have been seduced to join in this unnatural Rebellion, are hereby called to return to their duty to their Sovereign—to obey the Laws—and to live henceforward as good and faithful Subjects—and they will find the Government of their Queen as indulgent as it is just.

GOD SAVE THE QUEEN

Thursday, 3 o'clock, P. M.
7th Dec., 1837

☞ The Party of Rebels, under their Chief Leaders, is wholly dispersed, and flying before the Loyal Militia. The only thing that remains to be done, is to find them, and arrest them.

1
Rebellion

MONDAY NIGHT, 4 DECEMBER 1837

All night long the church bells of Toronto sounded the alarm. People of the city were in a panic. Rumours were flying about that the city would be attacked at any moment. Just a few kilometres north of Toronto, William Lyon Mackenzie gathered a small army of rebels at Montgomery's Tavern. Armed with muskets, rifles, pitchforks, and clubs, they were determined to attack the city and overthrow the government. Their plan was to march on Toronto, seize the Parliament buildings, take the Governor prisoner, and force him to bring about the changes that would give the people more influence in government.

Just before midnight, the sound of horses' hooves was heard along Yonge Street. Citizens hurried out as John Powell told his news. John Powell was an elected official in Toronto. Out of breath from a narrow escape, Powell could hardly speak. He described how he was stopped on Yonge Street about three kilometres beyond the city limits by Mackenzie and a number of armed rebels. Powell had fired some shots at the rebels. He missed Mackenzie, but managed to hit Anthony Anderson, one of Mackenzie's few experienced military leaders. Powell hid behind a log when chased by the rebels, and eventually made his way back to Toronto in the dark.

Escape of Mr. J. Powell.

About the same time, more bad news reached the city. Colonel Moodie, a retired army officer, lived north of Montgomery's Tavern. All day he watched with alarm the gathering of more and more rebel troops at the tavern. He was determined to get this information to the Governor. Colonel Moodie, accompanied by three gentlemen, set out by horse down Yonge Street. He approached Montgomery's Tavern and found the road was blocked. The fiery Colonel Moodie roared at the rebels, 'Who are you to stop me on the Queen's highway?' Shots were fired on both sides. When Colonel Moodie tried to charge through the barricade, he was shot and left to bleed to death. One of Moodie's companions, however, did escape and brought the news to the city.

TUESDAY, 5 DECEMBER 1837

Alarm grew in the city. Only three hundred trained fighters were available to defend Toronto. Most troops had been sent to Lower Canada to put down some trouble that had broken out there. Rumours spread quickly that the rebel force now numbered five thousand. The Governor of Upper Canada, Sir Francis Bond Head, placed his own family for safety on a steamer in the Toronto harbour. Sir Francis expected reinforcements from outside the city to arrive soon. In order to gain time, he sent a party of men to bargain with Mackenzie under a white flag of truce. The truce party met Mackenzie on Yonge Street at the top of Gallow's Hill. They told Mackenzie that Governor Head would pardon everyone who laid down his weapon. Immediately Mackenzie refused.

At six o'clock, seven hundred rebels gathered at the Bloor Street tollgate for a night attack on the capital of Upper Canada. In the pitch black darkness, they hiked south on Yonge Street. First came the rebels armed with rifles, led by Samuel Lount, followed by men carrying nothing more than sharpened sticks, clubs, and pitchforks.

In the vegetable garden of Mrs. Sharpe, where Maple Leaf Gardens now stands, Sheriff Jarvis and twenty-seven riflemen hid behind a fence. As the rebels reached the spot, Jarvis and his men ambushed them. There was a great flash and roar as the muskets went off. The rebels were caught by surprise, but Lount's riflemen fired back. Both sides panicked. Mackenzie's force turned and headed back to Montgomery's Tavern. Sheriff Jarvis' men fled into the city. In this skirmish, one member of the rebel force lay dead on the road.

WEDNESDAY, 6 DECEMBER 1837

Reinforcements began to arrive in Toronto to assist in the defence of

The death of Colonel Moodie.

the capital. Sixty men came by steamer from Hamilton under Colonel McNab, and one hundred men came into the city from Scarborough under Captain Maclean. The main buildings of Toronto — the City Hall, Houses of Parliament, Bank of Upper Canada, and many private houses — were barricaded with thick planks. Stores closed, and meat and bread became scarce.

About 6 km west of Toronto, Mackenzie and Lount held up the stage coach carrying the mail on Dundas Street. They seized money and letters that contained vital information about the defence of the city. Apart from this, there was little action in the rebel camp. Some of Mackenzie's supporters found there were no weapons for them, and went home. Two men, wounded in Tuesday night's battle, died from loss of blood.

THURSDAY, 7 DECEMBER 1837

Van Egmond, an experienced soldier, arrived this morning at Montgomery's Tavern and took control of the rebel forces. He was upset to find that he had only about five hundred poorly equipped men. Hundreds of Mackenzie's supporters from the outlying districts had not yet arrived.

At noon, Governor Head and Loyalist troops friendly to the government of Toronto moved north to fight the rebels. About six hundred soldiers marched up Yonge Street to the music of two military bands playing 'Yankee Doodle Dandy'. Two smaller groups of troops moved north through woods and ploughed fields to the west and east of Yonge Street. The three companies planned to attack the rebel headquarters at Montgomery's Tavern.

At one o'clock, rebel scouts sent word to Mackenzie that the government forces were marching up Gallow's Hill. Van Egmond and about two hundred armed men took up position in the woods south of the tavern on the west side of Yonge Street. Another sixty hid behind a rail fence east of Yonge Street. The unarmed rebels remained behind at the tavern.

As the rebels opened fire, Loyalist troops set up their two cannons and aimed into the woods. One of the rebels, Joseph Gould from Uxbridge Township, described the scene.

They fired over us into the tops of the trees cutting the dead and dry limbs of the hemlocks which, falling thickly among us, scared the boys as much as if cannon balls had been rattling around us.

The battle at Montgomery's farm.

The other gun was fired low, and so careless that I did not like it. One of the balls struck a sandbank by my feet and filled my eyes with sand, nearly blinding me.

At that moment the Loyalist troops advancing through the woods on the west side of Yonge Street closed in behind the rebels. The rebels dropped their rifles and ran. Then the cannons were moved up and pointed directly at the front of Montgomery's Tavern. A couple of cannon balls passed right through the tavern. The rebels inside poured out like bees from a hive and headed into the surrounding woods. Governor Head ordered a thorough search of the rooms of the tavern. In one of them, the soldiers found Mackenzie's papers, which included a list of the names of all supporters of the rebel cause. After the search, the tavern was burned to the ground.

The fighting lasted less than half an hour. One rebel died immediately and eleven rebels were wounded, four of them dying afterwards. Five Loyalists were wounded, none of them seriously. The Rebellion was crushed. Mackenzie and other rebel leaders rode off swiftly to the north to avoid being taken prisoners. Sir Francis Bond Head offered a reward of one thousand pounds for the capture and return of the rebel leader, William Lyon Mackenzie.

ACTIVITIES

1. Many of Mackenzie's supporters came in on foot to Montgomery's Tavern from their backwoods farms. Some walked 50 km in winter weather. What does this suggest about the loyalty and conviction of Mackenzie's supporters?

2. Compare the rebel forces and the loyalist forces in a chart under the following headings:
   a) size of army
   b) weapons available
   c) experience of the leaders
   d) experience of the troops

3. Creative Writing. Write an eye-witness account of the events of the Rebellion of 1837 from the point of view of:
   a) Mrs. Sharpe who was watching the events taking place at the bottom of her garden.
   b) John Montgomery, tavern owner, describing the rebels and their leader.
   c) John Powell relating his news to the citizens of Toronto.
   d) A member of the rebel force describing the burning of Montgomery's Tavern.

4. Susanna Moodie emigrated from England to Upper Canada with her husband in 1832 and settled near Cobourg. Her husband served with the government troops in putting down the Rebellion of 1837.

Buried in the obscurity of these woods [north of Peterborough], we knew nothing, heard nothing of the political state of the country, and were little aware of the revolution which was about to work a great change for us and for Canada. . . .

A letter from my sister explained the nature of the outbreak, and the astonishment with which the news had been received by all the settlers in the bush. My brother and my sister's husband had already gone off to join some of the numerous bands of gentlemen who were collecting from all quarters to march to the aid of Toronto, which it was said was besieged by the rebel force. She advised me not to permit Moodie to leave home in his present weak state; but the spirit of my husband was aroused, he instantly obeyed what he considered the imperative call of duty, and told me to prepare him a few necessaries, that he might be ready to start early in the morning. . . .

The honest backwoodsmen, perfectly ignorant of the abuses that had led to the present position of things, regarded the rebels as a set of monsters, for whom no punishment was too severe, and obeyed the call to arms with enthusiasm. The leader of the rebels must have been astonished at the rapidity with which a large force was collected, as if by magic, to put down the rebellion. . . .

From *Roughing it in the Bush: or, Forest Life in Canada* by Susanna Moodie.

QUESTIONS ON SUSANNA MOODIE'S DIARY (Susanna Moodie is not related to Colonel Moodie)
1.   Why would the Moodies 'know nothing of the political state of the country?'
2.   What side are the Moodies on? Pick out words and phrases to prove your opinion.
3.   Why do you think large numbers of people in Upper Canada marched to the defence of Toronto and the Governor?
4.   You are the wife or mother of a man who has just left home to join the forces of Sir Francis Bond Head *or* William Lyon Mackenzie. Write a diary. Tell:
    a) Why your husband or son decided to go.
    b) How he would get to Toronto.
    c) What he took with him.
    d) How you felt as you said good-bye.

5.   Draw a chart to trace the good or bad fortunes of the two sides in the Rebellion. Use one colour to indicate Mackenzie and his supporters, and another colour to show Bond Head and the loyalists. The top of the chart may represent success; the bottom may represent defeat. For each situation in the Rebellion, you must decide where the two opposing forces stand. These questions will help you to decide: who won or lost in this situation? Whose fortunes are rising or falling here? why?
The chart has been started for you:
Situation 1: Monday, 4 Dec. 1837.
    Mackenzie's fortunes are high. His rebel army is gathering with arms and is about to attack Toronto.
    The Governor's fortunes are low. The city is in a panic. Rumours are flying, and most troops are away in Lower Canada.

Situation 2: The John Powell incident.

Mackenzie's prisoner, Powell, escapes after shooting the most experienced rebel military leader. Therefore, Mackenzie's fortunes have fallen.

The Governor's fortunes have improved slightly because Powell flees back to Toronto to sound the alarm.

When you have examined all the situations, then link each set of dots together. You will have two lines when you are finished which graph the fortunes of the opposing sides.

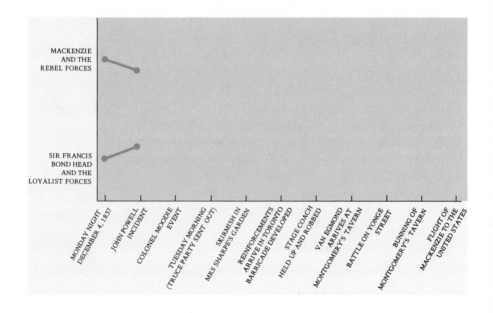

TORONTO FIELD TRIP

1. Montgomery's Tavern was located at Postal Station K, 2384 Yonge Street.
2. Toll Gate stood on Yonge Street just south of Bloor Street.
3. Location of the battle near Mrs. Sharpe's garden.
4. William Lyon Mackenzie's home in his later years, 82 Bond Street.
5. Old Toronto jail where Lount and Matthews were executed.
6. Necropolis: the burial place of Lount, Matthews, and W. L. Mackenzie.

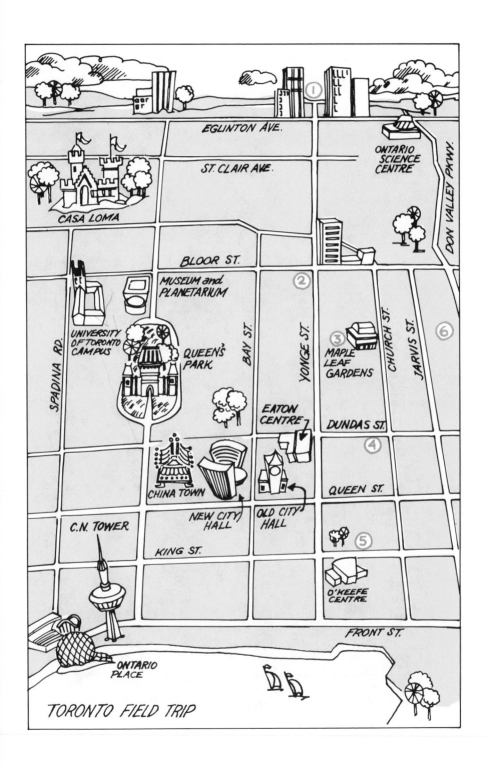

TORONTO FIELD TRIP

Queen Victoria.

2
Trouble in Upper Canada

Rebellion is an armed uprising against the established government. Usually there are serious problems causing discontent among the people. When the people cannot get these problems corrected, they feel they have no other choice than to take up arms and attack the government. In some cases the leaders of the rebellion try to establish a new and independent organization in place of the existing government.

For a few days in December 1837, rebellion raged in Upper Canada. Toronto, the capital, was a city with a population of between 10 000 and 12 000. It was under attack by a force of between 500 and 1000 armed men. The rebels marched on the city to overthrow the government and bring about changes they considered important. Why would formerly law-abiding citizens take such a desperate step? What were their causes of discontent? Why were they angry with the government? Why did they think the only way to bring about change in Upper Canada was to take up muskets and other weapons? Who were their leaders? What were the strengths and weaknesses of these leaders? Why did this rebellion fail?

CAUSES OF DISCONTENT

1. The Way the Colony Was Governed

Each British colony in North America had an Assembly of elected colonists. The colony was divided into voting districts, and each district could elect representatives to the Assembly. At Assembly meetings the elected representatives made plans for the colony, and wrote these plans down and called them bills. However, before a bill could become a law, it had to be approved by the Governor and his Councils. There were Executive and Legislative Councils whose members were appointed by the Governor. Often the Governor and this small group of people he chose to advise him did not approve of the Assembly's bills. When this happened they could simply toss the bills aside and ignore the wishes of the Assembly. Nothing could become law without the consent of the Governor and his Councils. In other words, the people the colonists elected to the Assembly only *helped* to make laws. The real power was in the hands of the Governor and the Councils. The Governor always appointed his Councils from among the judges, clergymen, bankers, lawyers, military officers, and leading businessmen in the colony. Since the Councils were chosen and not elected, they did not necessarily worry about carrying out the wishes of the people.

Today, in Canada, the Governor-General still must approve all laws passed by the Parliament of Canada. But the men who advise the Governor-General are chosen from among the peoples' elected representatives in Parliament. Today the Governor-General must listen to the advice of these elected members. Thus he is 'responsible' to the wishes of these members, and through them to the people who have elected them.

2. The People Who Ruled the Colony

At the head of the government in the colonies was the Governor. He was usually sent out from Britain since he was the personal representative of the King. He was told that he was responsible to no one but the King for his actions.

Usually the Governor came to North America for a short stay only and was totally unfamiliar with the people and the way of life in the colony. Therefore, he depended a great deal on the advice of the people in the Executive and Legislative Councils. The problem was that the advisors in these Councils were always chosen from among the wealthy and influential people. A few were Englishmen, but most were members of United Empire Loyalist families who had lived in the colony for many years. In most cases they were men who had always been close friends and were related to one another. The colonists nicknamed this small group of Loyalists the 'Family Compact'. They did not all come from the same family but all did belong to the highest social class. And they thought that because they were wealthy and better educated, they were much better able to govern the colony than ordinary people were.

COLONIAL GOVERNMENT

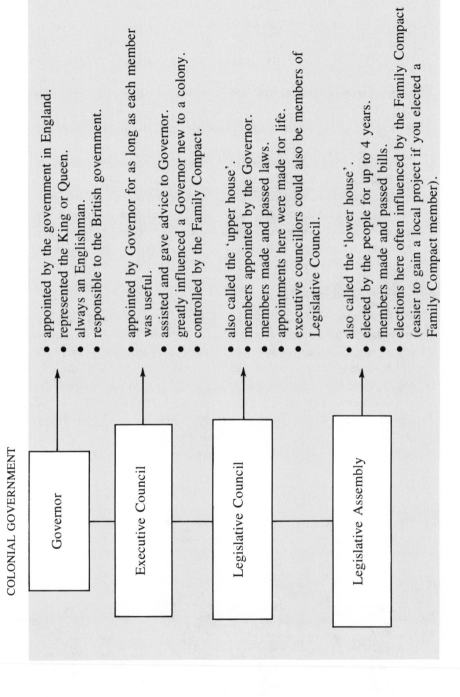

Governor
- appointed by the government in England.
- represented the King or Queen.
- always an Englishman.
- responsible to the British government.

Executive Council
- appointed by Governor for as long as each member was useful.
- assisted and gave advice to Governor.
- greatly influenced a Governor new to a colony.
- controlled by the Family Compact.

Legislative Council
- also called the 'upper house'.
- members appointed by the Governor.
- members made and passed laws.
- appointments here were made for life.
- executive councillors could also be members of Legislative Council.

Legislative Assembly
- also called the 'lower house'.
- elected by the people for up to 4 years.
- members made and passed bills.
- elections here were often influenced by the Family Compact (easier to gain a local project if you elected a Family Compact member).

Some of the members of the Family Compact were very capable, clever persons. One of the most powerful was John Strachan, who later became the Anglican bishop of Toronto. He insisted that the Anglican Church should have special privileges and position in the colony. For example, until 1831 only Anglican clergymen were licensed to perform marriages even though the majority of the colonists belonged to other churches. During his lifetime Strachan was very interested in education. He founded Upper Canada College, a school for Anglican boys. In 1827 he established a university that eventually grew into the University of Toronto.

Another prominent member of the Family Compact was John Beverley Robinson. He had been one of Strachan's pupils. Eventually he became a lawyer and Chief Justice of Upper Canada. In this position Robinson was able to exercise a great deal of power in the Councils and with the Governor. As long as the Family Compact could persaude the Governor to listen to their advice, the elected representatives of the people in the Assembly would not have much say in government.

3. The Problem of Land

Another cause of discontent among the people of Upper Canada was the unfair way that land was granted to settlers. The best farming areas were often given to members of the Family Compact or their friends and favourites. For example, a former officer, Colonel Thomas Talbot, received a grant of thousands of hectares along the north shore of Lake Erie. He had an arrangement with the government by which he got another 50 ha for himself every time he sold 20 ha to a settler! Bishop Mountain, an Anglican bishop, was granted 4800 ha. Executive and Legislative Councillors and their families controlled

An Ontario farm.

King Street, Toronto, in 1835.

75 000 ha of land in Upper Canada. The result was that less than one-tenth of land in the colony was cultivated and producing crops. Most of the best farm land in Upper Canada was in the hands of people who had neither the skill nor the intention of farming it. They were simply waiting for it to go up in value so they could sell it at a handsome profit.

Farmers also objected to the government practice of granting one-seventh of all surveyed land to the Anglican church. These huge tracts were known as Clergy Reserves. People said that it was not fair that other Protestant churches, such as the Presbyterians, Methodists, Baptists, and Lutherans, were not given equal grants. But more important, they complained because these 'church lands' were left uncleared for years, while new settlers had to be content with poorer land. A large uncleared church grant would often be between a settler and his nearest neighbour. It held up settlement because no roads were built through it. It harboured wolves which attacked the settler's flocks and herds, and weeds which contaminated his crops.

It seemed to the farmers of Upper Canada that they were being mistreated by the government's land policies. No wonder there were so many farmers in the ranks of William Lyon Mackenzie's rebellion!

4. The Problem of Transportation

Farmers need roads if they are to get their products to market. But in Upper Canada roads were terribly inadequate. For most of the year even the main roads were impassable. Only in the winter, when they were frozen over, were many roads easily travelled. The government, however, did spend large amounts of tax money building canals which

benefited the merchant members of the Family Compact and their business friends. One of their special projects was the Welland Canal. It would make passage from Lake Erie to Lake Ontario possible by passing around the rapids on the Niagara River and the Falls. A large grant of free land and huge sums of money were loaned to the private businessmen who undertook the Welland Canal project. To farmers it seemed that government granted money to everyone but them. They found it almost impossible to borrow money to buy land, improve their farms, or buy new farm implements. Bankers and merchants grew prosperous while farmers struggled just to keep their farms going.

5. Special Privileges for a Few People

The Governor in the colony had the right to appoint all officials. He selected the members of the Councils, judges, sheriffs and justices of the peace. Coroners, customs officers, postmasters, immigration officers and Indian affairs officials were also named by him. As head of the military forces he appointed 1500 officers. He could make land grants and spend crown money for pensions to reward faithful supporters. Obviously the British Governors relied heavily on the advice of the Family Compact when naming people to these positions. It was said that no one could obtain a government job unless he was a member or a friend of the Family Compact.

All these causes of discontent among the people of Upper Canada were the tiny sparks that burst into the flame of rebellion in 1837.

ACTIVITIES

1. Interview the following people for a newspaper article to determine their ideas about the Family Compact.
   a) Bishop Strachan
   b) Mackenzie
   c) a farmer in Upper Canada
2. Select a few people to play the roles of Governor and Council for the colony of Upper Canada. Let a larger group act in the Assembly representing the voters. Prepare a bill that suggests what to do about the Clergy Reserves. Try to make your bill law. Play your roles as they would have been in the 1830s.

3
Tories and Reformers

Friends and supporters of the Family Compact were known as Conservatives or Tories. Tories wanted to 'conserve' or keep the existing form of government more or less as it was. The Tories approved of England's way of governing her colonies. They claimed that the Governor should be responsible only to the King. Needless to say members of the Councils were nearly always chosen from among Conservatives.

But more and more people in Upper Canada began to disagree with the Family Compact. They wanted the system of government changed or 're-formed' so that the people would have more influence in government. Reformers claimed that the Governor should be responsible for carrying out the wishes of the majority in the Assembly. This would be known as 'responsible government'. The colonies should be allowed to grow up and manage their own affairs!

SOME FAMOUS REFORMERS

Early Reformers included Robert Gourlay, a Scotsman who had settled in Upper Canada in 1819. He pointed out abuses in the method of granting land and the need for roads. For doing this Gourlay was arrested, accused of stirring up the settlers, and banished from the country.

Dr. William Baldwin and his son Robert were among the most influential Reformers in Upper Canada. Though the Baldwins were wealthy, well educated, and members of the Anglican church, they were not Tories. The Baldwins believed strongly in reform though they never had any thought of Upper Canada breaking away from Britain.

Bishop John Strachan.

Robert Baldwin.

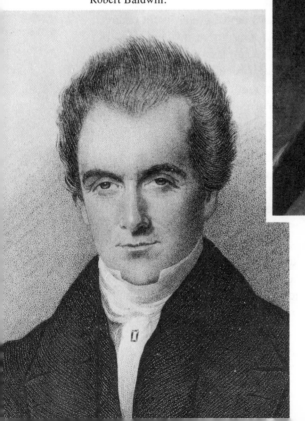

Sir Francis Bond Head.

They worked out their own plan for responsible government for Upper Canada. Put simply it would work like this: the Governor should not be allowed to have his own way. He should do what his Council or Cabinet advises him to do and he ought to pick that Cabinet from the largest party in the Assembly. In this way, the Governor would be carrying out the wishes of the largest number of voters. Upper Canada would then have responsible government as it was practised in Britain itself.

Of all the Reformers, William Lyon Mackenzie was the most outspoken. He was born in Scotland in 1795. His father died when he was only three weeks old, leaving Elizabeth Mackenzie, his mother, with very little to live on. By sheer hard work Elizabeth Mackenzie supported herself and her son. There was never money for luxuries in their home.

Young Willie was a keen reader and kept notes on the books he borrowed and read from libraries. Between 1806 and 1819 he read 957 books. In later life he was always able to quote famous authors to back up his opinions.

In 1820 Mackenzie set sail for Montreal. Two years later he was joined in Canada by Isabel Baxter, who soon became his wife. Over the years the Mackenzies had thirteen children. Five died in infancy and one at thirteen years; five daughters and two sons lived to be adults.

From the time he arrived in the colony Mackenzie had been complaining about the government he found there. In York he set up his newspaper, the *Colonial Advocate*. Now his complaint against the government could be read by a large number of people. In the *Advocate* he attacked the Family Compact and even the Governor himself. He dragged out family scandals and gossip about the Family Compact and printed them in his paper for all the colony to read.

Late one night some sons of the Family Compact members decided to end Mackenzie's attacks upon their parents once and for all. They broke into his newspaper office, smashed his press, and threw the type into the bay. Mackenzie learned the names of the young lawbreakers and brought them into court. He won the case and with the money received from his lawsuit he bought a better press and renewed his attacks on the Governor and the group of men around him.

In 1827 Mackenzie was elected to the Assembly as one of the representatives for York. He represented the people who lived from Lot Street (now Queen Street) in Toronto north to Lake Simcoe. In the

Assembly Mackenzie continued his fiery attacks on the government. Mackenzie was only 1.65 m tall, but people listened to him when he spoke. He was completely bald and wore a flaming red wig which he would sometimes toss into the air in front of the startled Assembly. He had bushy eyebrows and deep blue eyes, whose piercing gaze made his enemies nervous. Five times Mackenzie was expelled from the Assembly for his attacks on the government. Each time the people voted Mackenzie back into the Assembly as their representative. The attacks continued. In 1834 York became the city of Toronto and honoured Mackenzie by making him its first mayor. He was the mayor of Toronto when the Rebellion broke out.

As time went on, Mackenzie began to lose hope of the people ever gaining the right to make their own laws. More and more he doubted that Upper Canada could remain a British colony. He began to speak of breaking away from Britain as the Americans had done in 1776. When he started talking about independence, Mackenzie lost the support of many of the moderate Reformers. Men like Baldwin were as loyal to Britain as the Governor himself. They feared that Mackenzie had gone too far!

In 1836 a new Governor, Sir Francis Bond Head, arrived in Upper Canada. He knew nothing about Canada and little about politics. There is a story that his appointment was an error and that his cousin Edmund Head was the person intended for the post. As far as the Reformers were concerned Head's appointment was a mistake. They felt that in sending them Head as Governor, Britain as much as said there would be no self-government or reform in the colony. Sir Francis considered all Reformers, including Baldwin and the Moderates, disloyal traitors to Britain.

During the election of 1836 Sir Frances Bond Head did what no Governor-General would dare to do today. He went around the colony urging people to vote for the Tories. 'A vote for a Reformer,' he warned, 'is a vote against Britain!' The Tories won the election, and Mackenzie and many other Reformers lost their seats in the Assembly.

The time had come, radical Reformers decided, to take up arms. If they could not get reform by peaceful means, then they would fight for their beliefs. In late November 1837, Mackenzie published a bold call for independence from Britain. All over the colony people read his pamphlet.

Canadians! Do you love freedom? . . . Do you hate oppression?

Do you wish perpetual peace? . . . Then buckle on your armour,
and put down the villains who oppress and enslave our country.
. . . The bounty you must pay for freedom is to give the strength
of your arms to put down tyranny at Toronto.
   Up then, brave Canadians! Get ready your rifles and make
short work of it; . . . with governors from England we will have
bribery at elections, corruption, villainy and continued trouble in
every township. But Independence would give us the means of
enjoying many blessings.

This was Mackenzie's call to arms. In the backwoods of the colony
and in the Tory stronghold of Toronto itself, men shouldered their
muskets and prepared to overthrow the government of Upper Canada.
   As you have read, the Rebellion in Upper Canada was short-lived.
In a few days it was put down by Sir Francis Bond Head and the
Loyalists.
   After the burning of Montgomery's Tavern, William Lyon Mackenzie fled westward towards the American border at Niagara. For much
of the way he travelled on foot. At one point he waded across Sixteen
Mile Creek up to his neck in icy water. Even with the price of one
thousand pounds on his head, all along the way supporters risked their
lives to hide him from the approaching government search parties.
These supporters were proud to be able to help their hero in his escape.
One person who aided Mackenzie ordered these words to be printed on
his own gravestone:

> Up the hill stood the home of Samuel Chandler
> He guided Mackenzie to Buffalo
> And here they had supper
> Dec. 10, 1837

Four days later, frozen and exhausted, Mackenzie was rowed across
the Niagara River and stepped to safety on American soil.
   From Navy Island in the Niagara River, Mackenzie tried to keep his
rebellion alive. With about two hundred supporters he tried to conduct
raids along the border. When the officials of Upper Canada protested,
the American government arrested Mackenzie and put him in jail at
Rochester, New York, for eighteen months.
   Two of Mackenzie's leading supporters were not as lucky. They
were Samuel Lount, a blacksmith from Holland Landing, and Peter
Matthews, a farmer from Pickering. They had been captured after

several days of hiding and travelling in their attempt to escape to the United States. They were both convicted and sentenced to hang on 12 April 1838 for their leading roles in the Rebellion. Elizabeth Lount, Samuel's wife, was not prepared to accept the death of her well-respected husband without a fight. This brave woman visited the Governor and begged on her knees for her husband's life. She collected the signatures of thirty thousand people who urged the government to spare the lives of Lount and Matthews. The Governor refused to accept the pleas of Mrs. Lount. The execution was carried out at the Toronto Jail. Captain Matthews left a widow and fifteen children, and Samuel Lount left a widow and seven children.

The government refused to turn over their bodies to their families, and they were buried in unmarked graves near the intersection of Yonge and Bloor Streets in Toronto. In 1859, the bodies of Lount and Matthews were moved by William Lyon Mackenzie and others to the Toronto burial ground known as the Necropolis. In 1893 a monument was erected that carries the following inscription:

> This monument is erected to the memory of Samuel Lount of Holland Landing, County of York, born 24th September 1791,

Elizabeth Lount visits the Governor.

Died 12th April 1838, and of Peter Matthews of Pickering, County of Ontario, Born 1786, Died 12th April 1838. Erected by their friends and sympathizers, 1893.

Two months after the execution of her husband, Elizabeth Lount wrote in a letter, 'Canada will do justice to his memory. Canadians cannot long remain in bondage. They will be free.'

Ninety-two other rebels were sent to Van Diemen's Land. This was a British prison colony off the southeastern coast of Australia, today called Tasmania.

It is estimated that in the year following the failure of the Rebellion, 25 000 people left Upper Canada for the United States. Their hopes of change in Upper Canada had been dashed. At a time when the total population of Upper Canada was 300 000, this loss of 25 000 of its well-respected and hard-working citizens was a serious blow to the colony.

Eventually the British government gave in and accepted Mackenzie's request for a pardon. Twelve years after the Rebellion, Mackenzie was officially pardoned and returned in 1850 with his family to settle in Toronto. He lived in a house on Bond Street until his death in 1861.

William Lyon Mackenzie's daughter Isabel, the last born of his thirteen children, married John King in 1872. They became parents of a son whom they named William Lyon Mackenzie King. In 1921, Mackenzie King became Canada's eleventh Prime Minister. He was head of Canada's government longer than any other Prime Minister.

ACTIVITIES

1.   How important was the part played in the Rebellion by each of the following people? Try to decide how the events of the Rebellion might have been different if each of these people had not been there.

Major Characters	Minor Characters
Sir Francis Bond Head	Colonel Moodie
William Lyon Mackenzie	Anthony Anderson
Samuel Lount	Sheriff Jarvis
Robert Baldwin	Van Egmond
	Montgomery (innkeeper)

2.   Would you have supported or opposed Mackenzie in the Rebellion of 1837? Justify your position.

3.   In the election of 1834, the Reformers won a majority of seats in

the Assembly of Upper Canada. Suggest reasons why the Reformers did not then pass laws to improve conditions.

4. How did Robert Baldwin propose to alter the system of government in Upper Canada? Why would Britain find Baldwin's approach more acceptable than Mackenzie's approach?

5. Imagine you are Elizabeth Lount appearing before Sir Francis Bond Head to plead for the life of your husband. Write out the arguments you will present to persuade the Governor to spare Samuel's life.

6. Was the hanging of Samuel Lount justified? Would he be hanged for the same offence today?

7. Discuss Mrs. Lount's comments about the rebels: 'Canada will do justice to their memory. Canadians cannot long remain in bondage. They will be free.'

RADICALS, MODERATE REFORMERS, CONSERVATIVES

What do these words mean?

Radicals might say, 'We want changes in our colony. We will use all methods, including violence, to bring about the changes we want.'

Moderate reformers might say, 'There are many things that are unjust in the colony. However, changes will not happen overnight. We must attack the problems but realize that it may take years to bring about change.'

Conservatives might say, 'We don't want any changes at all. Things are fine as they are right now in the colony.'

Decide whether each of the following men is a radical, moderate reformer, or conservative. Explain your opinion.

William Lyon Mackenzie
Francis Bond Head
Robert Baldwin
Robert Gourlay

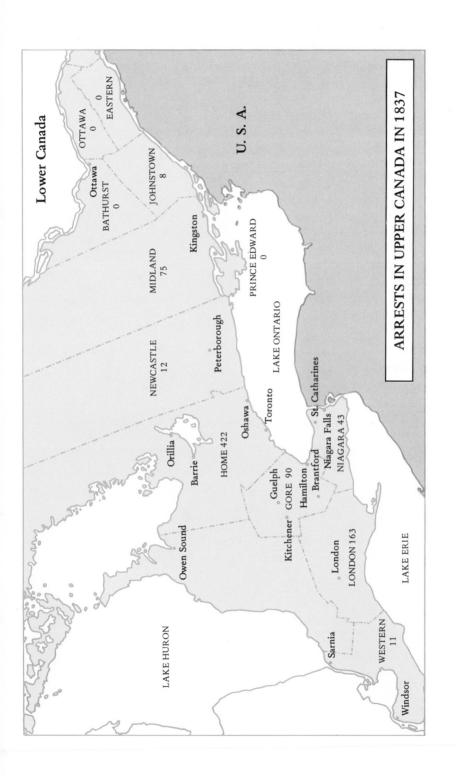

ARRESTS IN UPPER CANADA IN 1837

Lower Canada

OTTAWA 0

EASTERN 0

Ottawa 0

BATHURST 0

JOHNSTOWN 8

MIDLAND 75

Kingston

NEWCASTLE 12

Peterborough

PRINCE EDWARD 0

LAKE ONTARIO

U. S. A.

Orillia

Barrie

HOME 422

Oshawa

Toronto

St. Catharines

Owen Sound

Guelph

GORE 90

Hamilton

Brantford

Niagara Falls

NIAGARA 43

Kitchener

London

LONDON 163

LAKE ERIE

LAKE HURON

Sarnia

WESTERN 11

Windsor

ARRESTS BY OCCUPATION

small landowner or farmer	374
labourer	345
craftsman	72
hired farm hand	20
merchant	16
innkeeper	11
medical doctor	8
teacher	4
clerk	4
Member of Parliament, former Member of Parliament or son of same	4
gentleman	3
attorney	3
unlicenced medical doctor	3
land surveyor	3
bookseller	3
artist	2
preacher	2
magistrate or son of same	2
engineer	1
mariner	1
law student	1
unknown	3
TOTAL	885

QUESTION

From which occupational groups did Mackenzie receive the most support in the Rebellion of 1837? Suggest reasons for this.

4
Trouble in Lower Canada and the Maritimes

LOWER CANADA

During the 1830s there was also a growing reform movement in Lower Canada. In many ways the situation was similar to that of Upper Canada. It was also a case of the elected Assembly pulling in one direction, and the two appointed Councils pulling the other way. An added factor was that in Lower Canada the problem was complicated because two language groups, the French and the English, were involved.

Most of the people of Lower Canada were French-speaking and they dominated the elected Assembly. The French-speaking members of the Assembly were annoyed because they could not get the English Governor to agree to all the laws they wished to pass. They were concerned about preserving their French language, their religion, and their traditional agricultural way of life. But the Governor had chosen most of his Councillors from among the English-speaking merchants and bankers of the colony. These Councillors were interested in using tax money to build roads and canals which would improve their businesses. They were also anxious to bring large numbers of English-speaking settlers to Lower Canada from Britain. This ruling group was known as the 'Chateau Clique' because they met often at the Governor's residence at 'Chateau St. Louis'.

Rebels at St. Eustache.

The leader of the French-speaking majority in the Assembly was Louis-Joseph Papineau. Papineau was born in Montreal in 1786. Like his father before him, Papineau was elected a member of the Assembly for Lower Canada. In politics he was known as an outstanding and eloquent speaker.

In his early life Papineau was an admirer of Britain. But as he grew older he feared that the British intended to turn his people into English men and women. The rest of his life he dedicated to struggle to preserve the French language, law, and religion. Papineau and his supporters in Lower Canada came to be known as 'patriotes'. While Mackenzie was busy criticizing the Family Compact in Upper Canada, Papineau was leading attacks on the Governor and the English-speaking Chateau Clique in Lower Canada. As time went on these attacks grew more and more violent. Then in the fall of 1837 his followers took up arms against the government. Fighting actually broke out in Lower Canada before Mackenzie and his rebels marched against Toronto in December.

The Rebellion in Lower Canada started in Montreal when a few English officers, coming out of their club, got into a fight with a group of French-Canadian 'patriotes' in the street. During the following days hatred flared up in the city between the French and the English. The situation became so serious that troops had to be sent from Upper Canada to help put down the troublemakers.

On 23 November 1837 at St. Denis, a clash took place between the French-Canadian 'patriotes' and the government troops who were looking for Papineau. To avoid trouble Papineau fled to the United States before the battle took place. After seven hours of bloody fighting and fifty casualties, the government troops were forced to withdraw. It was a 'patriote' victory! Two days later a larger force of government troops raided nearby St. Charles. This town was burned and over fifty 'patriotes' were killed when the Loyalist troops stormed the barricades. On 14 December 1837 two thousand troops and Loyalist volunteers attacked the village of St. Eustache where the 'patriotes' had fortified themselves in the village church. The troops set fire to the church and more than sixty 'patriotes' were shot down as they fled from the burning building. Dr. Jean-Olivier Chenier, a patriote leader, leaped from a church window and died fighting. After the battle, the government troops cut out Chenier's heart and displayed it in a tavern for several days.

In the 'October Crisis' of 1970 in Quebec, the FLQ (Front de Libération du Québec) members who kidnapped and killed Pierre Laporte called themselves the 'Chenier cell' of the FLQ after Dr. Chenier.

During the 1837 Rebellion in Lower Canada, Papineau fled to the United States and then to Paris. He was eventually pardoned and

Soldiers leading prisoners in Lower Canada.

returned to Quebec in 1845. For a brief time he returned to politics, but soon retired to spend the rest of his life on his estate at Montebello. His last years were unhappy and full of personal grief as several of his children were stricken with illness. Papineau died at the age of 85 in 1871.

THE MARITIMES

In the Maritimes the struggle for reform was not as bitter as in Upper and Lower Canada. Nevertheless, in each colony the real power of controlling the government rested in the hands of a small influential group who worked closely with the Governor. However, Reformers were gradually elected to the Legislative Assemblies. Men like Joseph Howe in Nova Scotia, George Coles in Prince Edward Island, and L. A. Wilmot in New Brunswick worked to bring changes and pass the laws they felt people wanted. Gradually their patient struggle paid off. When responsible government was achieved, it came first to Nova Scotia. Reform had come to the Maritimes without rebellion and without bloodshed.

ACTIVITIES

1.   What were the causes of discontent in Lower Canada that led to the outbreak of Rebellion in 1837? Which of these causes are still causing unrest in Quebec today?
2.   An interesting historical exercise is to play the 'what if' game. 'What if' Mackenzie and his supporters had decided to move against Toronto at the exact same time as the outbreak of the Rebellion in Lower Canada instead of a few weeks later? Would the British have diverted a large portion of their troops back to Upper Canada? Would this have given the French Canadian revolutionaries a greater chance of victory? Would the history of the Rebellion have turned out differently? Would the history of Canada have been different?

5

Responsible Government at Last

After the rebellions in Upper and Lower Canada, the British government realized that something had to be done. The British government asked Lord Durham to go to Canada to report on needed reforms. In 1838 Lord Durham was named Governor-in-Chief of all the British North American colonies. Durham was known in Britain as a reformer himself. Although he belonged to the wealthy class, he supported reforms that would improve living conditions for the working people. Because of his political views, he had been nicknamed 'Radical Jack'.

Lord Durham set to work to find out as much about Canada as he could. He did not ask just the wealthy people, or those in government. He sent officials throughout the country to talk with ordinary people in the towns and with settlers in the backwoods. He himself went to Toronto to talk to Robert Baldwin and others who had been struggling for better government in the colony. Although he spent only five months in British North America, he was able to put his finger on the trouble. When he returned to England, he wrote a famous report, the Durham Report, for the British government.

Lord Durham made two main recommendations. The first was that the two colonies of Upper and Lower Canada should be joined into one province of Canada. The second main recommendation was that responsible government should be granted to British North America. Lord Durham thought the advisors of the Governor should be chosen from the largest party in the Assembly elected by the citizens of the colony. Then the Governor must be ready to sign his name to all the bills passed in the Assembly.

Lord Durham also made other suggestions, some of which have

Toronto Bay, Canada West.

been carried out. He advised that the Anglican church should have no
more privileges than any other Protestant church. Each colony should
also look after its own affairs, while the British government should be
responsible for the defence of the colonies. Lord Durham also suggested that some day all the British North American colonies might be
joined together.

Most of Durham's ideas were good. However, he made one very
unwise suggestion. Durham decided that the trouble in Lower Canada
had been caused by the French and English wanting different ways of
life. He thought that French Canadians should be made to speak English and live like the English. He failed to understand how deeply the
French Canadians of Lower Canada treasure their language and ways
of life.

On Lord Durham's advice, Upper and Lower Canada were united by
the Act of Union, 1841. Upper Canada became known as Canada
West, and Lower Canada was renamed Canada East. The new government first met at Kingston, and then the capital of the two colonies
was moved to Montreal.

Lord Durham's second recommendation, that of responsible government, was not granted until 1848. At that time the British government began to look more favourably on the idea of allowing the
colonies to govern themselves.

In 1846 a new Governor-General was appointed for Canada. He was
Lord Elgin, the son-in-law of Lord Durham. He shared many of Lord

Durham's ideas about how the colonies should be allowed to govern themselves. He believed in the idea of responsible government.

In the election of 1848, more Reformers than Tories were elected to the Assembly. Therefore, Lord Elgin asked the Reform leaders, Robert Baldwin and Louis Lafontaine, to recommend which elected officials should advise him. Of course they chose members of their Reform party in the Assembly. Lord Elgin promised that he would take their advice as long as the Reformers held a majority in the Assembly. Responsible government had arrived!

The showdown came in 1849 with the Rebellion Losses Bill. If this bill was passed and became law, a large amount of money would be paid to people whose property in Lower Canada had been damaged during the Rebellion of 1837. Tories voted against the bill. They feared that rebels, as well as Loyalists, would be paid for the losses they suffered during the Rebellion. The Tories called it 'a reward for those who rebelled.' Because the Reform party had the largest number of supporters in the Assembly, the Tories were outvoted and the bill was passed. It was then sent to Lord Elgin to be signed.

LORD ELGIN'S DILEMMA

In the carriage on the way to the Assembly, Lord Elgin knew that he faced a dilemma. Today, he would be asked to approve the Rebellion Losses Bill and make it law. Lord Elgin himself did not think the bill was wise. But the government of Baldwin and Lafontaine favoured the bill, and the peoples' representatives had passed it. Would the Governor-General then make it a law by signing his name to it?

Lord Elgin knew that he was being called upon to make an important decision. The Tories were violently opposed to the bill. Their leader had pointed out very strongly to Lord Elgin that there should be 'no reward to the rebels.' Furthermore, the Tory leader had hinted that if Lord Elgin did sign, more violence could break out.

What should the Governor do? He was following the advice of the leaders with a majority of supporters in the Assembly. But the thought of violence was disturbing. Lord Elgin's wife, Lady Mary, was about to give birth. According to her doctor, she and the baby were in some danger. Complete quiet was essential. Suppose a mob were to attack the Governor's mansion? On the other hand, Mary was the daughter of Lord Durham who originally suggested self-government for the colonies. Lady Mary supported the ideas of her father and urged her husband to sign the bill. What should Lord Elgin do?

1.   Decide what you would do if you were Lord Elgin. Write down your private decision on a piece of paper.
2.   Discuss with your class all the possible courses of action open to Lord Elgin.
3.   List the consequences of each possible course of action.
4.   Reconsider your original individual decision. What would you do if you were Lord Elgin?

When the bill was handed to him, Lord Elgin signed it immediately. What happened next was recorded by an eye-witness in a letter to his wife.

Montreal, April 25th, 1849

My dear wife:

I'll attempt to give you an account of what I am doing and what other people are doing for great things have been talked of today. I begin by saying that I am glad you and the children are not here, for we are on the eve of another rebellion . . . It was rumoured that the Rebellion Losses Bill was now to be signed. The report spread through town like wildfire. An immense mob assembled and surrounded Parliament to see what the Governor intended to do. When it was finally announced that he had signed the bill, there was trouble.

As his Excellency, the Governor, left Parliament, he was struck with stones, chips, and rotten and good eggs by thousands of people. He was struck in the face with an egg, his carriage windows were broken, but by the speed of his horses, he was able to escape with no injury except to his carriage.

I stop here, for the cry is raised that Parliament is on fire. "Fire!" is the cry. From my door, I can see the red flames lighting up the heavens — I go — more news after I see what the fuss is about.

April 26th, 1849

It is too true. Last night about eight o'clock, while Parliament was still sitting, a mob assembled and commenced the destruction of the building by breaking windows. (It can be called nothing but a mob, though composed of some of our most worthy Tory citizens.) Soon the doors were broken open and . . . fires were lit in a dozen places . . . Members barely escaped with their lives.

Your affectionate husband
Wm. Rufus Seaver

As Lord Elgin drove into Montreal five days later, he was once again attacked by Tories. Strange as it may seem, the Tories were attacking the Governor. In 1837 it had been just the other way around. Then the Tories had supported Governor Bond Head in putting down the rebels.

Lord Elgin twice risked his life by facing angry mobs. He did so to carry out the wishes of the elected representatives of the people and to give them responsible government. His carriage, which had been damaged by rocks and bricks, was never fixed. He wanted people to see it and to remember at what price responsible government had been won.

ROLE-PLAYING ACTIVITY

Purpose: To review and dramatize the development of responsible government in Upper Canada.

Procedure: Arrange desks in the following manner:

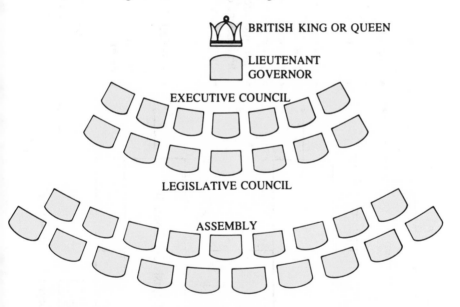

BRITISH KING OR QUEEN

LIEUTENANT GOVERNOR

EXECUTIVE COUNCIL

LEGISLATIVE COUNCIL

ASSEMBLY

1. The teacher represents the British King or Queen. Review the role of the colonies in the British Empire.

2. The teacher, representing the British King or Queen, appoints a Lieutenant-Governor for the colony of Upper Canada. Review the characteristics or qualities of a Lieutenant-Governor. Describe the powers of the Governor.

HOW THE COLONIAL GOVERNMENT WAS CHANGED: COLONIAL GOVERNMENT: 1849

Governor
- appointed by the government in England.
- represented the King or Queen.
- always an Englishman.
- responsible to British Government.

Executive Council
- chosen from the group (party) holding a majority in the Assembly.
- responsible to the Legislative Assembly.
- no longer held office for life.
- each member (Minister) given charge of a department of government.
- must defend government business in the Legislative Assembly.

Legislative Council
- also called the 'upper house'.
- members here were appointed by the Governor for life.
- members made and passed laws.

Executive Council

Legislative Assembly
- also called the 'lower house'.
- elected by the people for up to 4 years.
- members made and passed laws.

3. The teacher distributes cards labelled either TORY or REFORMER to the remaining students.

4. The Governor appoints his Executive and Legislative Councils. He chooses only TORIES. Review the characteristics or qualities of the members of the Councils. Outline their powers.

5. The remaining students take their places in the Legislative Assembly. The majority here are REFORMERS. Remember that the members of the Assembly are elected by the people of the colony and are responsible for making their views known.

6. Members of the Assembly should make a list of all the causes of discontent felt by the citizens of the colony. Make a list of the ways in which the Members of the Assembly might bring about reform.

7. Members of the Assembly should introduce a Bill to bring about reform, e.g. a Bill to Abolish the Clergy Reserves. Members state their reasons for introducing and passing this Bill in the Assembly.

8. The Governor and the Councils react to the proposed Bill to Abolish the Clergy Reserves. If the Bill fails to receive the approval of Governor and Councils the wishes of the elected representatives of the people have not been carried out.

9. If the Bill fails to receive approval, what choices for action are left to the Members of the Assembly and the citizens of Upper Canada? Consider all the alternatives, from the most peaceful to the most violent.

10. Now, introduce Lord Durham's reforms. Replace the Governor. Appoint members from the majority group in the Assembly to the Executive Council. Decide whether or not this is responsible government. Discuss the role of Lord Elgin.

ACTIVITIES

1. Suppose you are one of Mackenzie's supporters before the outbreak of the Rebellion of 1837.

    a) List the arguments you could give to your friends to show why the Rebellion is necessary at this time.

    b) List the requirements you think are necessary to carry out a successful Rebellion.

    c) Which of the requirements you mentioned in (b) were missing in Upper Canada in 1837? Why did the Rebellion fail?

2. What would be the reaction of the following groups to the recommendations made by Lord Durham?

Toronto, Canada West.

a) Tories in Upper and Lower Canada
b) French-speaking people in Lower Canada
c) English-speaking people in Lower Canada
d) Reformers in Upper and Lower Canada
e) Protestants other than Anglicans in Upper Canada.

3. Compare the Rebellions in Upper and Lower Canada under the following headings:

a) Causes of discontent
b) The personalities of the leaders
c) The battles fought
d) The results of the Rebellion on the government, on the leaders and the participants, and on the people of the Canadas.

4. Make a collection of pictures of riots or rebellions such as the Rebellions of 1837, the Riel Rebellions, riots on College campuses, race riots in South Africa or the United States, etc. Try to determine the ways in which all the pictures are similar and different. Answer these questions:

a) Why do people rebel or riot?
b) Do riots ever bring about needed social change?
c) When do people resort to violence in order to bring about social change?
d) Can you think of alternatives to riots as a means of bringing about social change?

5. In what ways were the Rebellions of 1837 a military failure but a political success?

6
John A. Arrives

In the summer of 1820 an event occurred that was to affect Canada for all time. At Quebec City a five-year-old boy ran down the gangplank of a sailing ship and stepped onto North American soil. The ship, *The Earl of Buckinghamshire,* had been on the Atlantic Ocean for forty-two days. It was carrying another load of new immigrants to Canada. Among them was this boy, his parents, and his brothers and sisters. They were a poor family from Scotland hoping to find a better life for themselves in the new world. The boy's name was John Alexander Macdonald.

Who could have known that this curly-haired boy from Glasgow would one day lead all Britain's North American possessions into a great union called the Dominion of Canada?

Who would have dreamed that this son of poor Scottish immigrants would become the first Prime Minister of Canada?

When he died more than seventy years later, one of his political opponents, Wilfrid Laurier, said of Macdonald, 'His life from the day he entered Parliament is the history of Canada.'

The Macdonald family eventually settled at Glenora in Upper Canada, west of Kingston. John's father took over the mill, but the business was not a great success. However, John's mother was determined that her son would get a good education. Like most Scottish immigrants of her day, Helen Macdonald placed a high value on learning to read and write. Though poor, the family managed to scrape together enough money to send John to a boarding school in Kingston. There he learned mathematics, Latin, history, and French. Young John

John A. Macdonald, 1858.

was something of a bookworm. He read wisely and became well-informed on many topics. This love of books stayed with him all his life.

By the time he was fifteen, Macdonald's schooling was over for good. His parents could not afford to send him to university. At that time universities were a long distance away in Montreal, Fredericton, or Halifax. It was decided instead that John would become a lawyer. It was possible in those days for a young man to work in a lawyer's office during the day and study law at night. After several years he could write the examination of the Law Society of Upper Canada. The fifteen-year-old John followed in this tradition and went to work for a prominent Kingston lawyer. In 1836, at the age of twenty-one, he opened his own law office in Kingston.

JOHN A. MACDONALD, ATTORNEY
has opened his office, in the brick
building belonging to Mr. Collar,
opposite the shop of D. Prestion, Esq.,
Quarry Street, where he will attend to
all the duties of the profession.
Kingston, 24th August

Gradually John A. Macdonald developed a prosperous and thriving law business in Kingston. Not only was he recognized for his excellent knowledge of the law, but he was also admired for his friendly manner and sense of humour. Macdonald was not a handsome man, but he loved stylish clothes and dressed well. He was tall and slender, with dark curly hair which hung down over his ears and collar. His nose was so large that it became a standing joke, especially in his later years, with newspaper cartoonists. Macdonald's sister, Louisa, was once told that she looked like her famous brother. She replied, 'That is no compliment because everybody knows that John is the ugliest man in the country.'

While his social and professional life was successful and happy, Macdonald's personal life was often sad. His wife, Isabella, whom he

Isabella Macdonald.

had married in 1843, was frequently sick, and confined to bed. They were often separated for months because Mrs. Macdonald had to go south to a warmer climate for the sake of her health. Their first baby, John Macdonald, born in 1847, died thirteen months later. A second son, Hugh John, was born in 1850. After his birth, Mrs. Macdonald was never strong again. Her illness became worse, and in 1857 she died.

It was during the years of Isabella's long sickness that Macdonald turned more and more to drink. Overworked and sick with worry about his wife, child, and mounting medical debts, John began to drink heavily. Overwhelmed by the loneliness and sadness of these years, unfortunately he turned more and more to alcohol. Heavy drinking was a habit that stayed with Macdonald for most of his life.

Later there were times as Prime Minister when his drinking habits and behaviour were scandalous to the country. Everyone knew when Macdonald was drinking heavily because some newspapers reported sarcastically that 'John A. was sick again.'

In spite of this weakness, the people of Kingston recognized qualities in the successful young lawyer that would make him a good politician. He was intelligent, charming, and witty, though occasionally hot-tempered. Once in Parliament his temper got the better of him. He was criticized by his former law student Oliver Mowat. John A. shouted to Mowat, 'You damned pup, I'll slap your chops.' This scrappy, tough Macdonald was exactly the type of dedicated politician needed to guide the new Dominion of Canada through the first shaky years of its life.

Macdonald's impressive skills as a politician were put to use as an elected member of Kingston's City Council, then as a Member of Parliament, and eventually in 1867 as the first Prime Minister of the Dominion of Canada. Because Macdonald's own life was filled with tragedy, he was always sensitive to the problems of the people he represented.

Once a Member of the Opposition gave out a long list of Macdonald's mistakes, misdeeds and bad habits. When he sat down Sir John rose and, with a grin, replied 'Ain't I the old devil, though?'

The following words were used by John A's friends and enemies to describe him. Use a dictionary to make sure you understand the meaning of all the words. Make two lists, one for those descriptions which are complimentary and another for those words which are not.

amiable	ingenious
cantankerous	persuasive
conciliatory	prophetic
crotchety	shrewd
dedicated	sly
drunk	stubborn
homely	studious

Which words would you use to describe Sir John A.? As you study the unit on Confederation, you may wish to revise your list, or add words of your own.

7
Political Deadlock

During the early 1860s the machinery of the government of Canada gradually ground to a halt. The wheels simply stopped turning; the engine sputtered and stalled. The battery was dead. It was 'political deadlock'.

In 1841 Upper and Lower Canada had been united into one province called the Province of Canada. Canada East and Canada West were given an equal number of seats in the Assembly or Parliament. Two main political groups were represented in the Assembly. One group was called Conservatives or Tories, also called Parti Bleu in Canada East. The other group was the Reform Party or Clear Grits, called the Parti Rouge in Canada East.

John A. Macdonald was a member of the Tory Party. Tories were intensely loyal to the Queen and proud of Canada's connection with Britain. Most Tories were well-educated, wealthy gentlemen who thought they were best equipped as the upper class to run the government. From the Tory Party the modern Progressive Conservative Party has developed.

The Reform Party was led by George Brown, a Scot who edited the *Globe*, a Toronto newspaper. Reformers wanted change for the better. They believed that the common man deserved more share in the running of the government. They found a great deal of support among rural people of Canada West. From the Reform Party developed the modern Liberal Party of Canada.

DOUBLE SHUFFLE

In 1857 Macdonald was the Prime Minister of the Province of Canada. Since the union of Canada East and Canada West in 1841, the Assembly had met at different times in Kingston, Quebec City, Montreal, and Toronto. It was time that the government of Canada had a permanent capital. Each of the four cities expected it would be chosen. London and Ottawa also requested the honour.

Where would the new capital be? This was the topic of conversation in barber shops, newspapers, taverns, and churches all over Canada East and Canada West. People in Toronto said that Montreal should not be chosen because riots had occurred there in 1849. The buildings where the Assembly met were burned down by the angry mob who objected to the Rebellion Losses Bill. This bill would have paid money to people whose property was damaged in the Rebellion of 1837. People of Quebec City said that the capital should be in Canada East and that Toronto or London were too far west. The people of Kingston thought that Quebec City was too far east to suit them.

Macdonald decided that the safest thing to do was to refer the whole matter to Queen Victoria in England. When the Queen announced that her choice was Ottawa, the other cities were in an uproar. They sneered that Ottawa was nothing more than 'a sub-Arctic lumber village.'

There is a story that Queen Victoria had been influenced by a painting of Ottawa sent to her by Lady Head, wife of the Governor-General, who was the Queen's representative in Canada. Lady Head was an amateur painter. She had painted the beautiful area where the Rideau River flows into the Ottawa River. It is more likely that Queen Victoria had been advised to choose Ottawa for reasons of defence. It was further from the American border in case of war with the United States. It had good water transportation routes for moving troops. It was connected to the St. Lawrence River by the Ottawa River, and to the Great Lakes by the Rideau Canal. Ottawa was also the only centre on the border of Canada East and Canada West, and the only city of which the other five cities were not extremely jealous.

Not everyone in the Assembly was pleased with Queen Victoria's decision. When a vote was taken to move the capital to Ottawa, the English-speaking Conservatives voted for the move. Macdonald said that to ignore the Queen's advice would be an insult. The Grits voted against having Ottawa as capital. Strangely enough, on this occasion the French-speaking Conservatives voted with the Grits. Probably most would have preferred to have the capital in Montreal or Quebec City. Macdonald's Conservative government had been defeated. It resigned and shifted to the Opposition benches.

George Brown's Grits became the government. Two days later the Conservatives moved a vote of non-confidence in Brown's new government. A non-confidence vote means that the Assembly is saying to the Government 'we no longer support you.' If the vote passes, the government must resign. This is exactly what happened to George Brown and the Grits. This time the French-speaking Conservatives voted with the English-speaking Conservatives. Brown was Prime Minister for slightly more than forty-eight hours. Macdonald and his Conservative government returned to power and joked about the 'double shuffle'.

So Ottawa did become the capital of the Province of Canada. Work was soon begun on the Parliament Buildings high on the cliffs overlooking the Ottawa River. They were built in grey limestone in the gothic style, meaning that the tops of doors and windows were pointed and the roofs were steep. Broad lawns, where parades could be held, stretched down to the street. The Assembly met in a spacious meeting room on the main floor for the first time in 1866. Upstairs were offices for members of the Assembly. Even George Brown was forced to admit that it was a beautiful building worthy of a great 'province'.

In the 1860s, the Government and the Opposition were so nearly even in number that measures were often passed or defeated by one or two votes. Canada West was represented in the Assembly by many Grits and a few Conservatives. Canada East was represented by many Parti Bleu and a few Parti Rouge. The Grits and the Rouges usually voted together against the Conservatives and the Bleus. The two groups were almost equally balanced. It was like two evenly-matched teams playing tug-of-war. It became impossible to get any bills passed through the Assembly, or to make any new laws. It was political deadlock. How had this come about?

When Upper and Lower Canada were united in 1841, each part of the new colony was given an equal number of seats in the Assembly. In the beginning this was unfair to Canada East because more people lived there than in Canada West. Naturally, the people of Canada East protested that there should be representation in the Assembly on the basis of population. They should have more seats in the Assembly in proportion to their extra population. This was known as 'representation by population'.

Ottawa and the Parliament buildings in 1866.

By 1861 things had changed. The population of Canada West was now greater than that of Canada East. This time many people in Canada West were demanding 'representation by population'. George Brown, leader of the Grits, said equal representation was not fair.

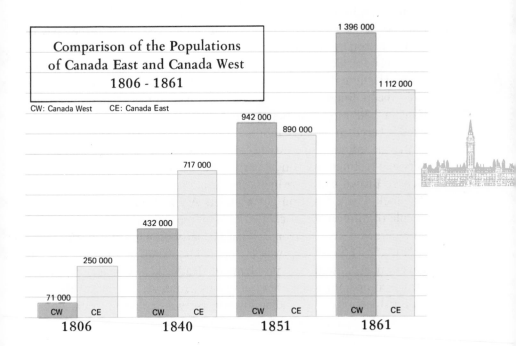

Comparison of the Populations
of Canada East and Canada West
1806 - 1861

CW: Canada West   CE: Canada East

	1806	1840	1851	1861
CW	71 000	432 000	942 000	1 396 000
CE	250 000	717 000	890 000	1 112 000

Canada West was larger than Canada East by almost 300 000 people. Canada West therefore should have more members in the Assembly. There should be representation by population. The people of Canada East, of course, would never agree to that! And so political deadlock continued.

In the three years before 1864 four governments resigned and there were two general elections in Canada. Neither side could get enough votes to carry on the work of government. The tug-of-war continued. About this time, John A. Macdonald talked of retiring from politics. Macdonald's wife had died in 1857 and his young son Hugh John was living in Kingston with his grandmother. The Conservatives begged John A. to stay on as their leader. Fortunately, he agreed to remain.

On 14 June 1864, Macdonald's government was defeated by two votes. Macdonald could call an election, but what good would that do? Another election would probably change nothing. Neither side could hope to win enough seats in the Assembly to get any bills passed. 'Political deadlock' had brought the government to a standstill. It was George Brown who saved the day.

George Brown was the enormously respected editor of the Toronto newspaper the *Globe*. He was also a member of the Assembly and a leader of the Grits. He hated the Conservative Party and had absolutely no use for John A. For years the two men had hurled many bitter remarks at each other across the floor of the Assembly. If they passed each other on the street, neither one would speak. Nor did Brown have much use for Georges Cartier, the leader of the French-speaking Parti Bleu. He thought the Roman Catholic Church had too much power over the politics of Canada East. He had argued that it was time Canada had representation by population so the French would be outnumbered in the Assembly.

But the future of his province meant more to George Brown than his personal feelings or political party. The idea that he suggested revealed George Brown's true greatness. He thought that the answer to political deadlock was a coalition government. A coalition was the joining of people of different political parties into one government in the time of an emergency to do together what no party could do by itself.

Now, in 1864, Brown was saying that he would co-operate with any government to settle the problems of deadlock in Canada. Even if it meant co-operating with his old enemy, John A.! In one of the most unselfish actions in Canadian history, Brown explained to the Assembly why he was prepared to co-operate:

George Brown.

For ten years I have stood opposed to the honourable gentlemen opposite in the most hostile manner it is possible to conceive . . . But I think the House will admit that, if a crisis has ever arisen in the political affairs of any country that would justify such a coalition, such a crisis has now arrived in the history of Canada . . . I do say, that if by any means we can find a solution to the difficulties, every man who has the slightest interest in the country will be grateful to those who accomplish it . . . I desire no greater honour for my children to remember than that I had a hand, however humble, in bringing about that great work.

After Brown had finished his speech, members of all parties burst into cheers. People flocked around the big Scot, shaking his hand and slapping his back. One French-Canadian member rushed over with tears in his eyes and kissed Brown on both cheeks. By his unselfish action, Brown had broken the deadlock!

Now the government of Canada could do something. Brown persuaded all forty of his Grit members to join him in the coalition government. Of the 130 members in the Assembly, there were at least 100 who would vote together.

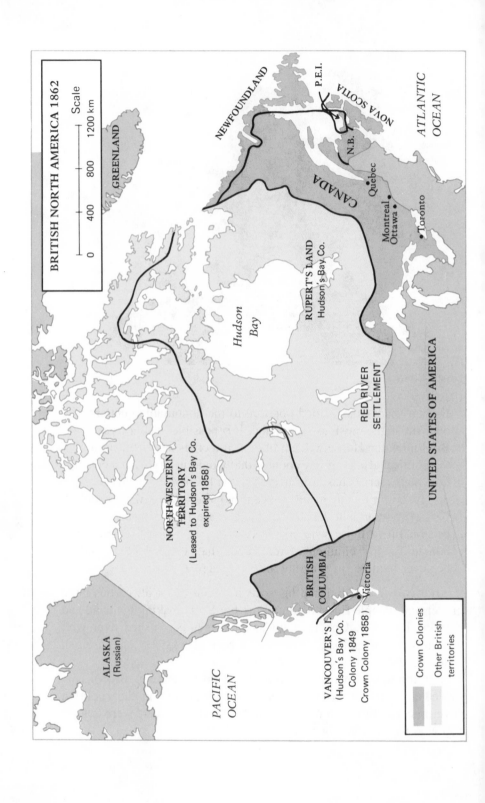

BRITISH NORTH AMERICA 1862

Scale

0   400   800   1200 km

GREENLAND

ALASKA
(Russian)

PACIFIC
OCEAN

NORTH-WESTERN
TERRITORY
(Leased to Hudson's Bay Co.
expired 1858)

Hudson
Bay

RUPERT'S LAND
Hudson's Bay Co.

NEWFOUNDLAND

P.E.I.

NOVA SCOTIA

N.B.

CANADA

Quebec

Montreal
Ottawa
Toronto

ATLANTIC
OCEAN

RED RIVER
SETTLEMENT

BRITISH
COLUMBIA

VANCOUVER'S I.
(Hudson's Bay Co.
Colony 1849
Crown Colony 1858)

Victoria

UNITED STATES OF AMERICA

Crown Colonies

Other British
territories

The coalition government had two plans. The first was that they would try to form a union or Confederation of all the British colonies in North America. These colonies included Nova Scotia, New Brunswick, Prince Edward Island, and Newfoundland, in addition to Canada East and Canada West. This was not a new idea. Sir Guy Carleton, William Lyon Mackenzie, and Lord Durham had all dreamed about some day uniting all the British North American colonies with a central government for all. If this failed, they would attempt their second plan. It was to split Canada again into two provinces (Ontario and Quebec). Each province would run its own local affairs but there would be a central government based on representation by population to look after matters of concern to both Canada East and Canada West. Other colonies could come in later if they so desired. The idea of Confederation was beginning to move ahead in Canada.

In the 1860s, a number of other factors were pushing British North American colonies closer and closer towards union. Some of these problems were coming from outside the colonies, and some were coming from inside. What were the common problems the colonies faced?

ACTIVITIES

1. Representation by Population
   a) Why didn't Canada West ask for representation by population at the time of union in 1841?
   b) Why did George Brown begin to demand representation by population for Canada West about 1853?
   c) Why would Canada East object to Brown's demand for representation by population? What reasons would they give?
2. In the period 1854-1864 there were ten different governments in the province of Canada. Compare these figures to the last ten years in Canada and in your province. What effects will these many changes have on the running of the province of Canada?
3. Explain the events in Canada that brought about the great coalition.
4. Why do you think Brown was cheered and congratulated after his speech?

8
Pushed Together

PROBLEMS WITH THE UNITED STATES

From 1861-1865, the Americans had been fighting a bloody Civil War. It was a battle between the states of the North and the South. The issue at stake was whether North and South should remain united together or separate into two countries. By 1865, the South had been defeated, and the United States remained one country.

The American Civil War had nothing to do with Canada or Britain, but wars have a habit of affecting many countries. Early in the war Britain appeared to support the Southern states, which were the great producers of cotton. The British textile factories depended on this supply of cotton. This did not make Britain popular with the northern states.

One incident almost drew Britain into war with the North. It occurred when a northern ship stopped the British vessel *Trent*. The Northerners went aboard and removed two Southerners and took them prisoners. The British government was angry and insulted. They said the Northern American states had no right to stop their vessel. It might have led to war, but Queen Victoria persuaded the British government to be satisfied with an apology from the Americans.

A second incident created tension between the British and the northern states. During the Civil War, British shipyards built armed cruisers for sale to the South. One of these, the *Alabama,* captured and destroyed northern ships, perhaps as many as sixty-five. The North demanded that Britain pay millions of dollars in damages. After the war, Britain did pay $15 500 000 to the United States to settle the claims for the damages.

In October 1864, about twenty-five southern soldiers made their way to Canada. From Canada they made a raid on the village of St. Albans in Vermont, a northern state. They robbed banks, set some houses on fire, and then dashed back across the border into Canada. The northern states were very angry with Canada for allowing this raid to be made from Canada.

When the North won and the war ended in 1865, Canadians really began to worry. They wondered whether the North would then turn their vast armies against Canada. Would they see an attack on Canada as a way of getting revenge on Britain?

A number of United States newspapers and politicians had been talking about the takeover of Canada. One American senator suggested that Canada should be turned over to the United States for the damage done by the British boat *Alabama*. Many Americans believed at this time in 'Manifest Destiny'. They believed that it was natural and expected that the United States would one day control all North America. In the summer of 1867, an American official, William H. Seward, had said in a speech,

I know that Nature plans that this whole continent, not merely these 36 states, shall be, sooner or later, within the American union.

In 1867 the Americans had purchased Alaska from the Russians. Now they began to crave the empty plains of the North-West of Canada. Many Americans hoped to make the Prairies part of the United States. American people, railways and trade were steadily pressing in on the Red River settlement near what is now Winnipeg. It looked as if the colony might be surrounded and become so American that it would be joined to the United States.

On the west coast, the same thing was happening. The discovery of gold in British Columbia had brought thousands of Americans into that colony. With the purchase of Alaska by the Americans, British Columbia was hemmed in to the north and south by the United States. If the colony of British Columbia and the empty plains were to be kept British, something would have to be done quickly. Thus, the threat of invasion from the United States and American expansion beyond their own borders were factors pushing the colonies together.

PROBLEMS WITH THE FENIANS

Canada was actually invaded by Irish-American troops after the Civil War was over. They were members of an Irish-American organization called the Fenians. During the first half of the nineteenth century, a large number of Irish had come to the United States. At that time, Britain controlled all of Ireland. Many Irish detested the British control, and they left Ireland to get away from it.

In the United States, they continued to look for a way to free Ireland of British rule. They thought that if they invaded Canada and captured it, it would be a way of getting back at Britain. If the Fenians controlled Canada, perhaps they could compel Britain to free Ireland. It may sound like a foolish plan, but the Fenians felt sure of success. Many of their men were soldiers who were experienced in fighting.

Fenian Marching Song

Many battles have been won
Along with the 'boys in blue',*
And we'll go and capture Canada,
For we've nothing else to do.

*(Northern army in the Civil War.)

They had just been released from the victorious northern army. Probably they thought that the American government, which was already hostile to Britain, would not try to stop them.

The Fenians planned to invade Canada at three points — in the Niagara region, along the St. Lawrence River, and in the Eastern Townships of Quebec. On one occasion in May 1866, about 1500 Fenians crossed the border at Buffalo, captured Fort Erie, and won a victory over a Canadian force at Ridgeway. Six Canadians were killed and thirty were wounded. Because American reinforcements failed to arrive, the Fenians turned back across the border. That same year British warships prevented a Fenian attack in New Brunswick. For the next several years, people along the border lived in fear and were always on the alert for Fenian raids. Raids did occur at several points along the border, including an attack on a Manitoba town in 1871.

The Fenian attacks had two major effects on British North American colonies. First, John A. managed to turn the raids to his advantage. He argued that a united country would be better able to resist such invasions. It was time, he said, that Canadians thought more seriously

Battle with the Fenians.

about defence. The governments of the provinces voted more money for defence and more volunteers were trained for the army. Second, there was a feeling of resentment on the part of Canadians against the United States government for allowing the Fenian raids to go on so long. Many felt that American newspapers encouraged the Fenians. They also believed that the United States government could have and should have stopped the Fenians at the border. Thus, the Fenians provided another push towards Confederation.

PROBLEMS OF TRADE

Another concern to the British North American colonies was the problem of trade. As members of the British Empire, the provinces had enjoyed a special position in trading with Britain. The British Corn Laws had allowed wheat and flour from the British North American colonies to enter Britain with a very low tax. This was called a 'preference'. Foreign merchants (for example Americans wanting to send their wheat and flour to Britain) had to pay a much higher tax to the British government. With the protection of the Corn Laws, the British North American colonies were doing a booming business with Britain.

Thousands of bushels of grain were shipped to Britain from Canadian ports every year. Canadians could import American wheat, grind it into flour, and ship the flour to England at the preferred rate.

Suddenly, in 1846, the Canadians heard the bad news. The British had decided to cancel the Corn Laws. No longer would Britain give special favours to goods shipped from her colonies in North America. Britain would start to have free trade, allowing goods from any country into her markets without paying tax. The Canadians, who had spent a great deal of money to build a canal system and flour mills so that American wheat and flour could reach British markets, now found themselves in financial trouble. After 1846, the Americans could ship their own goods to Britain more cheaply.

Cost of shipping 1 ton of wheat to Liverpool in 1849

From Chicago by way of Montreal $13.75
From Chicago by way of New York $10.50

Angry merchants, especially in Montreal, felt they would be better off breaking away from Britain and joining the United States. Eventually though, their anger cooled when the British colonies made a Reciprocity Treaty with the United States in 1854.

Reciprocity is an agreement made by two countries about tariffs or taxes on the goods they trade with each other. Each country agrees to allow certain goods from the other country to be brought in free of tariffs. With the loss of the 'preferred' market in Britain, the British North American colonies began to look towards the United States as a trading partner.

What did the Canadian provinces have that the Americans wanted? More than anything else, the Americans wanted to be allowed to fish in Maritime waters. What did the Americans have that Canada wanted? The North American colonies wanted to be able to send their farm and forest products to the huge markets of the United States without paying the tariffs. And so, a reciprocal treaty was worked out. It was agreed that both Canada and the United States could fish along the Atlantic shores. For the next ten years both countries would allow the products of farms, mines and seas to cross the border without tax. Fish, timber, grain, and cattle were sent from the colonies to the United States; American coal and pork were sent north to the colonies. Reciprocity did not include exchange of manufactured goods. After a ten-year trial, either country could break the bargain.

Strange as it may seem, at this time there was very little trading among the colonies themselves. When they did exchange goods with each other, they always charged high tariffs. When wheat was sent from Canada into the United States, it crossed tax-free into that foreign country. When the same wheat was shipped to New Brunswick or Nova Scotia, it was taxed. In view of the fact that all the colonies were British, this practice appeared odd and foolish.

During the 1860s the provinces began to worry that the United States might end the Reciprocity Agreement. Americans were saying they were losing thousands of dollars each year by allowing British North American goods into their country tax-free. There was a growing feeling of hostility during the Civil War between the United States and Canada because of the British involvement with the South. In 1865 the United States announced that it intended to end the Reciprocity Treaty.

The British North American colonies were thrown into a panic over the loss of the American market. The only solution seemed to be free trade between the colonies themselves. If the provinces were united, it would be easy and logical for them to trade with each other. Trade was another factor pushing the provinces closer together.

THE PROBLEMS OF RAILWAYS

If there was going to be trade between the colonies, there had to be a railway link. In 1850 there were only 106 km of track in British North

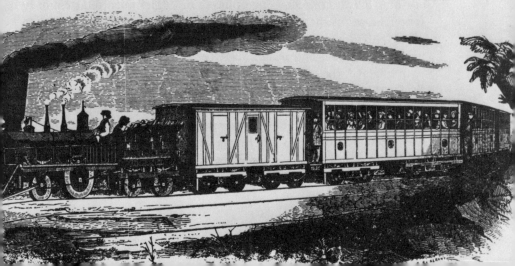

BYTOWN AND PRESCOTT RAILROAD.

America, while there were 14 484 km in the United States. Much of the railway business in the provinces was going to the American railways. It was time, Canadians thought, to build their own railways.

Between 1850 and 1867, 3 570 km of track were added in the colonies. In 1853, a railway line called the Saint Lawrence and Atlantic was completed to the ocean at Portland, Maine. Since Montreal port was ice-free for only six months of the year, this line linked Canada with an ice-free American port.

The most ambitious railway project of the 1850s was the Grand Trunk Railway. It was to be an all-Canadian route linking Canada West with the Atlantic Ocean at Halifax. By 1860 the Grand Trunk had stretched east from Sarnia to Rivière du Loup. But it cost a tremendous amount of money to build, and it was on the verge of being bankrupt.

Many people thought that the only way that the Grand Trunk could be completed to Halifax would be if the provinces were united. Then expenses could be shared. The railways would also provide a communication and trade link between the colonies. Some railroaders even dreamed of one day extending the railway right across the continent to the colony of British Columbia and the Pacific.

The railway connection with the Maritimes was essential for the defence of Canada. Suppose Canada was attacked by the United States during the winter. The St. Lawrence River would be blocked by ice. There would be no way British troops could be rushed to the Maritimes by rail without crossing through the United States. For trade and defence, a rail link between the colonies seemed to be essential. It was another reason for Confederation.

PROBLEMS OF THE CHANGING BRITISH ATTITUDE TOWARDS COLONIES

When the British government brought in free trade in 1846, it was a crushing blow to the economy of the colonies. In order to raise money for public works such as canal and road building, Canadians decided to place tariffs on all goods coming into the provinces. British manufacturers were furious at the Canadians for raising the costs of their goods.

In England, there was a small but noisy group of people who wanted to get rid of the colonies completely. They were known as 'Little Englanders'. They thought that colonies were a great expense and a great burden. One of the biggest expenses of colonies, they claimed, was their defence. The 'Little Englanders' believed it was time that the British North American colonies began to pay their own way. John

Bright expressed their views in the British Parliament with the following speech:

> I think it is natural and reasonable to hope that there is in the North American provinces a very strong attachment to Britain. But if they are to be constantly applying to us for guarantees for railways, and for grants for fortresses, and for works of defence, then I think it would be far better for them and us — cheaper for us — that they should become independent. They could maintain their own fortresses, fight their own cause, and build up their own future without relying on us. And we know, as everybody knows, that the population of Canada is much better off than most of the population of Britain. I say the time has come when it ought to be clearly understood that the taxes of England are no longer to go across the ocean to pay expenses of any kind.

Many people in Britain agreed with the 'Little Englanders'. They said Britain should not pay the heavy defence costs of the British North American colonies. This was bad news for the provinces at the very time that the Fenians were raiding their borders and the Americans were threatening to move into the West. The views of the 'Little Englanders' helped to push the Canadians towards Confederation.

ACTIVITIES

1.   Give the reasons for the bad relations between the Canadians and the Americans and between the British and the Americans in the 1860s.
2.   G.E. Cartier said: 'When all colonies are united the enemy will know that if he attacks any province he will have to deal with the combined forces of the Empire'.
   a)   Who was the enemy being referred to?
   b)   Who were the soldiers of the colonies?
   c)   Why were British troops stationed in the colonies?
   d)   Why would it be difficult for an individual colony to defend itself?
3.   a)   Who were the Fenians?
   b)   What were their goals?
   c)   How did they try to achieve these goals?
   d)   In which British North American colonies did the Fenians have the greatest effect on public opinion?

e) How did the Fenians help the cause of the union of the colonies?

4. What is 'neutrality'? Do you think that the seizure of the two southerners on board the *Trent* was an insult to Britain's neutrality? Why? Do you think that the building of the *Alabama* broke British neutrality? Why?

5. Students living in Canada-United States border areas should investigate the effects of the Civil War and the Fenian raids on their areas.

6. Make a list of the products which Canadians bought from other countries in the 1860s. From whom? Make a list of the products which Canada exported to other countries in the mid nineteenth century. To whom were they sold?

7. Explain how the British Corn Laws gave preference to Canadian flour over American flour in the British markets.

8. It was later said by Lord Elgin that when Britain cancelled the Corn Laws it had a disastrous effect on Montreal businesses. Elgin claimed that 75% of Montreal's commercial men went broke and property value fell by 50%. Explain why this happened.

9. What are the advantages and disadvantages for Canada of reciprocity with the United States? Does Canada have reciprocity with the United States today? Do the provinces have reciprocity with each other today?

10. Why was the building of a railway so important for New Brunswick? Why was the railway essential for Canada?

11. Explain what the 'Little Englanders' believed in. Why did their beliefs cause the Canadians to worry?

12. What advantages did the British North American colonies bring to Britain? What burdens did the colonies place on the mother country?

13. The population of the United States in 1861 was 31 000 000. The total population of the British colonies was 3 295 000. How will the great difference in population affect the colonies?

14. Summarize the common problems facing the colonies which helped to move them towards union. Rank these in the order of importance. Discuss your reasons for the ranking chosen.

9
Confederation

Suppose your family is trying to decide whether to buy a new house or fix up the old one. Faced with such a big decision, your family could make a list of the advantages and disadvantages of both alternatives. The disadvantage of the old house is that it needs many expensive repairs, such as a new furnace and a new roof. The advantage of the old house is that it is in a neighbourhood where the family has many friends and where the children like the school and their teachers. The advantage of a new house is that everything is modern and up-to-date. The disadvantages of a new house are that the children will have to go to a new school and father will have farther to travel to work. When the family has drawn up such a list, it will help them to make a decision.

In the 1860s, the British North American colonies had to decide whether or not to unite with each other. Each colony had to determine the advantages and disadvantages of such a union.

One way to understand the differing points of view in the colonies is for your class to role-play each of the British North American colonies.

John Gray.

John Galt.

Oliver Mowat.

Leonard Tilley.

Ambrose Shea.

Charles Tupper.

Thomas D'Arcy McGee.

George-Etienne Cartier.

SITUATION: THE BRITISH NORTH AMERICAN COLONIES IN THE 1860s

1.   Divide the class into six groups representing Canada West, Canada East, New Brunswick, Nova Scotia, Prince Edward Island, and Newfoundland. You may take the name of actual historical figures from each colony if you wish.

2.   Let each colony meet separately and study the material about itself on the following pages.

3.   The question for discussion is, 'What does your colony think about union?' Make a list of the advantages and disadvantages of remaining a separate colony, and a list of the advantages and disadvantages of uniting with the other colonies.

4.   On the basis of what you have read and discussed, make an 'educated guess' about what your colony will decide concerning union.

5.   Let each colony present its decision to the class, explaining its reasons for the decision.

6.   After the role-playing, discuss how you felt about your part in the proceedings.

7.   Keep track of what each colony in your class decided to do. Later compare your decisions with what actually happened in history.

CANADA WEST   ROLE CARD

Canada West is still very much a farming province. More than 80 percent of the people live outside the cities or towns. The wilderness is being pushed back and farms are becoming wider and more prosperous.

New farm machinery makes the back-breaking work of the farmers easier. Daniel Massey at Newcastle, and Alanson Harris at Beamsville, Canada West, are now producing ploughs and horse-drawn mechanical reapers. The two businesses will eventually form the large farm implement firm of Massey-Harris.

The cities of Canada West are growing rapidly. Toronto's main streets are paved and gas lamps provide little patches of light for evening pedestrians. The other streets are dirt and covered with horse manure. Sidewalks are made of boards that become treacherous and slippery when wet.

Open sewers and outdoor toilets are common, even in cities. Bathtubs are only for the rich. Most people wash their hands, face, and feet in that order. They deal with other body odours with perfumes and scented lotions.

An important natural resource has recently been found in Canada West. James M. Williams is developing North America's first oil well at Oil Springs in Canada West during the late 1850s. In 1862, oil is discovered at nearby Petrolia. Hugh Shaw hits the first free-flowing gusher. Oil flows out at the rate of 2000 barrels a day and brings a price of $10.00 a barrel. From the oil, kerosene (coal oil) can be burned in coal-oil lamps and asphalt made for paving the streets.

Toronto stagecoach.

CANADA WEST   FACTS AND FIGURES

Population: 1 396 000 (1861)

Largest Cities: Toronto population 56 000 (1861); Hamilton 26 700; Ottawa 21 500; London 15 826; Kingston 12 400; Brantford 8 100.

How People Make their Living: The largest part of the population is engaged in farming. In the cities, in 1861, the main occupations are clerks, carpenters, saddlers, brewers, shoemakers, blacksmiths, booksellers, bankers, grocers, hotel-keepers, and preachers.

Special Problems:

1. Good farm land in Canada West is becoming scarce. Young men who want to start farming often have to go to the American West to find available land. People are saying that it is time that the Hudson's Bay Company open up their western lands for settlement.
2. Political deadlock makes it impossible to get any bills passed through the Assembly, or to pass any new laws.
3. The population of Canada West is now greater than Canada East. People in Canada West want representation by population to gain a larger voice in the Assembly.

Railways: The St. Lawrence River has no year-round ice-free port. For half of the year goods in and out of the colony must be transported on American railways through American territory. A railway to Halifax through Canada East, New Brunswick, and Nova Scotia will provide an all-British route for trade and defence.

Defence: There is danger that the Fenians will attack along the Canadian-American border in the Niagara region and around Prescott on the St. Lawrence River.

Fathers of Confederation:

Canada West

John A. Macdonald	1815-1891
George Brown	1818-1880
William McDougall	1822-1905
Alexander Campbell	1822-1892
Oliver Mowat	1820-1903
James Cockburn	1819-1883
William P. Howland	1811-1907

CANADA EAST   ROLE CARD

The backbone of Canada East is the rural habitant. Habitants are the French-Canadian farmers whose farms hug the shores of the St. Lawrence and other rivers. They live in long, low, whitewashed stone houses. They are cheerful, God-fearing people. The habitants pride themselves on their French language, customs, and their unique way of dressing. In winter the habitants wear shaggy fur caps, loose, thick, blue woolen coats with hoods, and bright scarlet sashes tied around the waist. The women wear large straw hats or high white caps, and noisy sabots, coarse leather shoes with thick wooden soles.

The most important agricultural products produced by the habitants of Canada East are potatoes, rye, buckwheat, and livestock.

Montreal is the largest city in all of the British North American colonies. Some of the wealthiest people in Canada live there in elegant mansions. Many of the wealthy are Scots who have made great fortunes in iron and steel works, flour mills, steamship lines, and timber.

Montreal is a city of striking contrasts. There are thousands of French who cannot speak one word of English, and thousands of English who cannot speak one word of French. It is easy to trace the two main divisions of the population of Montreal. Taking St. Lawrence Street as a dividing line, all that is east of it is French, and all that is west of it is English-speaking.

Habitants playing cards.

CANADA EAST   FACTS AND FIGURES

Population: 1 112 000
Largest Cities: Montreal population 107 225 (1861); Quebec City 59 700 (1861)
How They Make their Living: Most of the rural population are engaged in agriculture. In the bush, hundreds of workers cut trees, square them with broad axes, and float them to the St. Lawrence during the spring floods. Sawmills turn the logs into planks and boards for sale in the United States. Factories in Canada East make shingles, furniture, matches, wash-boards, door-frames, and windows. Along the waterfront in Montreal, factories are springing up which provide many jobs. Montreal alone has twenty boot and shoe factories, as well as flour mills, woolen mills, foundries, and sugar refineries. In iron and steel works rails, spikes, nails and even locomotives are now being made.
Special Problems:
1. 'Political deadlock' is making it impossible to get anything done in the government in Canada East and Canada West. Both English-speaking people and French-speaking people are accusing the other group of always wanting their own way.
2. The loss of the 'preferred' markets in Britain means that the colony must look elsewhere for markets for its industrial and agricultural products.
3. In any union of colonies, the French-speaking people of Canada East feel they will be swamped by an English-speaking majority.
Railways: The St. Lawrence River has no port that is free of ice all year round. For half of the year goods in and out of the colony must be transported on American railways through American territory. A railway to Halifax through Canada East, New Brunswick, and Nova Scotia will provide an all-British route for trade and defence.
Defence: There is danger that the Fenians will attack along the Canadian-American border south and east of Montreal.
Fathers of Confederation:
    Canada East

Georges E. Cartier	1814-1873
Alexander T. Galt	1817-1893
Thomas D'Arcy McGee	1825-1868
Hector L. Langevin	1826-1906
Etienne P. Taché	1795-1865
Jean Charles Champais	1811-1885

NEW BRUNSWICK   ROLE CARD

In the 1860s, Saint John is one of the largest cities in the Maritimes. Saint John is an ambitious, commercial city. It often seems very American. The editor of a Kingston newspaper describes it like this: 'In Saint John, you see big men casually dressed, with their hats tilted at an angle of 45 degrees on the backs of their heads, smoking cigars in hotels on Sunday, and talking politics. There are more flashy-dressed ladies at theatres and concerts than in Canada.'

Few New Brunswickers know people of the Canadas very well. Therefore, Premier Tilley of New Brunswick arranges to have some members of Parliament and businessmen from Canada visit his province in order to get to know one another better.

The visiting Canadians are treated with a great deal of hospitality by the Maritimers. Tours of the province are arranged, as well as banquets, dances and picnics. The visit does a great deal of good. It convinces Maritimers that Canadians are not bad fellows, and not as foreign and strange as they have supposed. Canadians too enjoy good times, food, liquor, games, and laughs.

Both Canadians and Maritimers see they have many things in common. They speak the same languages, English or French. They fly the same flag, and share many of the same laws and customs.

There are differences though. Each colony has its own money and postage stamps. Each charges the others duty on all goods shipped in.

Saint John, New Brunswick, 1870.

NEW BRUNSWICK

FACTS AND FIGURES

Population: 252 000

Largest City: Saint John population 28 805 (1861)

How People Make a Living: In the woods of New Brunswick thousands of lumberjacks cut trees and float them down the rivers to the mills. In the mills the logs are cut into planks and exported to all parts of the world. Many of the ships in which they are transported are themselves built in the shipyards of New Brunswick.

Railways: Many New Brunswickers hope to connect Saint John and Montreal by rail through the Saint John River Valley. They hope for a rail connection with Nova Scotia too. Then they can build a trade with the markets of Canada to the west and Nova Scotia to the east.

Defence: New Brunswick shares a long border with the United States, and in the event of war, the colony will have difficulty defending this border. It will take a long time for British troops to arrive in New Brunswick if needed. Many fear that the Americans might invade New Brunswick to punish Britain for the British part in the American Civil War.

Special Problems:

1. Railways cost a great deal of money to build, and only Britain can supply the funds to carry out the job. For reasons of defence, the British want to keep any railway away from the American-New Brunswick border. But that is exactly where the railway is needed most, in the settlements of the Saint John River Valley. Without British funds, New Brunswickers can only afford to build a small railway from Saint John to Shediac.

Fathers of Confederation:

New Brunswick

Samuel Leonard Tilley	1818-1896
John M. Johnson	1818-1868
William H. Steeves	1814-1873
Edward B. Chandler	1800-1880
John Hamilton Gray	1814-1889
Peter Mitchell	1824-1899
Charles Fisher	1808-1880
R. D. Wilmot	1809-1891

NOVA SCOTIA   ROLE CARD

Halifax, the capital of Nova Scotia, is an impressive sight to see. The citadel is a fortress of great strength overlooking the harbour and city. Next to that of Quebec City, it is the strongest and best constructed fortification in all British North America. It is so high that, if attacked from the harbour, no damage could be done to its massive walls.

The harbour of Halifax never freezes. That is why it is the chief station for the British Navy in the west Atlantic. At almost any time you can see British battleships lying in the harbour. Young ladies of Halifax are often swept off their feet by the sight of the handsome British soldiers in their scarlet tunics. This 'excitement' among the young ladies is jokingly referred to in Halifax as 'scarlet fever'.

There is no railway connection between Nova Scotia and Canada East and Canada West. Few Nova Scotians know any people from these colonies and dislike them, sight unseen. Nova Scotians are ready, however, to talk to the other Maritime colonies about the possibilities of a Maritime union.

Curling on a lake near Halifax.

NOVA SCOTIA   FACTS AND FIGURES

Population: 331 000 (1861)

Largest City: Halifax population 29 580 (1861)

How People Made a Living: Nova Scotia faces the sea, and most families are connected with sea-faring in one way or another. In 1863 more than 150 000 Nova Scotians work as fishermen. Others sail on merchant ships transporting cod to the West Indies and the United States, coal from England to the Far East, or wool from Australia to Europe. Sometimes these ships carry immigrants to new homelands around the world. Other Nova Scotians build ships. The ships built in Nova Scotia, made of softwoods such as pine, spruce, or tamarack, are world famous. Even when fully loaded, these softwood ships are light, graceful and speedy.

Special Problems:

1. Nova Scotians are worried about the new steamships. They fear that these steam ships may some day take away all the business from their wooden sailing ships.

2. Since 1854, Nova Scotia has enjoyed free trade with the United States. What would happen to Nova Scotia if the United States put heavy taxes on goods coming into their country from Nova Scotia?

Railways: Some people suggest that an Intercolonial Railway should be built between Nova Scotia and the Canadas. Nova Scotia could then carry on trade with the Canadas.

Defence: Nova Scotia feels reasonably secure against an attack because of the large number of British soldiers and seamen stationed at Halifax.

Fathers of Confederation:

Nova Scotia

Charles Tupper	1821-1915
William A. Henry	1816-1888
Jonathon McCully	1809-1877
Adams G. Archibald	1814-1892
Robert B. Dickey	1811-1903
John William Ritchie	1808-1890

PRINCE EDWARD ISLAND   ROLE CARD

An Indian legend tells us that long ago the Great Spirit took some dark red clay and formed it into a crescent. He placed it on the blue waters of the Gulf of St. Lawrence and made it the most beautiful land in the world. Soon Micmac Indians from the mainland crossed the stretch of water in their canoes. In summer they built their wigwams in coves along the shore and fished in the rivers. In winter they found shelter in the forests and hunted for game and birds. The Micmacs loved their beautiful island. They called it 'Abegweit', which means 'cradle on the waves'.

Prince Edward Island is indeed 'a most beautiful land cradled on the waves' of the Gulf of St. Lawrence. Sandy beaches glisten in the sunshine. Neat houses and barns dot the landscape. Most of the forests have been cleared for farming.

None of the people of the island live more than one day's journey from the capital city of Charlottetown. Charlottetown is an impressive centre with its attractive churches and fine Legislature, built in 1847 to house the government of the colony.

In winter the people on Prince Edward Island move about easily in sleighs called cutters. A cutter is a very comfortable open carriage set on runners, which can whiz easily and rapidly over the snow or ice.

Farmer's sleigh.

PRINCE EDWARD ISLAND   FACTS AND FIGURES

Population: 80 000 (1861)

Largest City: Charlottetown population 7 000

How People Make a Living: Some Prince Edward Islanders are fishermen, but the main industry is farming. The rich, red soil produces excellent crops of potatoes, oats, and hay. The food not eaten on the island is exported to England, Nova Scotia, New Brunswick, and the New England states.

Special Problems:

1. In 1861, 60 percent of the farmers on the island are tenant farmers. Many farms are owned by landlords in Britain. Most farmers in Prince Edward Island are renters. They clear the land, plough it, but do not always own it. Each year they send their rent to the absentee landlord who lives in Britain and does not often come to the land. This has been going on for 100 years. The farmers want the British government to force the landlords to sell the farms at a fair price. In 1860, the government of Prince Edward Island had purchased land known as the Selkirk estates and sold it to the tenant farmers.

2. During the winter Prince Edward Island is completely cut off from the mainland. This means that all supplies are cut off as well as the mail. Sometimes an iceboat mounted on runners and propelled by sails manages to cross the Northumberland Strait with mail from England and the other colonies.

Railways: Since the colony is an island, a railway link with the other colonies does not make much sense.

Defence: Prince Edward Islanders do not worry about being attacked by the United States since they do not share a common border.

Fathers of Confederation:

Prince Edward Island

John Hamilton Gray	1812-1887
Edward Palmer	1809-1889
William H. Pope	1825-1879
Andrew A. Macdonald	1829-1912
George Coles	1810-1875
Thomas H. Haviland	1822-1895
Edward Whelan	1824-1867

NEWFOUNDLAND   ROLE CARD

In the 1860s most people in Canada East and Canada West know nothing about Newfoundland. Since it is an island, the only way to get there is by steamer. Newfoundland is nearly as large as the other three maritime colonies put together.

The coastline is rugged and indented with many bays and inlets. Most people live along the coastline. The rest of the island is dense forest, swamps, and rock. There are no roads across the island. When people want to visit their friends, they get into their boats and call in at the coves along the shore.

The fishermen live in plain, unpainted houses, on the cliffs over-looking the coves where their fishing boats are anchored. Beside their houses are wooden racks where they dry the cod fish they catch. They grow potatoes and turnips in small gardens, though the soil is not good for growing crops. Newfoundlanders have to depend mostly on the sea.

From the earliest days Newfoundland has traded fish with Britain, in return for British manufactured goods. People wear clothes and shoes made in Britain and read British newspapers and magazines. Since 1858 Newfoundland has been linked with Britain by a trans-Atlantic cable. This cable lies on the floor of the Atlantic Ocean, and provides Newfoundland with telegraph communication to Britain.

Bonne Bay, Gros Morne, Newfoundland.

NEWFOUNDLAND   FACTS AND FIGURES

Population: 122 000 (1861)
Largest City: St. John's population 30 475 (1857)
How People Make a Living: Almost everyone is connected with the fishing industry or seal hunting. Merchants buy the fishermen's catch and sell them the things they need, such as ropes, hooks, canvas, salt, barrels and sou'westers (oilskin hats with wide brims at back, worn by sailors and fishermen).
Special Problems:
1. All through the 1860s the fishing and seal hunting is bad. Many fishermen are hopelessly in debt to the merchants. By 1865, one-third of all money in the colony is spent on helping the poor.
2. Since 1713, French fishermen have been allowed to catch fish and dry them on the west shore of this island colony. Newfoundlanders fear that the French want to use this shore for more than their fishing stations. French warships are seen in the Gulf of St. Lawrence. In case of trouble with France, will Britain be prepared to protect them?

Railways: Railway links with other colonies do not interest them because they have the sea for their highway.
Defence: Newfoundland depends on the British navy which is second to none. Newfoundland has little fear of being attacked by the United States.
Fathers of Confederation:
Newfoundland
Frederick B.T. Carter   1819-1900
Ambrose Shea   1815-1905

ACTIVITY

PLAN A CANADA WEEK

Groups could find out what life is like today in each of the provinces of Canada. Research each province. Use library resources and write to provincial governments for information. (Tourist offices are helpful.) Find out as much as you can about such topics as:

industries	occupations
cities/rural areas	economy
cultural groups	recreation
sports teams	climate
landforms	transportation
languages spoken	important citizens
historical sites	tourist industry

What are the similarities and differences between that province in 1860 and today? Present your research to the class in an interesting way. Use a bulletin board display of pictures or simulate a TV report on the province.

10
Confederation Discussed

George Brown had joined John A. Macdonald in a coalition government to try to break the political deadlock in Canada. That government
had promised to work for some kind of federation. They hoped that a
union of all the provinces of British North America might help them to
solve their problems. All the Canadians had to do now was to convince
the Maritimes to join in! John A. and his colleagues had a monumental
task ahead of them!

The Canadians began on 30 June 1864, by asking permission to
attend a conference in Charlottetown on Maritime union. The three
Maritime provinces had been talking for several years about a union
among themselves. Finally they had decided to hold a conference to
discuss the matter. Now, here were the Canadians inviting themselves
along to talk about an even wider union — Confederation.

THE CHARLOTTETOWN CONFERENCE 1864

The *Queen Victoria* left Quebec City for Charlottetown on Monday,
29 August 1864. It was carrying eight Canadian Cabinet Ministers.
Among them were George Brown, John A. Macdonald, Georges Cartier, and two other prominent politicians, Alexander Galt and D'Arcy
McGee. After a sunny passage down the St. Lawrence and along the
New Brunswick coast, the *Queen Victoria* steamed into Charlottetown
on Thursday, 1 September.

The Canadians were all strong men with strong opinions. They had
the ability to speak and gain the attention of their audiences. They had
worked out their Confederation plan and the arguments for Confedera-

The Charlottetown Convention, September 1864.

tion that they were going to use. All eight men were highly familiar with the plan and had a clear idea of what each one would say. They shared a single powerful purpose, the union of all British North America.

George Brown, in a letter to his wife, described their arrival in Charlottetown harbour:

Our steamer dropped anchor magnificently in the stream and its man-of-war [a large armed vessel] style evidently inspired the natives with huge respect for their big brothers from Canada. I flatter myself we did that well. Having dressed ourselves in correct style, our two boats were lowered man-of-war fashion — and each boat was manned with four oarsmen and a boatswain, dressed in blue uniform, hats, belts, etc. In regular style, we pulled away for shore and landed like Mr. Christopher Columbus who, before us, had taken possession of portions of the American continent.

The Charlottetown Conference met that afternoon and promptly put aside their own plans to discuss a Maritime union. Instead, they agreed to hear the Canadians for four days. They listened while the Canadians put forward the reasons why the Maritimes should join in a union with Canada. From the program, you can see how the Canadians made their appeal.

Georges Cartier — speaker
topic: 'The Arguments in Favour of Confederation'
luncheon — buffet luncheon of lobster, oysters and other island
       delicacies at the home of Mr. W. H. Pope in Char-
       lottetown

Saturday, 3 September 1864
A. T. Galt — speaker
topic: 'How Finances Could be Arranged in the United Provinces'
luncheon — Canadians host a party on the *Queen Victoria*
Georges Cartier — speaker
topic: 'Canada of the Future'
George Brown — speaker
topic: 'The Dream of Canada Atlantic to Pacific'

Monday, 5 September 1864
George Brown — speaker
topic: 'The Powers of the General Government and the Powers of
      the Local Government in Confederation'

Tuesday, 6 September 1864
topic: 'Other Reasons for Confederation'

Wednesday, 7 September 1864
Maritime delegates report on their decision about Confederation

Thursday, 8 September 1864
Supper and Grand Ball — Parliament Buildings, Prince Edward
                Island   Speeches, dinner, dancing

A week later, the Saint John daily newspaper reported that the arguments of Macdonald, Brown, Cartier, and the other Canadians were 'almost irresistible'. They noted that the Maritime delegates were 'more favourable now to Confederation than they used to be and as they talked to the Canadians, the difficulties in the matter of detail vanished'.

The parties and social festivities that went on with the Conference certainly helped to convince people of the idea of Confederation. The luncheon on the *Queen Victoria* was the most important piece of shipboard hospitality in Canadian history. There were no papers signed, but most of the delegates decided that afternoon that Confederation was a real possibility. As the champagne corks popped, Macdonald, McGee and the others spoke with warmth and brilliant wit. Maritimers began to be converted to the idea that a Confederation of the British North American colonies could actually come to pass.

As a result of the conference the Maritime delegates abandoned any idea of a Maritime union. They agreed to meet with the Canadians for a further conference on Confederation in Quebec City in October. But before the Canadians left, there was still another banquet with each group toasting the others and singing 'For They Are Jolly Good Fellows'. Cartier wound up the celebrations by singing 'God Save the Queen' in English and French. Then the Canadians returned home to get ready for the Quebec Conference.

THE QUEBEC CONFERENCE 1864

In October, delegates from all the provinces gathered together again at Quebec City. There were 7 from New Brunswick, 7 from Prince Edward Island, 5 from Nova Scotia. Newfoundland, which had not been represented at Charlottetown, sent two officials. All were ready to sit down and talk business with the 12 delegates from Canada East and Canada West. Many of the Maritimers brought their wives and daughters with them.

A great welcome awaited them at Quebec City. Though the weather outside was wet and depressing, celebrations inside were warm and hearty. The Canadian government arranged for a grand ball. There were 800 guests. They danced quadrilles, polkas, and waltzes. The Canadian Cabinet Ministers danced with such enthusiasm that Edward Whelan, a delegate from Prince Edward Island, wrote:

> The Canadian Cabinet Ministers — the leading ones especially — are the most tireless dancers I have ever seen. They do not seem to miss a dance during the live-long night. They are cunning fellows; and there's no doubt that it is all done for a political purpose. They know that if they can dance themselves into the affections of the wives and daughters of the Maritimers, the men will certainly become an easy target.

In the 1860s, women in the British North American colonies did not have the right to vote and they did not take an active part in the official discussions about Confederation. However, the wives and daughters of the politicians obviously did have a great deal of indirect influence on the Fathers of Confederation.

Behind closed doors, though, all the politicians had a great deal of hard work to do. They had to work out all the details of a plan for the union of the provinces. All the Fathers of Confederation were agreed on one point. The union must be a strong one which could not be broken by any one province. In the Canadian Confederation, the central government must have great power. In fact, it must be more powerful in every way than the governments of the provinces.

There were other decisions to be worked out. How many representatives would each province have in the central government? Where would the money come from to run the central government? What powers would the governor have? Would they have two houses of Parliament as the British system does? Would there be an elected House of Commons to make the laws? Would there be an appointed House of Lords to double-check all laws passed by the House of Commons? Would other colonies, such as British Columbia, be able to enter Confederation in the future? When these and many other questions had been worked out, the Quebec Conference drew up the Seventy-two Resolutions. These resolutions provided a plan for the new partnership of the British North American colonies.

At the end of the month, the delegates moved west to Montreal. In Montreal there was another Conference ball. Then they took the steamer north to Ottawa where they lunched in the nearly-completed Parliament Buildings. This was followed by a train trip to Toronto. At Toronto they were met by four brass bands, blazing torches, firework displays, and thousands of people. The excitement in the streets of Toronto did not die down until well past midnight. Everywhere the delegates went, they were received 'like warriors returning from a great victory'.

After the Quebec Conference had ended, the various hotel claims for entertainment against the Canadian government totalled $15 000.00. But during that summer and fall, the idea of Confederation had caught on. Before that time, most of the politicians had been strangers to one another. Now they found themselves working together for something bigger than they had ever known before. For Confederation, there were still many hurdles ahead. But those months, July to November of 1864, were a sweet time to remember.

CONFEDERATION!

THE MUCH-FATHERED YOUNGSTER.

The 'father' of Confederation.

ACTIVITIES

1. a)   Before the Charlottetown and Quebec Conferences, many Maritimers were distrustful of Canadians in general. What were their reasons for feeling this way?

    b)   As the Conferences went on, Maritimers came around to the idea of Confederation. Why did they change their minds? What methods did the Canadians use to persuade Maritimers that Confederation was a good idea?

2.   What was the original purpose of the Charlottetown Conference? How important was the part played by Macdonald, Galt and Brown? Was the Charlottetown Conference a success? For whom?

3.   Cartoon Analysis. Canadians today consider John A. Macdonald as *the* Father of Confederation. In 1867 several authors made claim to the title, including George Brown and William McDougall, shown in this cartoon.

    a)   Identify John A. Macdonald and George Brown in the cartoon.

    b)   Why is Confederation shown in the cartoon as a young child?

    c)   Who is the cartoonist poking fun at? Why?

4.   Choose any Father of Confederation of interest to you. Do some reading and research about that Father's work. Then write a summary of that man's contribution to the confederation movement. Does he deserve the title — 'Father of Confederation'?

11
Confederation Delayed

The Quebec Conference was a fine beginning, but there was trouble ahead. The plan for union, the Seventy-two Resolutions, had to be accepted by the government of each of the provinces. The Fathers of Confederation went home to convince their people about the idea. Would the people of the provinces be as excited about Confederation as were the delegates to the Charlottetown and Quebec Conferences?

NEW BRUNSWICK

In New Brunswick, Premier Leonard Tilley was a staunch supporter of Confederation. Tilley had grown up in Gagetown in the beautiful Saint John River country. But at age thirteen, he said good-bye to his family and headed downstream to the bustling seaport of Saint John. He took little with him except ambition, good character, and a fair education for those times.

Tilley's first job was a clerk in a drug store. Before many years had passed, he was in the pharmacy business for himself. By the year 1858, he had been elected to the Assembly of New Brunswick and become premier of his province.

After the Quebec Conference, Tilley called an election in New Brunswick, and Confederation was the main issue. Those who were opposed to Confederation (the anti-Confederationists) made fun of the whole idea. At the Quebec Conference it had been decided that each province would receive each year from the Dominion government a sum of money called a subsidy. The amount of the subsidy was to be based on the population of the province. In the case of New Brunswick, the subsidy amounted to about $.80 per person. One opponent of Confederation, A.B. Wetmore, had this imaginary conversation with his son:

Son: What country do we live in, Father?
Father: My dear son, you have no country, for Mr. Tilley has sold
us all to the Canadians for 80¢ each.

On election day in 1865, the anti-Confederationists won easily, and Tilley and his supporters were defeated.

It was a black day for all those who dreamed of a great united

The Academy of Music, Saint John, N.B.

country. For without New Brunswick, there could be no Confederation. New Brunswick was the land link between Canada and the other Atlantic provinces.

But Leonard Tilley did not give up the idea of Confederation. He promised that he would travel house-to-house throughout the province and talk to the people. He wanted to explain Confederation to them, as he hoped that they would change their minds and vote for it. In the months that followed, he spoke in every part of the province on the subject of Confederation. Tilley's speeches were clear and easily understood. He was a sincere and honest speaker and his personal efforts helped to win people over to the side of Confederation.

Three other events helped to convince New Brunswickers that there could be no progress without Confederation. First, the United States ended free trade with the British North American colonies. No longer would New Brunswick's goods pass into the United States without tax being charged on them.

Second, the British government sent a message encouraging New Brunswickers to join Confederation.

Third, the Fenians attacked New Brunswick in 1866. These Irishmen, living in the United States, wanted to free Canada from Britain. The people of New Brunswick were terrified as word arrived of hundreds of Fenians gathering near the border. The New Brunswick militia was called out, and this volunteer army camped near the border. During the month of April 1866, small bands of Fenians did cross into the province. While the Fenian threat was present, another election was called in New Brunswick. The people had another chance to say if they wanted Confederation.

This time, New Brunswickers voted in favour of Confederation. The threat from the Fenians, the poor treatment by the United States, and the urging of the British government convinced them that Confederation with Canada was the only way. But above all, it was Leonard Tilley himself who led his province into the union.

Tilley was given the title 'Sir' by Queen Victoria when he was presented to her at Buckingham Palace. After Confederation he became a Member of Parliament for New Brunswick in the government at Ottawa. In 1873, Tilley was further honoured by being appointed Lieutenant-Governor of New Brunswick, the Queen's representative in that province. He remained in this office until 1878. Leonard Tilley, a Father of Confederation, and New Brunswick's most famous citizen, died in 1896.

Fenian raid volunteers.

CANADA

In Canada, the politicians spent more than a month debating the Quebec Conference Resolutions. Every member of the Assembly was allowed to speak as long as he wished. All the speeches were published. One of the best speeches was given by George Brown, who spoke for four hours.

Brown gave the six main reasons why he was in favour of Confederation:

1. Confederation would change them from five unimportant colonies into a great and powerful nation.

2. It would remove the barriers to trade between the colonies and provide a market of almost four million people.

3. Canada would become the third largest sea-going nation in the world, behind Britain and the United States.

4.   It would encourage people to come from other countries to settle in Canada.

5.   Since the United States had cancelled free trade with the colonies, Confederation provided another market for their goods.

6.   In case of a war, all the colonies would stand strong together.

The people of Canada listened to respected men like George Brown and John A. Macdonald. When the vote was taken, the Resolutions were approved 91 to 33.

At the time of Confederation, George Brown withdrew from politics and gave all his attention to the *Globe*. In 1873 he was appointed to the Senate, but he called it a dreary place because it was so quiet.

His life ended in tragedy. Brown had fired an employee for being drunk. On 25 March 1880, the employee burst into the *Globe* offices and shot the editor. George Brown was not killed in the attack. They carried him back to his home on Beverley Street. He never recovered, and died on 10 May 1880. The man who shot him, George Bennett, was executed for his crime.

Would Confederation have been possible without George Brown? He had sacrificed himself and his party to help bring it about. He was not looking for personal credit, but thinking only of the good of his country.

In Canada East there were some bitter critics of the plan for Confederation. A.A. Dorion complained that at the Quebec Conference only four of the thirty-three delegates were French-speaking. All the discussions had been carried on entirely in English. Dorion argued that Confederation would be a bad deal for Canada East. He suggested that Canada East was being sold out by Georges Cartier.

In Canada East however, most French-speaking Canadians were won over eventually to the idea of Confederation by Georges Etienne Cartier.

Georges Cartier was a descendant of the famous Cartier family of New France. He was one of the most popular men in Montreal. Like John A. he was trained to be a lawyer, and like Macdonald, he became the leader of the Conservative Party. For years, Macdonald and Cartier worked together to govern the united province of Canada.

Many French-speaking Canadians were afraid that they would be completely outnumbered in Confederation. After all, the new government would be based on representation by population. Cartier travelled around Quebec trying to persuade the French-speaking people they had nothing to fear. He explained that in Confederation French and

English would be equal partners. He promised they would not lose their language, their religion or their schools. He warned them that if they did not join Confederation, then Canada East could be swallowed up by the United States.

The people of Canada East trusted Cartier and supported him. The Roman Catholic Church added its voice in support of Confederation. But when it came time to vote, twenty-two of the forty-eight French-speaking members of the combined Assembly of Canada East and Canada West voted *against* Confederation. A. A. Dorion wanted the people of Canada East to be given the chance to vote on the question. His request was refused by Cartier and the supporters of Confederation. Macdonald said that if it had not been for Cartier, Confederation would never have passed in Canada East.

Another great champion of Confederation from Canada East was Thomas D'Arcy McGee. He was the best speaker in the Canadian Assembly, and he believed in the union of the colonies with his whole heart.

D'Arcy McGee was born in Ireland and had come to Canada as a newspaperman. Eventually he was elected as a Member to the Assembly from Montreal. All through the 1860s he travelled through the British North American colonies talking about the dream of Confederation. He was the eloquent spokesman of union.

Montreal, 1865.

McGee had attended the Charlottetown and Quebec Conferences, and in 1867 was elected to the Parliament in Ottawa. He was one of the most promising men of the new government. But McGee had made enemies — the Fenians. He had criticized his fellow Irishmen who wanted to free Ireland and Canada from Britain. The Fenians never forgave him.

About 2:00 a.m. on the morning of 7 April 1868, D'Arcy McGee was making his way back to Mrs. Trotter's boarding house through the streets of Ottawa. As he paused at the door to insert the key, a man came up behind him and fired a shot. McGee slumped to the ground. In a few minutes Dr. Robitaille pronounced McGee dead. The bullet had gone through the base of his brain and emerged from his mouth. Someone ran to Sir John A.'s house with the news. Macdonald hurried to the scene, and helped to carry the body of his friend into the house. McGee was the first Father of Confederation to be assassinated. He died at the age of forty-three.

The government offered $20 000 for information leading to the arrest of the assassin. A Fenian named Patrick James Whelan was arrested and charged with murder. It was suspected that the motive for the murder was Fenian revenge. The Crown had difficulty proving that Whelan was guilty. A detective testified that he heard Whelan tell another person:

I don't care! I'll either swing or go to the penitentiary for life. I shot that fellow like a dog. Whiskey is the devil. If it was not for whiskey, I would not have shot McGee. I was drunk as the devil when I did it. There were three of us, but the others skedaddled home.

On 11 February 1869, Patrick Whelan was hanged for the murder of D'Arcy McGee.

Sir John A. was on the verge of tears when he announced McGee's death to Parliament. 'If ever a soldier fell in the front of the fight, it was D'Arcy McGee. He deserves to be honoured by Canada. His hand was open to everyone. His heart was made for friendship!'

NOVA SCOTIA

Charles Tupper was born in Nova Scotia. Even as a boy he was brilliant. Before he was seven years old he had read the whole Bible aloud to his father. When he was twenty-two, he graduated from Medical School in Edinburgh, Scotland.

Tupper returned to Nova Scotia and established a busy medical practice. He became known throughout the district as he made his rounds on horseback or by sleigh to visit the sick. Eventually he entered politics and in 1864 became the premier of Nova Scotia.

Confederation won Tupper's interest. He arranged the Charlottetown Conference and there met Macdonald for the first time. Tupper was excited and enthusiastic about the possibility of a union of colonies.

But when he returned to Halifax from Quebec he found trouble. Opposition leaders, especially Joseph Howe, were stirring up a storm of hostility against union. They were objecting to the subsidy worked out with the Dominion government. In Nova Scotia this subsidy amounted to forty cents per person. Tupper had sold out to central Canada for a grant of forty cents per person — the price of a sheepskin, roared Joseph Howe. Tupper knew that if he tried to introduce the Seventy-two Resolutions in the Assembly, he would be defeated.

Instead, he stalled for time. He travelled up and down the province. Everywhere he spoke he tried to destroy the arguments of Howe and the anti-Confederationists.

This was the fight of Tupper's life. Bitter statements were written and spoken on both sides. The people of Nova Scotia were deeply divided. Friendships were broken up when the people disagreed violently over the need for union.

About that time word reached Nova Scotia of the Fenian threat to New Brunswick. Many thought that there was a real possibility that Nova Scotia would be invaded by Fenians too. New Brunswickers had started to talk seriously of joining Confederation. Some people in Nova Scotia began to hint that they might also join if they received a better deal from Ottawa. At that moment Tupper suggested that delegates from all the provinces should meet in London to work out a plan that would satisfy everybody. Tupper went to London, England in 1866. He worked there with sixteen delegates from Canada, New Brunswick, and Nova Scotia to plan the union.

While the delegates were in London, the stubborn Howe continued to stir up trouble. Nevertheless, Confederation became a fact and Nova Scotia was one of the colonies that entered the partnership.

Tupper's life continued to be marked by honours. He was Premier of Nova Scotia; he led his province into Confederation; he was an important Member of Parliament at Ottawa, and for a short time in 1896, he was Prime Minister of Canada. Sir Charles Tupper died in England on

Women's evening and day dresses.

30 October 1915 at the age of ninety-four. A battleship of the British Navy brought his body back to his native Nova Scotia.

PRINCE EDWARD ISLAND AND NEWFOUNDLAND

Prince Edward Island and Newfoundland flatly rejected the Quebec Resolutions. It was not until six years later, in 1873, that Prince Edward Island entered Confederation. Newfoundland waited eighty-two years before it joined Canada.

Prince Edward Island was in a huff because Charlottetown was not even considered as the new capital of Canada. Since the idea of a union had been born at the Charlottetown Conference, some residents thought that their city deserved the honour.

A more important reason for turning down Confederation was their fear of the sheer size of the new country. Their island was small, and they thought they would be swamped in the union. The Fathers had agreed on representation in the new Parliament according to the population. Prince Edward Island had a very small population, smaller than the city of Montreal. With representation by population Prince Edward Island would have only five members in the House of Commons of a total of 194 members. The island was discouraged at the prospect of having so few representatives. How could the voice of Prince Edward Island be heard across the new country with only five members in Parliament?

The people of the island listened to all the talk of a railway from Canada to the Maritimes. Since their province was an island, the railway was of no great interest to them. What they needed was a railway to join the places on the island, but there was no mention of that in the Quebec Resolutions.

Nor was there any mention in the Quebec Resolutions of buying out the absentee landlords of the island. Not until the last minute was it suggested that this should be done. In October 1866, when it appeared that Prince Edward Island would not enter Confederation, a last-minute promise was made. It was suggested that Canada would buy the land for Prince Edward Island from the landlords for $800 000. A newspaper outside Prince Edward Island joked that this would surely persuade the islanders to join:

> That eight-hundred thousand will surely suffice,
> To buy all those Islanders up in a trice [hurry].

But it was too late. The islanders had made up their minds. They wanted no part of Confederation; they thought they would gain very little.

Three of the Fathers of Confederation from Prince Edward Island tried their best to convince the islanders to join. But nothing that John H. Gray, William H. Pope, or Edward Whelan could do or say seemed to make any difference. The tiny island preferred 'to stand off and watch the game for a little while'.

Newfoundlanders had not sent representatives to Charlottetown. However, two delegates had attended the Quebec Conference. One of these men, F.B.T. Carter, became Newfoundland's Premier in 1865. Although Carter personally was in favour of Confederation, he could not convince his independent people. They were very proud of their historic ties with Britain and the fact that they were Britian's first overseas colony.

A wealthy St. John's merchant, C.F. Bennett, led the fight against Confederation. He warned the fishermen that the new Dominion would probably tax their boats, fish and fishing tackle. Goods from Canada, he said, would be so cheap that Newfoundland products would not sell. He hinted that young men from the island would be expected to give up their lives 'in defence of the desert sands' of Canada. He made that statement even though Canada promised that Newfoundlanders would not have to serve on the mainland.

The campaign against Confederation was noisy and rowdy. Lively songs were used to help defeat Confederation. An example of an anti-Confederation song from Newfoundland is as follows:

Hurrah for our own native isle, Newfoundland!
Not a stranger shall hold one inch of its strand!
Her face turns to Britain, her back to the Gulf,
Come near at your peril, Canadian Wolf!

Ye brave Newfoundlanders who plough the salt sea
With hearts like the eagle so bold and so free,
The time is at hand when you'll all have to say
If Confederation will carry the day.

Cheap tea and molasses they say they will give,
All taxes take off that the poor man may live;
Cheap nails and cheap lumber our coffins to make,
And homespun to mend our old clothes when they break.

If they take off the taxes how then will they meet
The heavy expense of the country's upkeep?
Just give them the chance to get us in the scrape
And they'll chain us like slaves with pen, ink, and red tape.

Would you barter the rights that your fathers have won,
Your freedom transmitted from father to son?
For a few thousand dollars of Canadian gold,
Don't let it be said that your birthright was sold.

Then hurrah for our own native isle, Newfoundland!
Not a stranger shall hold one inch of its strand!
Her face turns to Britain, her back to the Gulf.
Come near at your peril, Canadian Wolf!

On the night Confederation was defeated in Newfoundland a huge parade wound through the streets of St. John's. They pushed a large coffin labelled 'Confederation'. The coffin was buried in a fake funeral. Confederation was a dead issue in Newfoundland. It stayed buried until 1949 when the Newfoundlanders voted to join Canada as the tenth province.

ACTIVITIES

1. Suppose you were a French Canadian living in Canada East in 1865/6.

a) Why might you wish to leave the government of the province as it is? What might be the dangers of this arrangement?

b) Why might you prefer to divide up the province again into the separate colonies of Canada East and Canada West?

c) Why might you prefer to join with the Maritimes to form a new nation?

2. Why was Prince Edward Island opposed to representation by population?

3. Suggest reasons why the people of Newfoundland and Prince Edward Island rejected the idea of Confederation.

4. At first, many people in New Brunswick and Nova Scotia rejected the idea of Confederation. Account for their eventual change of mind.

5. Why did the people of the Canadas accept Confederation?

12
Confederation Won

THE LONDON CONFERENCE

Since the British North American colonies still belonged to Britain, the union of the British North American colonies could not become official until the British Parliament approved it. Therefore, sixteen delegates from Canada, New Brunswick, and Nova Scotia journeyed to London, England to talk over the matter with members of the Mother Parliament. Among those were Macdonald, Cartier, Galt, Tupper, and Tilley. They stayed in London's Westminster Palace Hotel, and so this conference is sometimes called the Westminster Conference.

During the Westminster Conference a particularly happy event happened to Macdonald, who had been a widower for nine years. He met Susan Agnes Bernard and often they were seen together in theatres and restaurants. They were married on 16 February 1867. Agnes Macdonald brought great joy to her husband's life and provided him with a much more secure home life than he had known for years.

Throughout the winter of 1866-67, the Fathers of Confederation worked in London with British officials in charge of its colonies. They were drafting a Confederation Bill to be presented to the British Parliament.

From the time of the Quebec Conference, Britain was all in favour of Confederation in Canada. If the colonies were united, the British hoped they could look after themselves. Many of Britain's responsibilities for the colonies would now be over. Of course, Britain would still have to help defend the North American colonies, but the colonies would play a much larger role in defending themselves. The fact that the Confederation idea was supported by people of different political parties in Canada also impressed the British.

In the spring of 1867, the British North America Act was introduced to the British Parliament. It passed very quickly without any major changes. Queen Victoria put her royal signature on it and 1 July 1867 was proclaimed as the day the British North America Act would come into effect.

An anti-Confederation group from Nova Scotia led by Joseph Howe had also come to London that winter. They fought the Confederation scheme right up until the last minute. But their attempt to stop it was hopeless. The British North America Act passed with scarcely any debate. It was said that the members of the British Parliament were more interested in the debate on a new dog tax which followed.

The London Conference.

John A. Macdonald meets Queen Victoria.

With all the talk about Confederation, there was much discussion of what the new country should be named. The Toronto *Globe* invited its readers to submit names and the newspaper received many suggestions. Among them were: British Esfiga (from the first letters of English, Scottish, French, Irish, German, and Aboriginal), Britannia, Cabotia, Laurentia, New Britain, Niagarentia, Transatlantica, Albertania, Canadia, Tuponia, and Kingdom of Canada.

Macdonald and his friends would have preferred to call the new country 'Kindgom of Canada'. They said that this would emphasize that this country was a monarchy, loyal to the Queen. This name was rejected by the British. It was feared that the word 'Kingdom' might be objectionable to the Americans. During the American Revolution the United States had abandoned the British monarchy and become a 'Republic' governed by a President. The British did not want to cause any more trouble with the United States over the name of the new country to the north.

Leonard Tilley is said to be one who came up with the idea of the name 'Dominion' of Canada. He got the name from a verse in the seventy-second Psalm of the Bible that states, 'He shall have dominion from sea to sea, and from the river to the ends of the earth.' The

Fathers of Confederation agreed that this verse did indeed describe their land. Soon, they hoped, Canada would stretch from the Atlantic to the Pacific, and from the great St. Lawrence River to the end of land on the shores of the Arctic Ocean.

1 JULY 1867

The church bells started to ring at midnight. Early in the morning guns roared a salute from Halifax in the east to Sarnia in the west. Bonfires and fireworks lit up the sky in cities and towns hundreds of kilometres apart. It was Monday, 1 July 1867, and the people of Ontario, Quebec, New Brunswick, and Nova Scotia were celebrating the birth of the Dominion of Canada.

All over the new country it was a day of blue skies and sunshine. People of all religious faiths gathered to offer prayers for the future of the nation and its people. Through the crowded streets of Ottawa, the new Prime Minister, John A. Macdonald and his government made their way to the Parliament Buildings. There the new Governor-General, Lord Monck, was sworn into office. Monck, the representative of Queen Victoria in Canada, then made an important announcement in the name of the Queen. Her majesty had decided to honour Macdonald for his leadership in Confederation by making him a Knight Commander. He was now 'Sir' John A. Macdonald. The Royal Proclamation, declaring that the British North American Act was now in effect, was read throughout the land. Cheers went up for Canada and Queen Victoria. Brass bands broke into 'God Save the Queen'. Union Jacks lined the streets. Banners everywhere proclaimed 'Good Luck to Confederation!' and 'Bienvenue à la Nouvelle Puissance!'

That day, most of the people in Canada took a holiday. In Toronto a great celebration took place at the Horticultural Gardens. The gardens were lighted with Chinese lanterns. Fresh strawberries and ice cream were served. A concert was followed by dancing. Tickets were 25 cents; children's tickets were 10 cents. In another part of the city a huge ox was roasted all day and the meat distributed to the poor.

The steamer *Princess of Wales* left the wharf at Hamilton early in the morning for an all-day trip to the beach. A great fireworks display followed at night. The fare to the beach and back was 25 cents.

In Quebec, boat races on the river, horse races, and a cricket match were held.

In all parts of the Maritimes families travelled to the sea for a day of swimming and a supper of salads, cold meat, pies and cakes.

Almost everywhere there was the feeling that this day was just the beginning of great things for Canada. George Brown in his editorial put it well:

With the first dawn of this gladsome summer morn, we hail this birthday of a new nationality. A united British America takes its place among the nations of the world.

Unfortunately, in some parts of the new Dominion the mood was not one of rejoicing. Anti-Confederationists displayed flags at half-mast and wore black clothes as a sign of mourning. A likeness of Dr. Tupper was suspended by its neck all afternoon on the spot known as the Devil's Half Acre at Yarmouth, Nova Scotia. In the evening it was burned side-by-side with a rat.

A New Brunswick newspaper carried a death notice on its front page 'Died — at her residence in the city of Fredericton, The Province of New Brunswick, in the eighty-third year of her age.'

THE BRITISH NORTH AMERICA ACT

The Dominion of Canada was created by the British North America Act. It united four provinces, New Brunswick, Nova Scotia, and the two Canadas, now Ontario and Quebec. The act was built on the Seventy-two Resolutions worked out at the Quebec Conference. It was entirely the composition of Canadian politicians. The Resolutions were polished up in London and presented to the British Parliament for its approval.

The Fathers of Confederation were trying to find a way to unite four separate, scattered colonies. In building the new nation they had two models they could copy — the British and the American. They decided to select what they thought were the best features of the governments of both countries.

WHAT THE FATHERS TOOK FROM THE BRITISH MODEL

The provinces to be joined were British North American colonies. They were loyal to Britain. Nobody was talking about independence from Britain, and nobody doubted that the new country would remain British. The Queen would continue to be the head of the Canadian government, but she could not make laws by herself. For hundreds of years the British Queen or King had been bound to follow the advice of the elected members of Parliament.

Canada would have a parliamentary government fashioned on the

The meeting of the first Parliament under Confederation.

age-old proven example of the British system. In Britain the Prime Minister and his Cabinet were members of the political party that elected most people to the House of Commons. There would be no need in Canada to work out a new system of government as the Americans had done after they broke away from Britain. The Prime Minister and Cabinet would be chosen from the political party that had the largest number of members in the elected House of Commons. They would be responsible or accountable to the House of Commons and to the people of Canada. If they lost the support of a majority of the members of the House of Commons, they could be voted out of power.

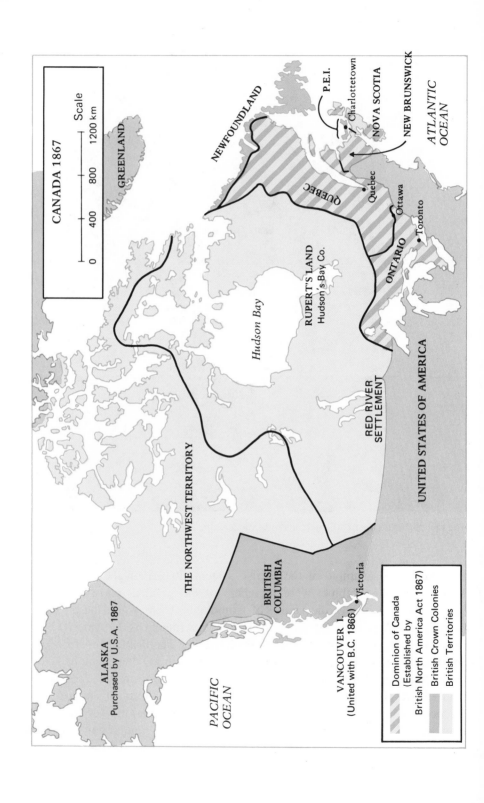

CANADA 1867

Scale

0   400   800   1200 km

GREENLAND

NEWFOUNDLAND

P.E.I.
Charlottetown
NOVA SCOTIA
NEW BRUNSWICK

ATLANTIC
OCEAN

QUEBEC

Quebec

Ottawa

Toronto

ONTARIO

Hudson Bay

RUPERT'S LAND
Hudson's Bay Co.

RED RIVER
SETTLEMENT

UNITED STATES OF AMERICA

THE NORTHWEST TERRITORY

BRITISH
COLUMBIA

Victoria

VANCOUVER I.
(United with B.C. 1866)

ALASKA
Purchased by U.S.A. 1867

PACIFIC
OCEAN

Dominion of Canada
(Established by
British North America Act 1867)

British Crown Colonies

British Territories

The House of Commons would consist of elected representatives from each of the provinces. Quebec would send sixty-five members. The other provinces would elect members on the basis of their populations. It was representation by population, George Brown's great principle. By promising Quebec sixty-five seats, they were guaranteeing that Quebec would not be swamped by an English-speaking majority. The tiny Prince Edward Island was discouraged however, with the prospect of having only five members.

Like the House of Lords in Britain, Canada would have a second house of Parliament. It would be called the Senate. The name was taken from the American system. There were to be seventy-two members, to sit for life in the Senate — twenty-four from Quebec, twenty-four from Ontario, and twenty-four from the Maritimes. The main function of the members of the Senate was to double-check all laws passed by the elected House of Commons.

WHAT THE FATHERS TOOK FROM THE AMERICAN MODEL

From the American system of government, the Fathers chose the pattern of a federal union. In a federal union there is a central government that deals with matters of concern to the whole nation. But each province or state also has a local government that deals with matters of concern to it alone. Britain is not a federal union; it only has a central government. For governing a large country, such as the United States and Canada, a federal union was considered to be a better form of government. The federal government is sometimes referred to as the central, the national, or the dominion government.

The questions then arose: What powers should the federal government have? What powers should the provincial governments have? Here again, the Fathers of Confederation learned from the American example.

In their federation, the Americans gave wide powers to the states and limited powers to the central government. They said that any powers that were not mentioned in their Constitution automatically belonged to the individual states. The bloody Civil War, which had just ended, arose out of the issue of states' rights. Macdonald thought that this was the great weakness of the American system. This mistake must be avoided in Canada at all costs. Canada must have a strong central government, and the provinces must be kept weak. John A. Macdonald, 1864:

In framing the Constitution, care should taken to avoid the mistakes and weaknesses of the United States system. Their primary error was reserving for the states all powers not given to the central government. We must reverse this . . . A strong central government is essential to the success of the experiment we are trying.

The Fathers of Confederation purposely set out to give as little power to the provinces as possible. They made a list of the powers the provinces could have. They were responsible for education, property rights, mines and forests, the licensing of businesses, raising money by taxes (such as a provincial sales tax) for provincial purposes, and other matters of provincial concerns. All other powers were to belong to the central government.

The Dominion government would control matters such as trade, defence, foreign affairs, banks, shipping, fisheries, and criminal law. It was also given the power to tax people and could disallow any law passed by the provinces.

FINANCES

 By the British North America Act, the central government would take over all the debts of the provinces. It would also take over most of the provinces' sources of income such as customs duties. Therefore, every province would be given a sum of money by the central government every year. The amount of money was based on the population of the province. The money was called a 'subsidy'.

The British North America Act promised that an Intercolonial Railway connecting the St. Lawrence River with Halifax would be begun within six months. It also allowed for other provinces to be admitted to the Dominion of Canada in the future.

The Fathers of Confederation were careful to protect the rights of the French-speaking people of Quebec. The French would keep their own province, language, religion, and schools. Both Roman Catholic and Protestant schools were guaranteed. English and French were to be used in the central Parliament, in the Parliament of Quebec, and in federal courts. Canadian historians cannot agree, however, on what the Fathers of Confederation intended. Were they limiting the French language to Quebec? Or, did they foresee a Canada of the future being fully bilingual (two languages) and bicultural (French and English)?

ACTIVITIES

1. How did your community celebrate on 1 July 1867? If your town or city is older than Confederation try to find out how the birth of Confederation was celebrated (or mourned).
Local libraries and old newspapers will help you. The 1 July 1867 issue of the Toronto *Globe* is available from the *Globe and Mail*, Education Department.
2. Discuss John A. Macdonald's statement at the time of Confederation, 'We are all mere petty provincial politicians at present; perhaps by and by some of us will rise to the level of national statesmen.'
3. People, events, feelings and physical features could help or hinder the cause of the union of the provinces. Make two columns. Label one 'factors which helped Confederation,' and the other 'factors which hindered Confederation'. Place each of the following factors in one or other column. Be prepared to defend your choice.
    — Joseph Howe
    — fear of a Fenian invasion
    — need for a railway to the Pacific
    — George Brown
    — the geography of the Canadian Shield
    — feelings of loyalty to Britain
    — larger population in Canada West than in Canada East
    — Georges Cartier
4. Do you think that the colonies got what they expected to get out of Confederation? Explain your answer.
5. On what kind of union did the delegates decide? Why? How was it different from the American one? Why?

13
Problems for the New Confederation

The first of July 1867 was a day of celebrations, picnics and speeches. There were editorials in many newspapers predicting a great future for the new nation. But there were also editorials forecasting problems and a terrible future ahead for Canada. Ahead lay some critical years.

THE PROBLEM OF JOSEPH HOWE AND NOVA SCOTIA

One of the first troubles facing the Fathers of the new country was Joseph Howe and Nova Scotia. Nova Scotia had come into the union kicking and screaming. No sooner was Confederation in force than Nova Scotia struggled to get out of it. In 1867, the first federal election in the new country of Canada was held. Of the eighteen members elected to federal Parliament from Nova Scotia, seventeen were anti-Confederationists. Sir Charles Tupper was the only member elected to the new Parliament from Nova Scotia who was in favour of Confederation.

The brilliant Joseph Howe was the champion of the Nova Scotia anti-Confederationists. He had fought to keep Nova Scotia out of the union. Now the British North America Act had been passed, Howe journeyed once again to London, England. He was going to try and persuade the British government to allow Nova Scotia to withdraw from Canada.

Many Nova Scotians appeared to support Howe when he said they had little in common with the Canadians. Nova Scotians were a prosperous, sea-going people. Most of their revenue had come from customs duties. The anti-Confederationists thought Tupper had sold out these sources of income and their independence when they joined

Canada. Nova Scotians would end up paying for the development of the West and for railways that would be of little use to them.

If there was to be a federation, Howe thought it should be a federation of the entire British Empire. He suggested a central government in London to which all countries belonging to the British Empire would send representatives. That kind of a federation would be more acceptable to the people of Nova Scotia than union with Canada. Howe thought that Nova Scotia was too small to have much influence in the Canadian Parliament, where membership was based on representation by population.

British officials in London listened politely to Howe's request to withdraw Nova Scotia from Confederation. Then they told him very firmly Nova Scotia was part of the Dominion of Canada now, and nothing could change that. Howe knew then that he was beaten. Confederation could not be shattered. Howe returned home to Canada a dejected man.

At that moment, Sir John A. Macdonald, on Tupper's urging, made a shrewd political move. He visited Halifax with Cartier, Tupper, and the Ontario Premier, John Sandfield Macdonald, a friend of Howe and a one-time anti-Confederationist. Together they reasoned with and coaxed Howe. Macdonald offered Howe a position in the Cabinet and

Confederation announced at Kingston, Ontario.

Halifax, 1887.

a larger subsidy for Nova Scotia. This allowed Howe to save his pride, though many anti-Confederationists called Howe a traitor.

In the next general election of 1871, Howe helped Tupper and supporters of Confederation to win in Nova Scotia.

In 1873 Howe was honoured with the post of Lieutenant-Governor of Nova Scotia, the province he loved so much. Three weeks after he took office, he died.

THE PROBLEMS WITH THE UNITED STATES

The Americans were giving Macdonald additional problems. Since the American Civil War, they had been demanding that Britain should pay for the damages caused by the *Alabama*. The *Alabama* had been built for the South by the British, and it was responsible for sinking a number of Northern ships. Several important American politicians suggested that if Britain turned over Canada to the United States, it would be an acceptable payment for the damages. At the very least the Americans wanted British Columbia or the North-West, or both. That would give them a handy land link with their new possession, Alaska.

Most people in the new nation of Canada were angered and insulted by the boldness of the American demand. In early 1869, the figure of 'Johnny Canuck' began to appear in Canadian newspapers and magazines. In the Montreal humour magazine *Grinchuckle,* he showed up as a clean-cut, square-jawed character in uniform. He resembled Hollywood's idea of a Royal Canadian Mountie. In his first cartoon, Johnny Canuck, then called 'Young Canada', kicked that American rascal 'Uncle Sam' out of Canada!

The same anti-American feelings ran high on the West Coast. In the *Sentinel*, published in Cariboo, British Columbia, 19 June 1869, this song was printed. It was sung to the tune 'Tramp! Tramp! Tramp!'

> Come boys, let's sing a song
> For the day it won't be long
> When united to our country we will be
> Then the Maple Leaf entwined
> And the Beaver too, combined
> With Old England's flag shall float upon the sea.
> Chorus
> Tramp! Tramp! Tramp! The New Dominion
> Now is knocking at the door
> So good-bye dear Uncle Sam
> As we do not care a clam
> For your greenbacks or your bunkum any more.

In 1871, Macdonald journeyed to Washington as a member of a British team to discuss problems between the United States and Britain and Canada. Because war had broken out in Europe, Britain was anxious for the friendship of the United States. The British were willing to give in to most of what the Americans demanded. As the only Canadian present, Macdonald was in a very awkward position. He had to fight very hard to protect Canada's interests and get a fair deal for Canada.

In this Treaty of Washington, Britain agreed to the United States' requests for:

1. free navigation of the St. Lawrence River
2. fishing rights in Canadian waters
3. a territorial claim for the island of San Juan off Vancouver Island.

Macdonald was not happy with the treaty. He thought it was dreadful from all Canadian points of view. But he did succeed later in getting the British to pay Canada for the damages suffered in the Fenian raids. Macdonald intended to use this money to build railroads in Canada.

People in the Canadian Parliament criticized Sir John A. for signing the Treaty of Washington. They felt that Britain had sacrificed Canada's interest for the sake of making friends with the Americans. But the treaty was important because it eased some of the tension between

Canada and the United States after the Civil War. It set a pattern for future co-operation between Canada and the United States. Instead of going to war over their problems, they would talk over and try to solve them. Also, by inviting Macdonald to join the British delegation, Britain was beginning to recognize Canada's position as a nation.

THE PROBLEM WITH THE INTERCOLONIAL RAILWAY

One of the biggest tasks facing the new government was to build the Intercolonial Railway. This rail link between the St. Lawrence and the Atlantic had been talked about for years. The British North America Act had promised that the building would begin within six months after the union. The first Dominion Parliament set out at once to start the project.

The new railway began at Levis, opposite Quebec City, and ran along the south shore of the St. Lawrence River to Rivière du Loup. Then it turned southward through 805 km of New Brunswick wilderness and mountains to Moncton. It was purposely built as far as possible from the American border so that it might be safe in case of war with the United States. Then it pushed on to Truro, and there joined track already completed to Halifax. From Moncton, the Intercolonial joined up with track laid to Saint John on the Bay of Fundy.

A nineteenth-century picnic.

On 1 July 1876, traffic was opened on the Intercolonial. The nine-year-old nation had its all-Canadian rail link between the St. Lawrence and the Atlantic. Although the Intercolonial Railway did not make money, the Canadian government made up its losses. That was the price Canada paid to bring the Maritimes into Confederation.

THE PROBLEM OF ACQUIRING THE WEST FROM THE HUDSON'S BAY COMPANY

Since the early 1850s, the people of Canada had dreamed of taking over the vast Hudson's Bay Company lands in the West. If the West was turned into farms, their sons could settle there under the British flag. No longer would they have to go to the United States to find available land, now that Canada West was filling up. Many people felt the Hudson's Bay Company had held the land for too long. They began to dream of a Canada that stretched right to the Pacific Ocean.

Settlers in the Red River had sent petitions to London complaining about the way the Hudson's Bay Company was ruling their settlement in Assiniboia. They felt they did not have the rights and liberties British subjects should enjoy. They said they would prefer to be joined to the Province of Canada.

How had the Hudson's Bay Company come to control their vast amount of land? In 1670, King Charles II of England gave the Governor and the Company of Gentlemen Adventurers the rights to thousands of square kilometres of land. In 1670, no one knew just how much land was included in this Charter. The Company was to have all the land drained by the rivers that empty into Hudson Bay. All this was granted for the sum of two beaver skins for the King whenever he visited this territory! The Hudson's Bay Company named this land Rupert's Land. Legally, Rupert's Land belonged to them.

For 150 years or so, no one cared very much about Rupert's Land. Then, around the time of Confederation, Canadians began to think about settling the West. It seemed that every year Canada began to want the West more. George Brown said in the *Globe* in 1856,

If Canada acquires this territory, it will rise in a few years from a position of a small and weak province to be the greatest colony any country has ever possessed, able to take its place among the empires of the earth. The wealth of this vast territory will flow through our waters and be gathered by our merchants, manufacturers, and agriculturalists. Our sons will occupy the chief places

of this vast territory. We will form its institutions, supply its
rules, teach its schools, fill its stores, run its mills, navigate its
streams. . . . We can beat the United States if we start at once.

John A. Macdonald said in a letter in 1865:

I am perfectly willing personally to leave the whole country as a
wilderness for the next half century, but I fear if the Canadians do
not go in the Yankees will, and with that fear I would gladly see a
crown colony established there.

Macdonald feared that Britain and Canada would lose the West as
Britain lost Oregon to the Americans. Britain had claimed Oregon, but
the Americans settled the area first, and simply took it over. When the
treaty was signed to settle the border between British and American
land, Oregon went to the United States. The same thing could happen
north of the border if the land was not settled.

At the Westminster Conference a clause was written into the British
North America Act to say that there would be room in the new Confederation for Rupert's Land and beyond. Canada also sent delegates to
London, England, to see if the Hudson's Bay Company would sell its
whole empire to Canada.

Of course, the Hudson's Bay Company was not in any hurry to give
up its claims to the land, and negotiations dragged on. Besides, the
Company wanted a great deal of money — one million pounds for its
rights. Finally, a price was agreed upon. The Hudson's Bay Company
would be paid £300 000 and be allowed to keep one-twentieth of all

the fertile land between the North Saskatchewan River and the Ameri-
can border. Some day it would sell some of those 2½ million hectares
to settlers. The Company kept their 120 posts and the land around each
of them. The whole region was to be passed to Canada on 1 December
1869, and re-named the North-West Territories.

Of course, the Hudson's Bay Company continued to flourish. It still
owned its posts and millions of hectares of land. Around its old fur
trading posts, towns such as Winnipeg and Edmonton sprang up. Although the fur trading days were drawing to a close, the Company
branched out into new ventures. They built a chain of department
stores where the new settlers could buy everything from hardware to
furniture. As the old Hudson's Bay Company trading posts provided
blankets, beads, and guns, so today do the Bay department stores
provide everything for modern living.

Thus one of the greatest land deals in history was completed. Before her third birthday, young Canada would stretch almost from sea to sea.

Now that Canada had the West, it had to be looked after. Even before the transfer took effect, Canada decided the North-West Territories would be ruled by a Lieutenant-Governor and Council appointed by the Federal government. In the first step to take over the new territories, Canada sent out surveyors to map the new lands.

ACTIVITIES

1.   Outline the factors that caused Joseph Howe to change his mind about Confederation. Some of the opponents of Confederation called Howe a traitor. Was this charge justified?

2.   Draw an outline map of western Canada. Draw in all the rivers that flow into Hudson Bay. Include the river systems which flow into the western shore of the Bay as well as the rivers flowing in from south and east. Now encircle the rivers with a line to show the size of Rupert's Land.

3.   Debate: The Hudson's Bay Company got a better deal than Canada in 1869.

14
Confederation Extended

LIFE AND POLITICS IN BRITISH COLUMBIA IN THE 1850s AND 1860s

In 1856 and 1857, Indians on the Thompson River in British Columbia presented gold nuggets for goods in the Hudson's Bay store at Kamloops. Donald A. McLean, the Hudson's Bay Company official, did not know the value of the mineral offered in barter. So he sent the gold nuggets to Victoria to James Douglas, his boss of the Hudson's Bay Company. Douglas sent word back to McLean to get all this metal that he could, as it was gold.

In February 1858 the Hudson's Bay Company steamer *Otter* left Victoria for San Francisco with the gold on board. The gold was being sent to the mint in San Francisco to be weighed and made into souvenir coins.

In no time the word spread through San Francisco that gold had been found in the north. Superintendent of the mint happened to remark at the volunteer fire department, 'Boys, the next excitement will be to the Fraser River.'

Gold on the Fraser River! Men who had been digging in the gold mines of California packed up and headed north. Businessmen sold out and joined the crowd going to British Columbia to get rich. In 1858 every available space on ships heading north was booked. Men took passage on steamers to Port Townsend in the state of Washington, and then on to Victoria, before crossing to the Fraser River. The gold rush in the valley of the Fraser River had begun.

A man who was there recounted his experience:

We camped for lunch on a sand bar about 16 km from Hope, British Columbia, to cook lunch. While we were doing so, one of our party noticed particles of gold in the moss that was growing on the rocks. He got a pan of this moss and got a good prospect. After lunch, we all prospected at the sand bar and found it a bar rich in gold. With our crude way of working, we made an average $50 per day per man. We named this bar in honour of the man who washed the first pan of moss — Hill's Bar. We located this claim on the 23rd of March, 1858. I remember the date, because it was my 26th birthday.

From 'The Discovery of Hill's Bar', *British Columbia Historical Quarterly.*

Since 1849, Vancouver Island had been a British Crown colony. The Hudson's Bay Company was responsible for settling the island and bringing people to it. The Company was really interested in the fur trade and did very little to encourage settlement. There were only 253

Mule team on the Cariboo Road.

white people in Victoria in 1853, and most of them worked for the Hudson's Bay Company.

When the gold rush broke, James Douglas, the Hudson's Bay Company's Chief Factor, was Governor of Vancouver Island. Douglas was a strong, wise man. He had left his native country, Scotland, when he was barely sixteen years old. Some reports say he brought his school books with him. He went to work as a fur trader for the North-West Company. Eventually, at age twenty-seven, he became assistant to the Chief Factor for all Hudson's Bay Company posts on the West Coast.

Douglas was put in charge of selecting the site and building the headquarters for the Company on the coast. The spot he chose for Fort Victoria was near the wharves of present-day Victoria. Douglas believed that Fort Victoria should be a place of comfort and culture. He saw to it that money was spent on furnishings, that the tables were covered with fine white linen, and that everything was spotlessly clean. He provided Scottish and English magazines, as well as books for the men to enjoy. He believed that if the surroundings of the fort were civilized, his men would do their best work. In 1851, James Douglas had been appointed Governor of Vancouver Island as well as keeping his position with the Hudson's Bay Company.

In 1858, Fort Victoria was a pretty little village of a few hundred people. Suddenly that summer, more than twenty thousand miners swarmed into town. Twenty-eight hundred arrived on one day alone. Strangers piled into the trading post to buy food and equipment. They wanted salt pork, pick-axes, flour, and frying pans. The little town of Victoria was changed into a bustling city of tents, shacks, and over two hundred stores. The price of lots in Victoria skyrocketed from $50 to $1500.

The men left from Victoria for the mouth of the Fraser River on anything that would float. Fist-fights broke out for places on the steamers. Those who were too impatient to wait for the steamships set out in canoes, rowboats, or even rafts.

At sandbars along the Fraser River near the town of Yale, men began 'panning' or 'rocking' for gold. The easiest and simplest method was to pan for gold. The miner used a metal pan with sloping sides about 36 cm across. He loosened the gravel in the stream bed with his pick-axe and shovelled it into his pan. Then he filled the pan with water and tilted it away from himself slightly. Since gold is so heavy, in a mixture of sand, gravel and water, the gold sinks to the bottom of the pan. The miner kept tilting the pan until all the light gravel had

Dawson City.

washed out. All that was left was fine black sand, and if he was lucky, flakes of gold.

A faster method of mining gold was to use the rocking method. The miners would build a box about 1.2 m long. It would be wide at the top and slope in at the bottom. It was built on rockers much like a cradle. While one man shovelled sand and gravel into the box, the other poured in water to wash it through. At the top was a screen where big nuggets of gold were caught. Below that, a solid board covered with a piece of blanket cloth caught the gold that sifted through from above. The heavier gold would be caught along the bottom of the box, and the sand and the gravel would be washed out.

Mining in this way, one rocker might produce gold dust worth $100 a day. By the end of the summer of 1858, about $500 000 worth of gold had been taken out of the Fraser River area. Many of the people who came looking for gold went home then, thinking it all had been found.

James Douglas, as Governor of Vancouver Island, had no power on the Fraser River. But he believed that as the Queen's representative he had to do all he could to keep law and order. He demanded that every miner buy a licence costing $5 a month. Every boat entering British territory was charged $6. During that summer, as miners crowded

Men playing tug-of-war in Dawson City.

north, Douglas made several trips up the Fraser, when he heard there was stealing and quarreling over claims. He was accompanied by a group of Royal Engineers armed with a cannon. He told the miners that they were in British territory and they must obey British law, or be punished. The British Parliament, hearing of the gold rush, passed an act creating the colony of British Columbia on the mainland. James Douglas was appointed Governor of British Columbia as well as Vancouver Island. He was, however, expected to give up his connection with the Hudson's Bay Company. At the same time, the British appointed Matthew Baillie Begbie, nicknamed 'The Hanging Judge', as judge in British Columbia. Together, James Douglas and Judge Matthew Baillie Begbie kept the gold rush in British Columbia from being as violent as the gold rush in California in 1849.

A few years later a great new gold find was made farther up the Fraser River in the Cariboo Mountains. Once again American miners began pouring into British Columbia. In 1861 gold had been taken out of the Cariboo by the ton. The estimated yield that year alone was $5 000 000! In 1862, a British sailor named Billy Barker arrived in the Cariboo. He was late getting there, and the entire bank of Williams Creek had already been claimed. So Billy Barker headed farther up the creek. Experienced miners laughed at him as he and his friends started digging in a mine shaft. They were digging down through the earth to reach the bedrock, where they hoped the gold rested. At 16 m they hit paydirt. Billy kept on digging. Eight metres farther down he found a rich vein of gold in the rock. In the first forty-eight hours, he took out $1000 worth of gold. Soon other people along Williams Creek hit gold too. The Boom was on!

Within a few weeks a collection of shanties and offices sprang up around the Barker claim. It was named Barkerville in Billy's honour, and grew into a town of 10 000. In Barkerville, gold flowed freely. There were hotels, music halls, dance halls, saloons, gambling houses and stores. Prices were sky-high! A barrel of flour cost $300 and potatoes cost $9.00 a pound. A pint of champagne sold for two ounces of gold. A quick dance with a dance-hall girl cost $10.00.

For ten years the Cariboo boomed. British Columbia became world famous as miners rushed in hoping to strike it rich.

Governor Douglas decided that a good wagon road was needed along the Fraser River to Barkerville. And so the Cariboo Road was begun. It was to run 645 km upriver from Yale, the farthest point the steamboat could reach. The road would be almost 6 m wide, and gravel-surfaced so that even the heavy spring floods would not stop traffic.

The Royal Engineers who built the road had an almost impossible task. In places they had to blast through solid rock. They had to span the river with high bridges on wooden trestles. Where the rock did not give way, they had to build the road out over the roaring river supported on cribbings. The cribbings were huge trees piled on top of each other to provide a solid base for the road.

By the time the road was finished, it provided an easy route north for the prospectors. It also lowered the cost of goods in the Cariboo towns since supplies could be brought in much more cheaply. But more important, it opened up the entire Cariboo for settlement. Miners began to bring in their families, and they settled there. Ranchers drove herds of cattle north and began an important industry that exists even today.

The Cariboo Road cost almost one million dollars. It was more than the new colony could afford. As the gold began to run out, hundreds of people left the country. Both colonies, Vancouver Island and British Columbia, suffered with financial problems. They saw that it would be cheaper if they had one Assembly and functioned as one colony. In 1866, they came together as British Columbia.

Although conditions improved a little after the union, the people of

British Columbia realized that they would probably have to be part of a larger country if they were going to prosper. There appeared to be three possible choices open to British Columbia.

First, British Columbia could remain a British colony. This was the choice of the Governor and some of the leading officials of the province. In this way they could keep their positions of power and their prestige. However, many of the people felt that the colony was too far from Britain and too weak on its own.

The second group of people in the colony thought it should join the United States. Many of the miners who had come to the Gold Rush had come from the United States, and they brought American ideas and a love of the United States with them. But, when a petition was circulated in 1869, only 104 of 10 000 people in the colony signed it to say they wanted to join the United States.

A third choice open to British Columbia was to join the Canadian Confederation. The British government favoured this, and so did many people in the colony. Its supporters formed a Confederation League and meetings were held to explain the advantages of joining with Canada. In Canada, they could live under the British flag, have their own provincial Assembly, and elect representatives to Parliament in Ottawa. They also saw that Canada had gained control of all the Hudson's Bay Company lands right up to their eastern border.

So on 10 May 1870, three delegates left Victoria for Ottawa. They travelled by steamer to San Francisco, and there they boarded the Union Pacific, America's newest railway, and headed east. When they arrived in Ottawa, they met with Sir John A. Macdonald and his officials. They told Macdonald that British Columbia was interested in joining Confederation if proper terms could be worked out.

British Columbia asked for responsible government as the other provinces had. It also wanted Canada to take over its heavy debts, especially those connected with the building of the Cariboo Road. Finally, Canada would have to build a wagon road across the Prairies and through the mountains to link British Columbia to the East.

The Canadian government discussed the proposal in Parliament. It had long been Macdonald's dream to link Canada to the Pacific. The new province would also provide Canada with tremendous amounts of natural resources, such as gold and lumber. Therefore, Canada finally agreed to accept British Columbia on its own terms. To everyone in British Columbia's surprise, Macdonald went even further. He promised it more than it had originally asked for.

British Columbia had asked for a wagon road; Macdonald promised it a railway. The railway would be started in two years and completed within ten. The new province would be linked to the East by steel.

On 20 July 1871, British Columbia entered the Dominion of Canada.

Today British Columbia and Canada joined hands and hearts across the Rocky Mountains. At midnight last night, there were signs of great rejoicing in the city. Bells were rung, guns fired, blue lights and Roman candles burned and firecrackers snapped. And people met on the streets and shook hands with and congratulated each other, and cheered, and cheered, and cheered. . .

From the *Daily British Colonist*, Victoria, 20 July 1871.

JUDGE MATTHEW BAILLIE BEGBIE

Begbie was a tall, dignified man who looked in every way like a British judge. He was the man chosen to be sent out from England to bring law and order to one of the toughest and most lawless groups of men — the American gold miners who had come north from California.

Begbie was a 'rough and ready' person himself. He would hold court in a saloon, a miner's cabin, or, if necessary, on horseback in the middle of the wilderness. Then, after a fair trial, he would give the order to string the murderer on the nearest tree.

Begbie was the only judge in an area hundreds of thousands of square kilometres in size. His main task was to protect the Indians who resented the appearance of the miners in their land, and to keep law and order among the miners. The legend of Judge Begbie soon spread around the campfires and the saloons. It was said that he was a 'hanging judge'.

On one occasion, a prisoner was on trial for murder. It was very obvious to the judge that the only possible verdict was 'guilty of murder'. But when the jury returned, they announced their verdict—'not guilty'. Judge Begbie was furious with the jury. 'Gentlemen of the jury,' he roared, 'you are a pack of horse thieves. It would give me great pleasure to see each and every one of you hanged for declaring a murderer not guilty!' To the prisoner the Judge said, 'Your crime was a devilish murder. You deserve to be hanged. If the jury had performed their duty, I would have the satisfaction of condemning you to death!'

Often Begbie ordered the prisoners to be whipped. He explained it like this. 'If a man insists on behaving like a brute, after fair warning, and won't leave the colony, treat him like a brute and whip him.'

Sometimes Judge Begbie's punishments seemed too harsh. It must be remembered that he was dealing with a very unruly group of men. Most were armed with pistols, bowieknives, and other weapons. The fear of being brought before Judge Begbie kept many possible law-breakers out of trouble. In his colony, violent crimes became very rare and highway robberies scarcely took place at all.

In 1870 Matthew Baillie Begbie became Chief Justice for British Columbia, and in 1874 he was knighted by Queen Victoria for his work.

THE GREAT CAMEL CAPER

In the 1860s a herd of twenty-three camels were imported to haul freight into the Cariboo goldfields. That was before the Royal Engineers carved out the Cariboo Road. The trail was steep and difficult and wound along the rocky sides of the Fraser Canyon.

John C. Calbraith paid $300 each for the animals, which were imported from Central Asia. It was said that the camels were capable of packing very heavy loads. A camel could carry a half tonne while a mule could only handle about one-fifth of that. These camels were supposed to be able to live in extreme summer heat and excessively cold winters. Also, camels could survive on a meagre diet when necessary because they could live off the fat stored in their humps.

The experiment seemed doomed from the beginning. No sooner were the animals unloaded in Victoria than two broke loose and wandered for months in the lush forests. They caused panic among the settlers and the death of an aged Indian who met one on a lonely trail and dropped dead from a heart attack.

The three frontiersmen who purchased the animals from Calbraith found a full quota of trouble ahead of them. Soon they discovered that the camels were unable to travel the rocky trails with ease because their feet were used to desert sands. And their drivers did not like the camels because the stench of them stuck to their clothing. The owners hoped that the camels' long legs would permit them to wade through the deep snow. But it didn't work. Several camels and drivers were lost in fierce blizzards.

When spring came, there was more trouble. The camels spooked the mule trains and caused some of the mules to plunge to their deaths in the deep canyons. The owners of the mule trains were outraged. Be-

Klondikers making sourdough bread.

fore guns started blazing, the camel project was abandoned and the animals were sent back to Victoria. On the way, some broke loose and wandered about in the Okanagan Valley until hot-headed settlers destroyed them. The last remaining camel in British Columbia died on a farm in 1905. Only ten camels reached the coast. These were put on auction and eventually were shipped to California. Their new owners displayed them at local fairs and exhibitions.

In California the owners arranged a show which was billed as 'The Great Dromedary Race — Absolutely the Most Thrilling Spectacle to be Seen on the Continent — Fifty Cents.' However, on the day of the race, the awkward-appearing camels, frightened by the crowd, stampeded. It seemed that the camels were no better in show business than they were in hauling freight to the Cariboo gold fields!

SOURDOUGH

Lonely bachelor prospectors in the Cariboo were a long way from bakeries and store-bought bread. Yet they longed for fresh bread, cakes, and sweet things to eat. However, it did not take them long to master the art of sourdough baking. All that was needed was flour, water, and a 'starter' containing yeast to make the dough rise. As long as they kept a little 'starter' in their sourdough crock, they could produce good things to eat for breakfast, lunch and supper.

Even if the 'starter' froze it could be re-activated by warming it up and adding flour and water. Miners' cabins along the trail were always equipped with a crock of frozen sourdough. As a traveller came along the trail all he had to do was to start a fire, mix up the thawed 'starter' with flour and water, and make his bread. Then he left a bit of the 'starter' to freeze again for the next man along the trail. Stories are told of miners who took the 'starter' to bed with them when camping outdoors. This way they could be sure that the 'starter' would be ready for pancakes in the morning.

During the goldrush days miners used to make sourdough bread in the same vessels they used for panning gold. A shallow hole was scooped in the ground. A fire was lit in this cavity and allowed to burn down to coals. Meanwhile, the sourdough was rising between two gold pans. Then some embers were raked out, the pans put into the hole and covered with coals. In one hour's time the prospector had a golden loaf of crusty bread.

Recipe for Sourdough

You can do sourdough cooking once you have a 'starter'. You can make a 'starter'. In a crock or a glass jar put one cup of unsifted flour. Dissolve one package of dried yeast in one cup of warm water. Add the yeast mixture to the flour, and stir well. Cover, and store overnight in a warm place (26°C). In the morning the 'starter' will be covered with bubbles. Add another cup of flour and one cup of warm water, stir, and leave for 24 hours. Now the 'starter' is ready to use in recipes.

Sourdough Pancakes

The night before, add two cups of flour and two cups of warm water to the 'starter'. Stir well and place in a warm spot overnight. In the morning pour all but one cup of 'starter' into a large bowl. (Feed the remaining 'starter' with equal amounts of flour and warm water before beginning the pancakes.) Use a deep bowl because the batter foams up. To the bowl add two eggs, two teaspoons of salt, one tablespoon of sugar, two tablespoons of cooking oil or bacon drippings. Blend, and stir well. The batter should be thin. (You may need to thin it with a little milk.) Fry pancakes on a lightly greased, hot griddle. Serve with butter and syrup.

Vancouver, 1885.

PRINCE EDWARD ISLAND JOINS CONFEDERATION

In 1867, Prince Edward Island had turned Confederation down flat. During the next six years, islanders began to have second thoughts.

The island had refused to enter Confederation because talk of an Intercolonial Railway simply did not interest the province. It decided instead to build its own railroad along the length of the island. But the railway caused all sorts of problems and bitterness. Each little town wanted to make certain that it had a track linkup with the main line. That meant all kinds of detours and branch lines that the railway planners had not counted on. Besides, when the island government tried to borrow money, they discovered that being small and alone made them a poor risk.

By 1873, the railway was hopelessly in debt, to the amount of $3 250 000, or about $35 per islander! When the people of Prince Edward Island heard that they would have to pay heavier taxes, or join Canada, the prospects of joining Canada started to appear very good.

Indeed, Canada was still interested in having Prince Edward Island as part of the Confederation. As long as it was outside of Confederation, Prince Edward Island could be used as a base for an attack on Canada. There was also the possibility that it might be used as a haven for smugglers.

In 1873, Prince Edward Island approached Ottawa and asked if it could enter Confederation. By the terms of the agreement, Canada provided $800 000 to the government to buy the land from the absentee landlords. Canada took over the province's debts, most of which had been caused by the new railway. It promised, too, that there would be a year-round ferry boat service from the mainland to the island, as well as a telegraph service.

On 1 July 1873, Prince Edward Island joined Confederation:

On Tuesday, July 1, for better or worse, Prince Edward Island became a province of the Dominion of Canada . . . . But among the people who thronged the streets, there was no enthusiasm. A minute before twelve, Mr. Sherrif Watson stepped forward on the balcony of the Colonial Building and read the Union Proclamation. . . . The audience within hearing consisted of three persons, and even they did not appear to be very attentive.

From *The Patriot*, Charlottetown, 3 July 1873.

Less than three weeks later the Canadian Governor-General arrived on the island on a state visit. The procession passed under an archway which was marked 'Long courted, won at last!' Later, the Governor-General told a friend that the islanders seemed to feel that 'it is the Dominion that has been annexed to Prince Edward Island!'

THE ARCTIC ISLANDS

In 1880, Britain presented to Canada the Arctic Islands. There were dozens of islands named and unnamed in the frozen north. These now became part of Canada. It had taken only thirteen years for Canada to fulfill the dream of 'stretching from sea to sea', and from 'the river to the ends of the earth.'

THOUGHTS ABOUT GOLD

People have always been excited by the prospect of finding gold. Columbus sailed across the ocean looking for gold. Kings promised rewards to anyone who could change less valuable metals into gold. Here are some thoughts that men have had about gold through the centuries:

All that glitters is not gold. (Proverb)

Gold is good and learning is much better. (Proverb)

Gold — a metal men dig out of holes for dentists and governments to put back in. (Anon)

It is observed of gold that to have it is to be in fear, and to want it is to be in danger. (S. Johnson)

Gold dust blinds all eyes. (Proverb)

Where the pale children of the feeble sun
In search of gold through every climate run;
From burning heat to freezing torrents go,
And live in all vicissitudes of woe. (Chatterton)

Though wisdom cannot be gotten for gold, still less can be gotten without it. (S. Butler)

Gold begets in brethren hate,
Gold in families debate,
Gold does friendship separate,
Gold does civil wars create. (A. Cowley)

Gold hath been the ruin of many. (Ecclesiasticus)

I despise gold; it hath persuaded many a man to evil. (Plautus)

Explain what each of these quotations means. Which quotations do you agree with? Why? Which quotations do you disagree with? Why? Find other sayings about gold or make up a short saying about gold.

ACTIVITIES

1. What were the three choices open to the colony of British Columbia in 1870/1? What were the advantages and disadvantages of each choice?
2. What had happened between 1867-1873 to cause Prince Edward Islanders to change their minds about Confederation?
3. British Columbia and Prince Edward Island entered Confederation late. For each of these colonies answer the following:
    a) Why did this colony not enter Confederation in 1867?
    b) What promises, if any, did Canada finally make to cause this colony to enter Confederation?
4. Make a time chart to show when each province became part of Canada.
5. Try to make sourdough pancakes as the miners did.
6. Discuss: 'To what extent would British Columbia and/or Prince Edward Island have been better off joining the United States in the 1870s rather than Confederation?'

WILL CONFEDERATION SURVIVE?

From the very beginning, there were groups in Canada who opposed Confederation. Some were in the Maritimes. As early as 1868, on the first birthday of Confederation, the city of Halifax draped its main street in black to show its opposition to the union. At other times groups in the West complained about the union. Some people in British Columbia would have preferred to join the United States. It is possible that British Columbia would have left the union if Macdonald's promise of a railway had not been kept.

In the 1970s the strongest feeling for separatism exists in Quebec. Separatism is the desire of a province to break away from the Canadian union.

On 15 November 1976, the Parti Québécois won an overwhelming victory in the Quebec provincial election. The Parti Québécois, under its leader René Levesque, believes that Quebec should separate from the rest of Canada. Quebec would then become a separate and independent country. This decision will be reached after the people of Quebec are allowed to vote on whether or not to leave the union.

Questions:

1. Based on your study of Confederation, do you think that the Fathers of Confederation intended that any province should be allowed to leave the union? Explain your answer.

2. Réne Lévesque has said that the people of Quebec alone should have the right to decide whether or not the province should stay in Confederation. Do you agree or disagree with René Lévesque, or do you think that people in other parts of Canada should have a say in this decision too?

3. What are your feelings about French Canada and your impressions of it?

4. How would you feel if Quebec or any other province of Canada did leave Confederation? Why?

5. What are your feelings about the future of Quebec?

6. Would the separation of any province lead to war with the rest of Canada? Explain your reasons.

7. If one or more provinces left the union, would the rest of Canada fall apart? What do you think would happen to Canada?

8. Some French-speaking students from Quebec were talking with some English-speaking students from the Prairies. They said to each

other, 'We don't know you! You don't know us!' What do you think
the students meant by this remark? Is it true? How well do you know
what other regions of Canada are like? Why is it important for Confederation for Canadians to understand how fellow Canadians think and
feel?
9.   What do you think must be done to keep Canada together, one
country sea to sea?
As a class, make some 'guesses' about problems that will face Canada
after 1867.
>   a) Will French Canadians remain happy with the way they are
>   governed in the new nation? Why or why not?
>   b) Which areas of Canada will be the most prosperous in the next
>   few years? Why?
>   c) What problems of transportation will have to be solved in
>   Canada?
>   d) Will Canada be able to live in peace side by side with the
>   United States? What possible problems could develop between
>   them?

WHO'S WHO IN CONFEDERATION

A good review exercise is to prepare your own 'Who's Who'. List all
the names you can remember discussing in this unit on Confederation.
In a sentence or two summarize the importance of each name. Then
use your list to quiz other members of your class.

Collect information from newspapers and magazines on the question of
Confederation today. Watch for references to dissatisfaction felt by
regions of Canada (Quebec, the Maritimes, and West) with the Confederation agreement.
>   a) display the articles on a bulletin board.
>   b) discuss the current issues involving the provinces and the fed-
>   eral government.
>   c) make a scrapbook on the theme Confederation Today.

15
Conditions of Work

Before Confederation, Canada was largely a country of farms and villages. In 1851 only 13 per cent of Canadians lived in towns or cities. Most Canadians were farmers raising their own food and making their own clothing. They had very few machines to help them in their work. About the time of Confederation this began to change as more and more people found jobs in the factories of the growing Canadian cities.

What brought about this change in the way of living? There are many reasons, but the most important was the invention and use of new machines. This great change was called the Industrial Revolution. Machines were invented that could do much of the work formerly done by human hands and muscles. As more farmers began to use machinery, fewer workers were needed on the farms. Therefore, they moved to the growing cities and towns looking for work in the factories. At the same time, large numbers of immigrants were coming to Canada, settling in the cities, and finding jobs in the factories. The growing number of factories in expanding cities soon brought many new problems.

Conditions for factory workers in the late 19th century were much different than they are today. There were no such things as unemployment insurance for the workers who lost their jobs or workmen's compensation if they were hurt in the factory. When they got sick there were no medical schemes to pay doctors and hospital bills, nor were there pension plans to provide an income when they were too old to

Slum district in Winnipeg, Manitoba.

work. Coffee breaks and paid holidays were unheard of! All these things are fairly recent improvements in working conditions.

Hours were long and wages were pitifully low. A typical ten-hour day ran from 7:30 a.m. until 6:00 p.m. six days a week. The half-hour lunch break was not paid for. An average wage for an industrial worker in the 1870s ranged from $185 per year in Quebec to $245 per year in Ontario. Even though prices also were very low, it was barely enough to live on. Some employers were kind to their employees, but many were not. Most owners saw nothing wrong with such working conditions. Today such long hours and low wages would shock us.

Near the end of the 19th century, the Canadian government appointed a Royal Commission on the Relations of Labour and Capital. This group was authorized to travel across Canada to investigate the conditions under which people worked and lived. They listened to evidence given by both industrial workers and employers. Their report, published in 1889, is one of the best sources of information about the hardships of working people.

Probably the worst off were the men who worked underground in mines. Daily they risked their lives in poorly lit mine shafts far below the surface of the earth. Sometimes these shafts collapsed, crushing and suffocating helpless workers. Other miners developed lung diseases owing to coal dust and the dampness of the mines. It was risky and dangerous work yet miners were very poorly paid.

ROYAL COMMISSION ON
THE RELATIONS OF LABOUR AND CAPITAL IN CANADA
1889: NOVA SCOTIA

Q. You are a coal cutter? A. Yes

Q. About how many hours a day do you work? A. We generally go down about 6 o'clock in the morning and come home sometimes as early as 4 o'clock. We generally come home from 4 to half-past 5 o'clock.

Q. Are you able to tell us how much you earned last year? A. I cannot exactly say, but I can tell you how much I earned for several months.

Q. State that? A. The figures are: For April, $22.51; May, $27.87; June, $38.50; July $25.13; August, $33.94; September, $40.67.

Q. Was this what you made clear? A. No; powder, oil, doctors, school and rent were to be deducted.

Q. Did you get some work every month? A. No.

Q. Some months you were idle for the whole month? A. Yes.

Q. How much time have you worked since last September? A. We worked October fairly steady, I think, and the best part of November, and I think a little in December. In January I think I was idle altogether; in February we were idle; in March we worked.

Q. Did you get a full month's work? A. No.

Q. How many days have you worked during the present month? A. Very few; in March I earned $25 or $26.

Women and young children were also required to work long hours. Ten-hour days were a common practice in all parts of Canada. Most workers were expected to work at least half a day on Saturdays as well.

ROYAL COMMISSION: NEW BRUNSWICK 1889

MISS ELLEN MCLEAN, Operator in Park's Cotton Mill, called and sworn.

Q. In what department are you employed? A. In the reeling-room.

Q. Are many workers employed there? A. There are about twenty workers

Q. Are they mostly ladies? A. Yes.

Q. About what would be the fair average wages a week in that room for skilled workers? A. About $6 a week.

Q. How long must a person work at that particular branch before being expert at it? A. Well, about two or three years.

Q. What would they be able to earn when beginning in the reeling-room? A. One dollar and fifty cents.

Q. And then their wages are advanced according as they become more expert? A. Yes.

Q. How many hours a day do you work? A. Eleven and a-half.

Q. Do you have any time out of that eleven and a-half hours for meals? A. Three-quarters of an hour for dinner.

Q. Do you work the same hours on Saturday as on other days? A. Half a day on Saturday.

Q. What would be the ages of the youngest girls you have known to work in that department? A. Nine years old.

In many factories workers were fined as a kind of punishment for breaking the rules. Money was deducted from their wages for talking at work, working too slowly, or sitting down on the job. There were fines for theft, wastefulness, or for making a mistake. Workers who left to get a drink of water too frequently could have ten or fifteen cents deducted from their small daily wage. It sometimes happened that these fines amounted to a high percentage of earnings so that workers had little left in their pay envelope at the end of the week.

ROYAL COMMISSION: QUEBEC 1889

Q.—What is, to your knowledge the highest fine that has been imposed? A.—I believe that it was five dollars.

Q.—All at once? A.—All at once. It was imposed on a boy for having broken a roller.

Q.—Had he broken it on purpose? A.—No; it was an accident.

Q.—How much, to your knowledge did that boy earn a day? A.—That boy, I believe earned fifty or fifty-five cents per day. I cannot say exactly what were his wages. . .

WOMEN AT WORK

Women frequently had to work in the same harsh conditions in the factories as men. However, they often received less money than the men for doing the same work.

BOSS: I had a girl who could do as much work, and as good work
as a man; she gets $5 a week. The man who is standing
next to her gets $11. The girls, however, average $3.50 a
week, and some as low as $2.

Many women however, did not work in factories, but in private
homes or shops. Women could turn out at home on a sewing machine
garments such as skirts, blouses, suits, and topcoats for the big clothing manufacturers. The manufacturer provided the material but the
women had to provide their own thread, sew up the garments, and
deliver the finished products to the factory. They received a few cents
for each completed garment (for example, 26¢ for a jacket and 17¢ for
a vest). This system allowed women to stay in their own homes with
their families, but it paid so poorly that they usually had to work from
sunrise until late at night.

Sometimes a businessman contracted with the large clothing manufacturers to sew garments for a certain price. He in turn hired a few
women, often immigrants, to sew these garments in his home or shop.
He paid the women less than he received from the manufacturers. Thus
the contractor hoped to make a profit. Frequently the women worked
in dark attic rooms in conditions as bad as the factories. Quickly these
house-shops earned the name 'sweatshops'. The term 'sweating'
suggests a condition of labour in which a maximum amount of work is
performed for a minimum wage and in which ordinary rules of health
and comfort are disregarded.

In 1897, writers from the Toronto newspaper *Daily Mail and Empire* visited some of the sweatshops. The newspaper described for its
readers the conditions of the shops and the desperate situation of some
of the women who worked there.

The next shop entered was one in which a man, his wife, two
children, and a hired woman were busily engaged making
button-holes in cloaks and overcoats. For the large two-inch
button-holes they were receiving a dollar a hundred, or one cent
each; for the others they got 50, 60, and 75 cents a hundred,
according to size. They had to furnish the thread and silk themselves. The woman who was working said that she received only
$1.50 a week, and out of this paid 75 cents a week for a room.
She was entirely dependent upon herself, and had been forced to
take this wage rather than starve to death. When asked how she
could possibly live on 75 cents a week she replied that it would

not be long before she would have to give up altogether. The hours were long, from eight in the morning until six every night; incessant work; no one to talk to, for the Polish Jew who was employing her did not know much of English, and she had scarcely enough to eat. Later on she said that she had been driven to crime to supplement her wages, but she called God to witness that the fact of her working steadily week after week at whatever she could get was evidence enough to prove that she was an unwilling party to it.

CHILD LABOUR

Thousands of families were so poor that they had no choice but to send their children out to work too. Any little bit of added income a child could earn helped to feed poverty-stricken families. The smallest children were sometimes sent into the mines to work as trappers. The trapper's job was to open and shut the doors in the mine shaft to allow the coal cars to pass. This was a lonely job for a child sitting huddled in the dark for hours on end deep below the ground. For this he received about 25¢ a day.

A fourteen-year-old coalminer.

Child workers were frequently mistreated and sometimes beaten by their bosses for petty offenses.

ROYAL COMMISSION: QUEBEC, 1889

Q. Have you ever seen boys or girls getting whipped? A. Yes.

Q. What for? A. For playing.

Q. Who beat them? A. The boss.

Q. Would that be the foreman or the manager? A. The foreman.

Q.—Have you seen other children beaten? A.—Yes, sir.

Q.—Did you see them beaten worse than yourself? A.—No, sir.

Q.—Do you know of a factory where there is a blackhole? A.—Yes, sir.

Q.—Have you seen children put in that blackhole? A.—Yes, sir.

Q.—How old were these children? A.—I could not tell the age.

Q.—Younger than yourself? A.—No, sir.

Q.—Why were they put into the blackhole? A.—Because they lost time.

Q.—Who put them into the blackhole? A.—The man who kept the press.

Q.—Do the children cry out? A.—No, sir.

Q.—Were they taken to the blackhole brutally? A.—No, sir.

Q.—How long did they stop in the hole, as a general thing? A.—Some of them stopped there till seven o'clock.

Q.—When were they put in? A.—In the afternoon.

Q.—Was it seven o'clock in the evening or seven hours of time? A.—Seven o'clock in the evening. They put them in during the afternoon until seven in the evening.

Q.—At what time do the men leave the factory? A.—Generally at five o'clock and sometimes at six.

Q.—Do you mean to say that those children were kept in the blackhole after the men had left the factory? A.—Yes, sir.

Q.—Who let them out? The same that put them in? A.—Yes, sir, I think so, but I never saw him.

Q.—Was this blackhole heated? A.—I don't know, sir.

Q.—In what floor of the factory is this blackhole? A.—In the cellar.

Q.—Is there a furnace in the cellar? A.—Yes, sir.
Q.—Is the blackhole near the furnace? A.—No, sir.
Q.—Is there a window therein? A.—No.
Q.—When children were shut in there, you never heard them cry to get some one to let them out? A.—No, sir.

Children who worked in factories faced all the perils adults did. They had to operate dangerous machines that had few safety features. Frequently fingers and hands got caught in the machinery.

ROYAL COMMISSION: NOVA SCOTIA

JOSEPH LARKINS, biscuit maker, sworn:

Q. How old are you? A. I am 11 years.

Q. What is the matter with your hand? A. It got hurt in the machinery.

Q. How? A. It got caught in the rollers.

Q. What rollers? A. The rollers of a cracker machine,—a biscuit machine.

Q. How long were you working in the biscuit factory? A. About seven weeks.

Q. Was it part of your work to look after the machinery? A. No; I was taken in as a packer and was then put to work on the machinery.

Q. How much wages did they give you? A. A dollar a week first, and then a dollar and a-quarter.

Q. How much do they give you now? A. Nothing at all.

Q. How long is it since you were hurt? A. Nine weeks Thursday.

Q. And have they not given you anything? A. No; except for the week when I was hurt.

Q. Did you ask for employment? A. My mother asked for a job for me, and they said I could get a job biscuit packing; then they changed me to where the machinery was.

Q. How long were you working at the machinery before you were hurt? A. I could not say.

Q. What were you doing at the machinery? A. I was brushing the dough off as it came through.

Q. Did you lose any fingers? A. I lost one.

Q. Did you lose any of the joints of the others? A. I think I will lose a second finger.

LIVING CONDITIONS

The conditions in which the working man and his family had to live were equally shocking. To own a house was out of the question. It was almost impossible for an industrial worker to save the $2500-$4000 that houses cost. Therefore most workers rented small dwellings or shabby apartments in cheap row housing. Rent for four rooms (a kitchen plus three other rooms) was as follows:

Locality	Four Rooms
	$
St. John	3 to 6
Halifax	10
Montreal	6 to 8
Toronto	10
Ottawa	8 to 12
Belleville	3

These living quarters were freezing cold in winter and stifling hot in summer. Outdoor toilets had to be shared with several other families. There were few facilities for bathing. Diseases often spread rapidly through the crowded, filthy streets.

Not only were living conditions for the working people drab and unpleasant, they were also dangerous. Fire was a constant danger. Many Canadian cities were partially destroyed by fire during the 19th century.

By comparison with today, prices in the 1880s do not seem high.

flour per hundred weight	$3.00
turkeys, each	$1.50
potatoes, per bushel	$ .35
apples, per bushel	$ .50
butter, per pound	$ .25
cheese, per pound	$ .17
eggs, per dozen	$ .25
wood, per cord	$5.00
molasses	$ .50
tea, per pound	$ .60
tobacco	$ .50
honey	$ .25
grey cotton, per yard	$ .10
nails, per pound	$ .04

Slums in Montreal.

It must be remembered, though, that salaries were very low too. Most working class families could barely make ends meet. Holidays were unheard of. Theatres, tobacco, and even 3¢ newspapers were luxuries for many. By far the cheapest form of entertainment was the tavern. Whiskey was only $1.40 per gallon and Toronto had a tavern for every seventy adults. Even the most shabbily dressed workers felt at home in the taverns. They were welcome as long as they had money to spend. Drinking became a cheap way for many workers to forget their troubles and to escape the horrible conditions of their lives.

But drunkenness soon became a national social problem. Drunks accounted for more than half the arrests. Families who were already poor were often reduced to near starvation because fathers squandered their income on liquor. By custom, women did not drink very much liquor. The women were often seen as victims of their drinking husbands who had control over the lives of their wives and children.

Clearly the time had come to do something about the depressing conditions under which many people had to live and work. But what could the worker do? What action could he take to improve his situation?

Perhaps this would be a good time for you to have a class discussion. You have examined a great deal of evidence about working and living conditions. Put yourself into the position of an industrial worker in the 1870s. Discuss what action you could take to solve your problems.

Here are some of the possible ideas that you have probably come up with. Each has some advantages and disadvantages. Which idea is best?

1. *You could go to your boss and complain.*

advantage
If you are lucky your boss might listen to your request. He may even give you a raise in salary. If he does not listen to you you could threaten to quit.

disadvantage
If you work in a factory where there are 100 workers, the boss probably will not care if you quit. He will still have 99 other workers and can easily find someone to replace you. Many new immigrants are so desperate for a job that they will work in your place for next to nothing. Your employer may warn other factory owners not to hire you because you are a 'trouble-maker'. This process is called 'blacklisting' a worker.

2. *You could quit your job and look for another with better conditions.*

advantage
If you are very lucky you may find a job that pays more and offers better working conditions.

disadvantage
Chances are that you will find no job at all. Jobs were scarce in the 1870s. The evidence of the Royal Commission showed that conditions were pretty bad in all parts of the country. Few industrial workers could afford to quit. They had no money saved up to support them until they found new jobs.

3. *You could bring your complaints to the government.*

advantage
If you are lucky the government may listen to your complaints.

Eventually they might pass laws to force factory owners to pay their workers more money and improve working conditions in the factories.

disadvantage
Members of Parliament are likely to have more friends who are factory owners and managers than friends who are factory workers. Politicians are probably going to take the side of the employer.

In Ontario, few industrial workers are even qualified to vote in the 1870s. Only men who earned more than $400 per year could vote. Women could not vote at all. Will governments be very concerned about problems of people who do not have the right to vote them in or out of power?

4. *You could join together with other workers to form a union.*

advantage
If all workers in a factory join together and demand the same thing, the employer will be more likely to listen to your demands. There is strength in numbers. Aesop, the Greek writer, has a story about this. A father asked his sons to break a single twig. That was easy. It was just one twig. Then he asked them to break a bundle of twigs. They could not do it. That is what is meant by the slogan 'in the union there is strength'. A single worker is like a single twig. He is weak and easily broken. But together with his fellow workers he gains strength and power to deal with his employer.

disadvantage
In the early 1870s in Canada it was still against the law to try to get better wages or working conditions. Members of unions could be arrested and treated as criminals.

It is not surprising then that more and more workers began to see the value of coming together in unions. Their main purpose in organizing themselves was to improve their working conditions. As early as 1800 skilled workers of the same trade or craft joined together in Canada. Shoemakers joined with other shoemakers, carpenters with carpenters, stone-cutters with stone-cutters. Since these workers shared the same skills and many of the same problems in their jobs, their groups were known as craft unions. Unions could speak to employers with one strong voice about the interests and needs of their members.

Unions fight for better wages, hours and conditions of work. Their leaders speak for all the members. When union leaders meet with employers to talk over their problems the process is called collective bargaining. The workers try to persuade the employer to make the changes they feel are necessary. If collective bargaining does not bring an agreement, each side may take other action. The workers may simply refuse to work until their demands are met. This is called a strike. During a strike, the employer may decide to close down his factory and refuse to talk with the workers. This is known as a lockout. To stop a strike, the employer may ask for a court injunction. This is an order from a court which forbids a strike and orders the workers to return to work.

Employers, of course, did not want to be told how to run their businesses. They claimed the right to hire and fire workers and set their wages. Often employers threatened to get rid of any employee who joined a union as a 'trouble-maker'. Because they were so poor and frightened of losing their jobs, some workers were afraid to complain or join unions. In spite of the opposition to unions from employers, the union movement grew steadily in numbers. By 1872 the printers' union in Toronto was ready to test its strength in the demand for a nine-hour working day. The story of that conflict will be told in the next chapter.

ACTIVITIES

1. Look at the pictures of early industrial conditions in Canada.
   a) What sort of work is being done?
   b) How might those working conditions be harmful to a worker's health?
   c) What do you see in the pictures that could cause accidents? What would have to be done to make the factory a safer place to work?
   d) What action could workers take to improve their position?
2. Child Labour:
   a) What sort of jobs did children do?
   b) How many hours each week did children work?
   c) What would happen to their education?
   d) Why was it necessary for children to work?
3. What evidence can you find to support the workers' charge that some owners were both greedy and lazy?
4. These words have been used in this unit. Do not define the words, but use each word in a sentence or short paragraph to show that you

Slum district.

understand its meaning: union, strike, trappers, collective bargaining, fines, craft union, sweatshop, lockout, blacklist, injunction.

5.   Diary. Using the information found in the documents, write a diary of a day in the life of a boy or a girl employed in a factory in early Canada.

16
The Beginning
of Industry

Toronto had never seen a parade quite like it. It was 15 April 1872 and Canadian working people were preparing to march to the provincial Parliament at Queen's Park to demand a shorter work week. Working people were protesting the fact that they were expected to work ten hours each day or sixty hours a week. What they wanted was a nine-hour working day or fifty-four hours a week, with no loss in pay.

At noon thousands began lining up for the march. There were bricklayers, iron workers, cigar makers, blacksmiths, machinists, bakers, barrel makers, masons, and others who did not belong to any union. All of them were there to support the printers who, two weeks before, had gone on strike until their demands for a shorter working day were met. The owners of the newspapers, led by George Brown of the Toronto *Globe*, had turned down the workers' demands. Brown and the others were bitter foes of unions. Perhaps they were afraid of the combined strength of working people. They believed it was their right to produce goods in the cheapest ways. If a worker objected to unhealthy conditions, long hours, and low wages, he could simply be replaced. That is exactly what newspaper owners did. They started to hire workers who did not belong to the printers' union.

The marchers, four abreast, set out through the main business section of Toronto. Several brass bands joined the parade and hundreds of spectators lined the sidewalks to cheer them on. As they passed the *Globe* building they maintained a scornful silence.

At Queen's Park the marchers and crowd numbered about 10 000. Even though a spring snowflurry swirled around them they listened to speeches by their leaders and some politicians. 'Fifty-four hours a week is enough for any one to work!', they were told. The vast crowd of workers cheered the speakers. It seemed that labour had won a victory that day.

The Toronto Printers' Strike forced the Canadian government to act. George Brown was formerly the leader of the Liberal Party and a long-time rival of Macdonald. Now the crafty Sir John A. saw this as a chance to discredit Brown and the Liberals. At the same time he hoped to gain popularity for the Conservative Party among the workers. Macdonald quickly had a law passed in Parliament that legalized unions. The charges against the striking printers were dropped. Canadian workers could now legally form unions to better their working conditions. From this time on strikes spread rapidly as workers protested the conditions under which they had to live and work.

Another important effect of the Toronto Printers' Strike was that it strengthened the bonds between various groups of workers. In the past workers with the same special skills had formed their own craft unions. There was one for tailors, another for carpenters, and so on. Gradually various groups of craft unions began to come together in Trades Assemblies in Canadian towns and cities. Workers were realizing that if unions stood together, they could demand greater changes from employers and government.

Daniel O'Donoghue was a printer who played an important part in union history at this time. O'Donoghue was often referred to as the Father of Canadian unionism. He came to Canada from Ireland as a small boy. To help support his widowed mother, Daniel became a printer's helper when he was eleven years old. He learned the trade and became a leading organizer of the printers' union in Canada.

In 1873, O'Donoghue began a practice which still continues. He led a delegation of workers to talk to Prime Minister Sir John A. Macdonald. In those days it was referred to as a cap-in-hand delegation because of the cloth caps the workers carried. It gave the workers a chance to present their point of view to the government. Today in Canada labour no longer has to approach government cap-in-hand. All political parties listen respectfully to the ideas and opinions of union members. In all parties there are representatives who speak for the working people of Canada.

THE ONTARIO FACTORY ACT 1884

The Factory Act of 1884 in Ontario began correcting problems of the Canadian worker. Eventually, other provinces brought in similar laws to protect their workers.

By the Factory Act:

1) No child under twelve years of age could be employed in a factory except on the possession of a certificate stating his/her age.

2) No child, girl, or woman could be employed where there was danger of injury to health.

3) No child, girl, or woman could be employed more than ten hours in one day, or more than sixty hours in one week.

4) No less than one hour may be allowed for dinner.

5) Employees injured by machinery must be allowed to make up their lost time by working overtime.

6) Buildings where women and children work must be kept clean and safe.

7) Inspectors would be appointed to check factory conditions.

The Factory Act was not totally effective in improving the workers' conditions. For one thing, the government had to appoint inspectors to check factory conditions and there was a limited number of inspectors. They only had time to check the worst abuses in factories. Also, small factories that employed less than twenty persons did not come under the Act. Sometimes employers and employees made a deal to get around the Act. Sometimes, just to keep their jobs, employees agreed to overlook factory abuses and did not report terrible conditions to the inspectors. Similarly, employers were often glad to break the law and employ young children simply because they were cheaper to hire. 'Why pay a man a dollar,' they asked, 'when you can hire a boy for a dime?'

In spite of these shortcomings, the Factory Act of Ontario was a good law. Ontario was beginning to do something to solve the problems of working people in an industrial age.

By 1886 a National Trades and Labour Congress of Canada was formed to try to speak as one voice for workers. The union song *Solidarity Forever!* illustrates their belief that strength comes with a united effort.

Members of the Western Federation of Miners, Ferguson, B.C.

A new kind of union was organized in the 1880s, called the Knights of Labour. Previously craft unions were limited to skilled workers of the same trade. Now, the Knights of Labour, an American organization, opened union membership to all workers whether or not they had a special skill. Women as well as men were allowed to join. The Knights of Labour was a secret society with elaborate and involved ceremonies for its members. It stressed good health and education for members. The Knights believed in trying to persuade employers to resolve their differences with employees. They tried hard to avoid strikes whenever possible. They demanded equal pay for both sexes and an end to child labour. While they expanded quickly in the 1880s, the Knights came into conflict with other labour groups and disappeared after the turn of the 20th century.

In 1889 the Royal Commission on the Relations of Labour and Capital investigated and reported on the conditions of labour all across Canada. It discovered that employers were exploiting their workers. Workers could be fired without warning, conditions were unhealthy, wages were low, and child labour was common.

In 1894 the government decided to honour the Canadian worker. Labour Day was established as a compulsory holiday. The contribution of working people to the growth of Canada is remembered on that day.

The Child Labour Act of Ontario was passed in 1908. This Act prevented children under twelve from working in stores and children under fourteen from working in factories. A federal act was passed somewhat later.

Poor people sleeping on the sidewalk in Toronto, about 1903.

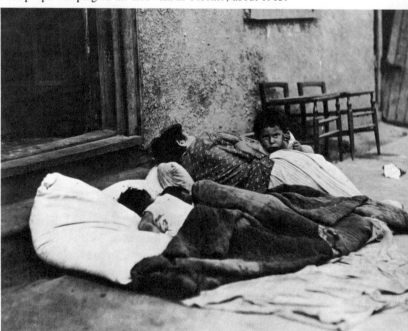

The movement of workers to improve working conditions is one of the earliest examples of social reform, or changes in the way people live. Other groups such as native peoples and women soon joined the struggle to bring about social reforms in their own lives.

ACTIVITIES

1. Discuss the first verse of the song *Solidarity Forever*. Practise this song to the tune *John Brown's Body*. Make a tape recording of the song when you have learned it. Why would this song appeal to people in the early days?

2. Write slogans and make posters to encourage workers to form a union.

3. Re-read the workers' evidence before the Royal Commission. Make two columns. In the left-hand column list specific evidence of hardship and suffering that workers experienced. In the right-hand column list the act or law which attempted to do something about the problems. Which abuses were still not solved by 1919?

4. On what grounds do you agree or disagree with this position: 'The employer who owns the plant and property may establish whatever wages and working conditions he wishes. If workers don't accept the employer's terms, they can go elsewhere'.

5. In each of the following situations, a property owner justifies his action by saying 'Although people may not like this, it is my property and I will do what I want on my property.' Which of the following do you think should be prohibited by law? Give your reasons.

    a) A factory owner refuses to hire women workers.

    b) A factory owner forbids any gathering of more than four employees during coffee breaks or lunch hours.

    c) A restaurant owner bars all people under 16 from his place of business.

    d) A factory owner orders scrap burned in open incinerators behind his shop.

    e) A restaurant owner bars all men from his place of business who are not wearing jackets and ties.

6. Discuss the statement: 'Why pay a man a dollar when you can hire a boy for a dime?' Is this statement still true today?

7. Why would factory owners be unwilling to recognize unions as legal?

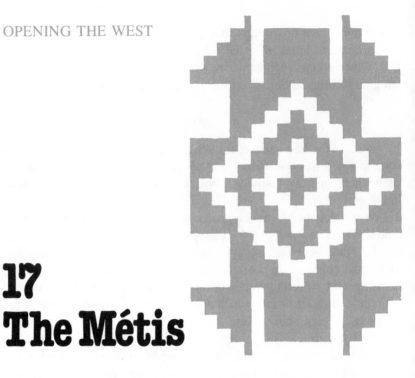

17
The Métis

The greatest land deal in Canadian history was completed in London, England in 1869. The Hudson's Bay Company sold Rupert's Land to the British government for £300 000. The British government then transferred the land back to Canada.

Even though this territory consisted of millions of hectares, not many people lived there. There were some wandering Indian tribes in the area. They lived by hunting buffalo and trapping fur-bearing animals. There were a few Hudson's Bay Company men at lonely, scattered trading posts. Their job was to buy the Indians' furs in exchange for the Hudson's Bay Company goods. Only at the Red River colony was there a large number of people. About 12 000 settlers lived in the colony around Fort Garry (near the present city of Winnipeg). Some of these people were white men. They were the original settlers or their descendants who had come with Lord Selkirk when he established the colony after 1811. The majority of these white people in the settlement were either farmers or merchants.

The largest number of people living in the Red River colony were known as Métis. The Métis were mixed-blood people — neither white nor Indian. When the white men came to North America, they often married Indian women. Less frequently an Indian man married a white woman. The children of these marriages were known as Métis. These Métis were not a tribe of Indians. Their ways were not entirely Indian, nor were they white men's ways either. They developed for themselves a whole new way of living. It was a mixture of white ways and Indian ways. They even called themselves the 'Métis Nation'.

THE MÉTIS WAY OF LIVING

In the early days the Métis formed the backbone of the fur trade. They were able to act as middlemen between the Indians and the Europeans. From their mothers, the Métis learned the Indian languages. From their fathers they learned French or English. This meant they could act as translators for both sides in the fur trade. The Métis were in a lucky position. They could buy the furs from the Indians who could not speak English or French. They could then sell these furs to the Hudson's Bay Company men, many of whom did not understand the different Indian languages.

In many ways the Métis took the customs of both worlds, the world of the white man and the world of the Indian. For example, in dress they used animal hides as Indians did, but they made them in the style of white man's clothing. Their vests and trousers were made of leather, decorated with beads and trimmed with fringes.

Métis traders, 1874.

Dancing, which the Métis loved, was also a mixture of styles. From their Scottish grandfathers, they took the 'reel' and 'square dances'. To these they added the fast footwork of Indian dancing. The result was called the Red River Jig:

Two dancers face each other 1 to 1.5 metres apart. The jig starts with a single shuffle with the right foot and then a single shuffle with the left foot. The foot is raised backward every third shuffle to miss a beat of music. Dancers may change sides or move in a circle. The object of the dance is to have perfect shuffling in a variety of steps with the change of steps being made at the end of a bar of music. A good dancer has a great variety of steps.

The winner of a contest is the one who best shows grace, perfect timing and the greatest variety of steps.

From *Cuthbert Grant and the Métis* by D.B. Sealey.

Even the language of the dances was mixed. The square dance call 'à la main gauche' became 'à la main left'. This call is still used today in square dancing as 'allemande left'. The music for these dances was provided by fiddles made in Canada of maple wood and birch bark.

There is a humorous story that shows the Métis love of dancing. The distance between two towns was once the cause of an argument. To settle the argument, a Métis was hired to walk the distance wearing a pedometer strapped to his leg. A pedometer is an instrument that measures how far you have walked. The distance between the towns was 22 km. The Métis was gone all night. When he returned, the pedometer read 157 km. It seems the Métis had arrived at the town just in time to enter a jig contest. The more he danced, the greater the distance that was added to the pedometer. Even after a 22 km walk a Métis could dance 135 km in a Red River jig.

Some Métis earned their living hauling goods in carts for the trading companies. These were the days before the railroad reached the West. The Métis developed the unusual Red River cart. These carts were very suitable to the prairie region.

THE RED RIVER CART

The Red River cart was a sturdy, two-wheeled vehicle. It was made entirely of wood. Its parts were held together by wooden pegs and strips of rawhide. The wheels were about two metres across. The

Maxim Marion, a Métis guide.

The Red River cart.

height of the wheels prevented tipping. Strips of buffalo hide could be wound around the wheels to soften the bumps. A simple box sat on the axle between the wheels. The cart was usually pulled by an ox. To cross rivers and streams the wheels were removed and attached to the bottom of the box. Then the cart was floated across the river like a raft. These carts usually travelled together in groups or trains. Sometimes there were 500 carts in one train.

Old-timers who recall the Red River carts remember their horrible, shrieking noise. Ungreased wheels grinding against wooden axles sounded like a 'thousand fingernails being drawn across a chalkboard'. The Indians sometimes joked that the reason the buffalo left the plains was that they were trying to get away from the noise of the Red River carts!

These carts played an important role in opening up the Canadian West. They could carry heavy loads, up to 450 kg. Many of the early cart trails became today's roads and highways of the Prairies.

The Indians who lived on the vast western plains passed on to the Métis their skill as horsemen and their love of racing horses. This meant the Métis were excellent buffalo hunters and spent part of each year in the hunt. The rest of their time they farmed small plots of land like their white ancestors.

JOIN THE MÉTIS ON A BUFFALO HUNT

The following is an imaginary letter in which a young man describes a Métis buffalo hunt. It took place on his trip to the Red River colony in the mid-1840s:

4 June 1846

Dear Mother and Father,

I have just returned to Fort Garry from the spring buffalo hunt. Hundreds of hunters set off in search of the buffalo. We were joined by Métis women and children in their creaking Red River carts. When a great herd of these mighty animals was spotted, the hunters jumped onto their horses. They set off in a cloud of dust towards the herd.

I wish you could have seen, Father, how the Métis rode their horses between the buffalo. They picked out the best animals in the herd, usually the cows, which have the most tender meat. Then, riding beside the animals at top speed, they aimed their guns at their hearts and fired. The huge brown beasts fell to the ground with a thud!

You can understand how dangerous it could be for the Métis hunter. If he was thrown from his horse, he would surely be trampled. What a thrill it was to experience the excitement of the hunt!

Then the Métis women took over. The animals were skinned and the hides spread out on the ground to dry. The meat was cut in strips and hung up on racks in the sun. The dried meat was made into pemmican. Perhaps Mother would like the recipe. It tastes much better than it sounds. Recipe for pemmican:

1) pound dried buffalo meat into shreds
2) mix in hot buffalo fat
3) add berries for flavour
4) store in bags made of buffalo hide
5) when hard, cut off chunks with an axe and eat raw or boiled.
P.S. It keeps for years!

The Métis sell pemmican to the fur traders who carry it with them on their long camping trips. It is light and easy to carry. Perhaps I will bring a sample with me when I come home in October.

Your loving son,
George

ACTIVITIES

1.   Compare the ways in which the lives of white settlers and the lives of Métis in the Red River settlement differed. Which life style would you prefer? Why?

2.   The buffalo was important to the Métis and the Indians of the Prairies. Do some research to discover the uses they found for the buffalo. Summarize your findings in a data retrieval chart under the following headings:

USE		PART OF THE BUFFALO
Food	Weapons	
Shelter	Transportation	
Clothing	Ceremonies	
Tools	Other uses	

3.   Study the picture and information in the text about the Red River cart. Use an old cardboard box to construct a model of a Red River cart.

4.   Collect information about modern Métis in Canada. Make a bulletin board display that describes their major problems and the government and self-help programs which are trying to assist them. How successful are these programs?

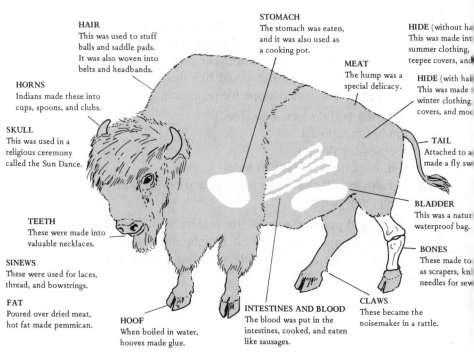

HAIR
This was used to stuff balls and saddle pads. It was also woven into belts and headbands.

HORNS
Indians made these into cups, spoons, and clubs.

SKULL
This was used in a religious ceremony called the Sun Dance.

TEETH
These were made into valuable necklaces.

SINEWS
These were used for laces, thread, and bowstrings.

FAT
Poured over dried meat, hot fat made pemmican.

HOOF
When boiled in water, hooves made glue.

STOMACH
The stomach was eaten, and it was also used as a cooking pot.

MEAT
The hump was a special delicacy.

INTESTINES AND BLOOD
The blood was put in the intestines, cooked, and eaten like sausages.

HIDE (without ha...
This was made int... summer clothing, teepee covers, and...

HIDE (with hai...
This was made ... winter clothing covers, and moc...

TAIL
Attached to a... made a fly sw...

BLADDER
This was a natur... waterproof bag.

BONES
These made to... as scrapers, kn... needles for sew...

CLAWS
These became the noisemaker in a rattle.

18
Trouble at Red River

On sunny June days in 1869, strangers appeared on the farms of the
Métis in the Red River settlement. These strangers were crews of
Canadian surveyors. The Canadian government was anxious to make a
survey of the land recently bought from the Hudson's Bay Company,
which would be turned over to the government on 1 December 1869.
These young men were carrying odd-looking surveyor's tripods as they
crossed the Métis fields. They were setting up the tripods, looking
through the glass at the top and waving their arms as signals to their
fellow workers. Then stakes were driven into the ground. This was
ground the Métis people thought they owned. They did not understand
the methods and reasons for the surveys. They had never seen surveyors before, and it greatly upset them.

The Métis were frightened when they were told by the surveyors that
the land would be marked out in large squares as it was in Ontario.
This would mean an end to their narrow river farms. These Métis
farms were laid out in narrow strips facing the rivers, as the people of
New France had laid out farms along the St. Lawrence. A typical Red
River farm ran more than 3 km back from the river. The custom was to
use a further 3 km for grazing cattle. This grazing area was called the
'hay privilege'.

Métis people were worried because they had no papers to prove they
owned their homes and their lands. The thought of settlers coming in
and taking over their lands alarmed them. They were also upset by the
rumours that the Canadian government was planning to build a railroad
right through their buffalo country. They were ready to fight to keep
what they thought rightfully belonged to them.

The Métis of the Red River gathered in a council meeting, Indian fashion. They were not sure what to do. They turned for leadership to a twenty-five-year-old Métis man, Louis Riel.

Louis Riel was born in 1844 at St. Boniface, across the Red River from the main settlement. His mother was the daughter of the first white woman in the North-West, and his father was an important Métis. Local priests arranged for the clever young Louis to be sent to school in Montreal. His mother hoped that he would become a priest. Though he trained to become a priest, he eventually gave up this idea. Instead, he turned to work in a law office and became deeply involved in the struggle to improve the lives of his people.

When he returned to the Red River in 1868, Riel was probably the best educated Métis man in the settlement. He could speak well in both French and English. This speaking ability and his hot temper made him an outspoken defender of the Métis cause. Riel was able to give confidence to his frightened Métis people.

On 11 October 1869, the crew of Canadian surveyors trespassed on the hay privilege of André Nault. Nault was a cousin of Louis Riel. The French-speaking Nault tried to stop them, but the English-speaking surveyors did not understand him. So he put a saddle on his horse and rode for help. Nault returned with Riel and sixteen Métis. Riel placed his moccasined foot on the surveyor's chain and said in excellent English, 'You go no farther.' Riel was asked later why he had done this. He said that the Canadian government had no right to make surveys before the land had been transferred to Canada. In addition, these surveys were being done without the permission of the people of the settlement.

So we see Louis Riel now coming onto the stage of Canadian history. That daring act of putting his foot on the surveyor's chain marked him as the champion of the Métis. He would speak for the Métis and was prepared to defend their rights. The Red River uprising was about to begin. Where would it eventually end?

THE RED RIVER REBELLION

One week after Louis Riel stepped on the surveyor's chain, he formed the National Committee of the Métis. The purpose of the Committee was to act as an Indian council and to decide how to protect Métis lands. Shortly afterwards, this National Committee heard that William McDougall was coming to Fort Garry to govern the new territory. McDougall had been appointed by Sir John A. Macdonald as

Louis Riel and his Council.

lieutenant-governor for the North-West Territories. His orders were to make arrangements to set up a Canadian government for the territory.

Mr. McDougall was travelling to the settlement through the United States because there was no road joining Ontario and the North-West Territories. When he arrived in late November at the border of the settlement, he found the road to Fort Garry blocked. A band of men was sent by the National Committee of the Métis to stop McDougall from entering the settlement. These armed Métis handed him a letter and told him to return to Ottawa. The Métis said they would not have any governor without being consulted first. They were also upset with the rumour that McDougall was bringing cases of rifles and ammunition with him. McDougall had no choice. He turned back to Pembina, the closest American frontier town. Here he waited for orders from Ottawa.

In the meantime, Louis Riel and the Métis seized Fort Garry and the Hudson's Bay Company there. Armed Métis slipped into the fort through the unguarded gates in groups of two and threes. Since they were the only armed group in the settlement, no one could challenge them. A short while later they set up a government of their own to replace the Hudson's Bay Company rule of the colony. It was known

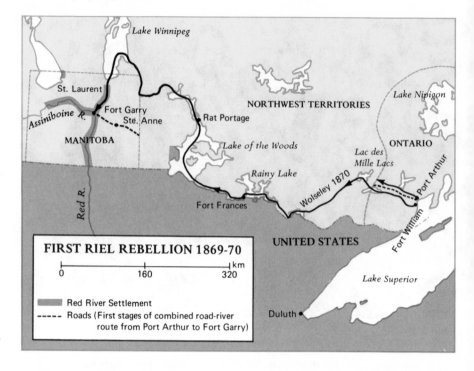

FIRST RIEL REBELLION 1869-70

as the Provisional Government and Riel said it would speak for their area in any dealings with the Canadian government. Some people in the settlement thought that this was an act of rebellion. Riel never thought of himself as a rebel. His people were loyal citizens of the Queen. All they were fighting against were two things. First, the Hudson's Bay Company sold them to Canada without telling them. Second, the Canadian government was taking them over without consulting them.

Everyone thought that Macdonald would rush troops to the Red River to remove Riel from Fort Garry. But Macdonald was too wise. The Red River colony did not belong to Canada until 1 December 1869. Canada would not accept the region before there was peace in it.

Actually, most of the people of the Red River colony liked Riel's government. Only a small group in the colony were opposed to it. They were a group of settlers who had come from Ontario and were known as the Canadians. They wanted to see the North-West become part of Canada. They had little respect for the Métis people. The Canadians sneered at the Métis and called them lazy and careless because of their carefree lifestyle. One of these Canadians was an Irish man named Thomas Scott from Ontario. The Canadians refused to accept Riel's Provisional Government. Riots broke out. A number of Canadians, including Thomas Scott, were put in jail by Riel.

In the meantime, Macdonald sent a messenger, Donald A. Smith, to explain how Canada intended to govern the colony. Smith would also report back to Ottawa on what the people of the Red River wanted. A Métis bill of rights was drawn up and sent to Ottawa. The major demands were as follows:

1. the territories must have the right to enter Canada's Confederation as a province;
2. they wanted to send four Members of Parliament to Ottawa;
3. they wanted to be able to control their own local affairs;
4. they wanted French and English languages to be equal in schools and law courts;
5. above all, they wanted to keep their customs and their Métis way of living.

These ideas were considered fair in Ottawa.

It was now that Louis Riel made a very serious mistake. He lost his temper over Thomas Scott. Scott was in jail on the charge of taking up arms against Riel's government. Scott continued to stir up trouble by striking his guards, calling the Métis a pack of cowards, insulting their Roman Catholic religion, and threatening to murder Riel. In a fit of anger, the young and inexperienced Riel ordered Scott brought to trial. The French-speaking court sentenced him to die. Within twenty-four hours, Thomas Scott was brought before the firing squad.

Why would Riel allow such a sentence to be carried out? Riel had to prove to the Canadians in the settlement that his Provisional Government must be obeyed. He also had to show the Canadian government in Ottawa that he was in charge in the settlement. Ottawa would have to work out with the Provisional Government the terms of the colony's entrance into Confederation.

It was a particularly cruel execution. Scott was led out to the wall of the prison. He was ordered to kneel down in the snow, and a white blindfold was wrapped over his eyes. His hands were tied behind his back. Rifle shots rang out. Scott was hit by three bullets, but none of them killed him. He lay there on the ground bleeding. Another Métis had to run up with a revolver and shoot him in the head.

The body of Thomas Scott was buried secretly and has never been found. For years rumours continued that his body had been sewn in

The tragedy at Fort Garry.

canvas, weighted down with chains, and dropped through the ice of the Red River.

When the news of the execution of Thomas Scott reached Ontario, the uproar started. Because Scott was English-speaking and a member of the Protestant religion, people in his home province of Ontario were outraged by his death. Newspapers throughout the province called for revenge. They claimed Scott had been 'butchered in cold blood'. The people of Ontario demanded that Riel should be hanged for Scott's murder. They even offered a reward for Riel's arrest.

On the other hand, in the Roman Catholic province of Quebec, people said Riel had done the right thing. They felt sympathy with Riel and his government because they were also French-speaking. They placed the blame for the problems in the Red River on the trouble-makers from Ontario.

The execution of Thomas Scott certainly aroused bitter feelings between the English and French. It would be a long time before the bitterness over the case of Thomas Scott would be forgotten.

THOMAS SCOTT

In 1869 Thomas Scott was 26 years old. He had set out from Ontario to seek his fortune in the West. On his way to British Columbia he stopped in the Red River Settlement to earn some money. At this time the Red River still belonged to the Hudson's Bay Company and Canadians were thought of as foreigners.

Scott found work on a road project with some other Canadians. Here he was the ring-leader in a dispute between the workers and their employer, John Snow.

When Snow refused to raise their wages, the workers threatened to drown him. Scott was brought to trial and fined £4 for assault. On leaving the courtroom Scott declared, 'My only regret is that we didn't give him a ducking and get our money's worth!'

Thomas Scott.

AFTERMATH OF THE REBELLION

By 15 July 1870, Riel's Provisional Government had worked out an agreement with Ottawa. On that day the Red River settlement entered Confederation. According to the Manitoba Act, it would be called Manitoba and would be the fifth Canadian province. Only the small settled part around Winnipeg was actually the province of Manitoba — the rest was still known as the North-West Territories. Sir John A. Macdonald had listened to the Métis Bill of Rights. The new province would be allowed to send four members to the House of Commons in Ottawa and also two members to the Canadian Senate. The people of

Manitoba would be allowed to use either English or French in schools and government.

By the bill, the Métis would be treated very well. Land, about 560 000 ha in total, was set aside for the Métis. The head of each Métis family received scrip, a certificate saying he owned 96 ha ,of land.

In time though, many Métis became more and more dissatisfied as white settlers moved into Manitoba in greater numbers. Some Métis sold their scrip for money and moved farther west. Many moved to the area of Canada we now know as Saskatchewan. Here they hoped to hunt buffalo and live the free life they had known.

Riel was pleased with the Manitoba Act. He considered that he had fathered a new province. He had won for his people the right to be represented in Ottawa. He had received the promise from Ottawa of land, French schools and French language for his Métis. Now he was prepared to turn over control of the settlement to the new lieutenant-governor sent from Ottawa.

Meanwhile, Sir John A. Macdonald decided that troops should be sent to the Red River area. The troops would be made up of British and Canadian men headed by Colonel Garnet Wolseley. They would be in Manitoba in case of further trouble. With the troops there, it would also be clear to the United States that Canada was claiming the West.

It took thirteen weeks for Colonel Wolseley and his troops to reach Manitoba. Since there was no railroad, the soldiers had to build a road as they went along. As the troops marched closer and closer to Winnipeg, Riel began to fear that he might be seized and punished for the death of Thomas Scott. When the fires of Wolseley's camps could be seen from Fort Garry, Riel's followers begged him to flee. He leaped on his horse and rode away to the United States.

In fact, some of the troops from Ontario were determined to get revenge for the murder of Scott. Some had openly vowed before leaving home that they would shoot any Frenchman involved with Scott's death. A number of Métis were beaten. One member of the Métis court that had sentenced Scott was driven by soldiers into the Red River and drowned. Riel's uncle was chased, stabbed and left on the Prairie for dead. It was obvious that Riel's life was in a great deal of danger.

On his way to the United States, Riel muttered bitterly, 'He who ruled in Fort Garry only yesterday is now a homeless wanderer with nothing to eat but two dried fishes.' It would be nearly fifteen years before the Métis would see their leader again.

Colonel Wolseley.

ACTIVITIES

1.   Why were the surveyors laying out land in squares? How do you think the surveyors felt when they were stopped at the farm? Why did the Métis resent a change in their way of living?

2.   Pretend you are a white settler in the Red River colony in 1869. You are writing a letter home to your relatives in Ontario. Tell about the problems white settlers face in the Red River area.

3.   Pretend you are a Métis person sent to Ottawa from the Red River colony. Make a list for the government of the problems faced by Indian and Métis people in the North West in 1869.

4. Write an article for an Ontario newspaper describing how Thomas Scott got into trouble with Riel. Be sure you describe:
   a) the problem of Scott's 'big mouth',
   b) what Scott, the Irish man from Ontario, thought about Riel,
   c) what most westerners felt about 'the Canadians' from Ontario who lived in the Settlement,
   d) the religion of Scott and the religion of Riel and most Métis,
   e) the way Scott died,
   f) the failure to punish Riel for Scott's death.
5. Suppose Riel had not put Thomas Scott to death but had simply sent him out of the Settlement. Do you think this might have been a better solution to the problem? Why or why not?
6. Outline the effects of the Red River Rebellion on a) Manitoba, b) the Métis, and c) the relations between Ontario and Quebec.
7. Whose side would you be on in the Red River Rebellion if you were:
   a) a Roman Catholic, French-speaking person living in Quebec,
   b) a person belonging to the Protestant religion living in Ontario?
Explain your reasons.
8. Because of the Riel Rebellion, Manitoba was brought into Confederation. Does Riel deserve the title 'Father of Confederation' in Manitoba? Explain.

DOCUMENT STUDY

In 1869, the Canadian government sent William McDougall to be Governor of the Red River Settlement. As he crossed the border into the Settlement from the United States, he was met by armed Métis. He was handed a letter written in French. Test your French by trying to read the letter. It is translated for you below.

Monsieur,

Le Comité National des Métis de la Rivière Rouge intime à Monsieur W. McDougall l'ordre de ne pas entrer sur le Territoire du Nord-Ouest sans une permission spéciale de ce Comité.

Par ordre du President,
JOHN BRUCE
LOUIS RIEL, Secrétaire.

daté à St. Norbert,
Rivière Rouge,
ce 21e jour d'Octobre, 1869.

1. Is this letter a primary or secondary source document? Explain.
2. Who wanted to keep the Governor out of the Red River Settlement and why?
3. How would you react to this letter if you were:
   a) William McDougall?
   b) the Canadian government?
   c) one of the 'Canadians' from Ontario living in the Red River?

The translation:
Sir,
    The National Committee of the Métis of the Red River notifies Mr. W. McDougall of the order not to enter the North-West Territory without special permission of this Committee.

                    By order of the President,
                    JOHN BRUCE.
                    LOUIS RIEL, Secretary.

dated at St. Norbert,
Red River,
this 21st day of October, 1869.

19
The North-West Mounted Police

If people around the world were asked what they knew about Canada, many would probably first mention the Mounties. A scarlet-coated member of the Royal Canadian Mounted Police is the mark of Canada. He is known even more than the maple leaf or the beaver. The famous force was organized on 20 May 1873. Why did it come into being?

Early in May 1873 a quarrel broke out over the theft of some horses. The scene of the trouble was the Cypress Hills. These hills are in the south-west corner of the present province of Saskatchewan. The quarrel was between a party of American wolf hunters and a band of Assiniboine Indians under Chief Little Soldier. The hunters were from Montana and were known as 'wolfers'. The 'wolfers' were men who killed buffalo and poisoned the remains as wolf bait. Because Indian dogs ate the poison, the 'wolfers' were hated by the Indians. The cruelty of their hunting method caused white fur traders to hate them also.

The battle started when a 'wolfer' accused Little Soldier's Indians of stealing his horse. (Later the horse was found — it had just strayed away.) A fight broke out when 'wolfers' burst into the Indian camp where they killed thirty-six men, women, and children. This event became known as the Cypress Hills Massacre.

When the news of this massacre reached Ottawa, Macdonald decided that it was time to act.

For years visitors to the North-West had complained about the number of outlaws and illegal whiskey traders in the area. Many of the whiskey traders were Americans. They cheated the Indians out of their furs in return for whiskey. They were destroying the Indians by providing them with endless amounts of liquor.

Fort Whoop-Up was the centre of this outlaw activity. Its proper name was Fort Hamilton and it stood near the present-day city of Lethbridge, Alberta. But its nickname, Whoop-Up, gave a much better idea of the kind of men who lived there. Most were American smugglers and traders. They flew the American flag over the fort, even though it was in Canadian territory.

The Reverend John McDougall has left a vivid description of what he saw of the whiskey trade.

Many thousands of buffalo robes, and hundreds of thousands of wolf and fox skins, and most of the best horses the Indians had were taken south into Montana. The chief article of trade for these was alcohol. In this trade very many Indians were killed and also quite a number of white men. That winter of 1873-74 forty-two able-bodied men within a few miles of us were killed in drunken brawls. These were Blackfoot Indians. There was no law but force. Some terrible scenes occurred when whole camps went on a spree, shooting, stabbing, killing, freezing, dying.

The situation in the west was becoming desperate. Parliament decided to form the North-West Mounted Police. The duties of the force were to keep peace, prevent crime, and catch criminals. It would be a mounted force of riflemen. A chain of posts would be built from Manitoba to the Rocky Mountains. The troops would wear bright scarlet coats. It had been suggested that the Indians had been im-

Fort Macleod.

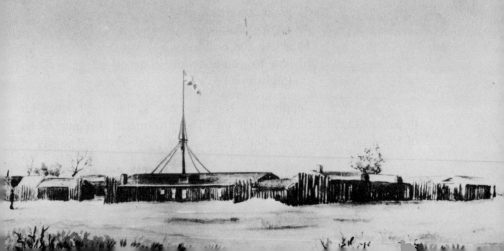

Blackfoot Indians, Calgary, Alberta.

pressed by the scarlet-coated British soldiers who had been at Fort Garry twenty-five years earlier. Scarlet tunics would help gain the respect of the Indians.

Recruiting began at once. Three hundred men were hired in the first group. Advertisements like the following appeared in towns and cities in eastern Canada.

WANTED

MEN TO JOIN THE NEWLY-FORMED NORTH-WEST MOUNTED POLICE

MEN MUST BE

1) between the ages of 18 and 40
2) at least 183 cm in height
3) good horsemen
4) of fine character
5) active and healthy
6) able to read and write either English or French

The government supplied free room and meals, clothing, boots, a kit of personal items, fuel, and lighting. The government also gave 64 ha of free land to each man after three years of good service. The pay of

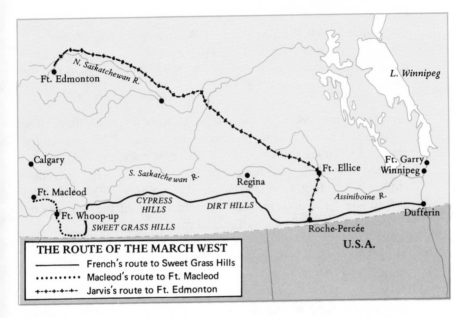

THE ROUTE OF THE MARCH WEST
——— French's route to Sweet Grass Hills
•••••••••• Macleod's route to Ft. Macleod
+-+-+-+-+- Jarvis's route to Ft. Edmonton

each constable was set at the magnificent sum of $1 a day! A sub-constable received 75¢ a day!

There was no shortage of recruits. Young men seeking adventure flocked to join the force. By summer 1874, 300 men were gathered in Manitoba to be sworn in as Mounties.

THE GREAT MARCH

The new force was faced with an almost impossible task. Three hundred men had to police six million square kilometres and thousands of Indians.

Colonel French, the first Commissioner or Commanding Officer of the North-West Mounted Police, wanted to let the people of the Territories know that the Mounties had arrived! He decided to make a long patrol with his men. They would march from Manitoba to Fort Whoop-Up near the Rocky Mountains. Here they would build a police post. Another group would head north to Fort Edmonton and set up a post there. Then some men would return to Manitoba and establish headquarters. He hoped that word would spread that 'The Law has arrived in the West!'

Plans were made for the Great March West. Many of the men kept diaries as they travelled. From these we can get a good picture of what the country was like and the problems they faced.

8 July 1874

The Great March West has begun! What a sight! 300 officers and men, 142 oxen pulling Red River carts and wagons, 93 head of cattle, 310 horses, 2 nine-pounder field guns, a hay-mowing machine, and portable kitchens!

9 July

Weather is hot. Men and horses are tortured by mosquitoes. The column is 3 km in length when there are no gaps. Col. French has arranged us in six divisions riding different coloured horses. "A" division ride dark bay horses (reddish brown). "B" ride dark browns. "C" follow on chestnuts. "D" on greys, "E" on blacks and finally "F" division ride on light bays. At the rear are the slower ox carts, wagons, cattle, and machines.

10 July

Already some men have deserted! They ran away in the night. This journey is going to be harder than we thought!

13 July

Heat is becoming unbearable. The supply wagons and oxen cannot keep up with the men and have fallen behind. So no food for us tonight.

16 July

Started to march at 4 a.m. and travelled 19 km before breakfast. Marched until 9 p.m. Men and horses are all tired.

18 July

Temperatures today over 32°C. Rained all night. Mosquitoes very bad.

21 July

Many horses are tiring out and are sick. Had to leave some horses to be brought along in carts. Not much grass for them to eat because grasshoppers have eaten everything in sight.

24 July

Sixteen days on the march and we have only covered 430 km. The worst part of the march is still ahead of us! Col. French has decided to send "A" division and the weaker horses north to the Hudson's Bay post at Edmonton. Supt. Jarvis will be in charge. They will be able to get supplies at Hudson's Bay posts along the way.

29 July

Water is very scarce. Horses are very tired and thirsty.

2 August

Twenty-two men are sick today from drinking swamp water. It was the colour of black ink!

First uniform of the RCMP, 1874.

3 August

A tremendous thunderstorm struck. All tents were blown down. Fortunately horses were prevented from stampeding. Unusually high hills are ahead of us.

7 August

Crossing the Dirt Hills. Every day tests the endurance of men and animals.

8 August

Had to stop to rest the horses today. The lack of feed and water have left the animals in a bad way. Some are dying of starvation and exhaustion.

23 August

We are coming close to the Cypress Hills. We killed some antelope. How delicious fresh meat smelled roasting over the open fire!

24 August

We are now deep into Indian country. From now on extra precautions are being taken to safeguard the camp. Have increased the number of sentries at night. Men have been told to sleep in their clothes and to keep guns ready for instant use.

Fort Walsh, 1878.

2 September

Buffalo were sighted and a few killed. This lessens the food shortage for the men. But the poor horses have nothing to eat! The prairie has been stripped bare of grass by the wandering herds of buffalo.

10 September

Weather has turned cold and wet. Each man gave up a blanket last night to cover the animals, but five horses were dead anyway in the morning.

14 September

We saw vast herds of buffalo as far as the eye could see. Many thousands of them were in sight. The prairie seemed covered with them!

16 September

Cannot go much farther!

18 September

Sighted the Sweet Grass Hills and found good grass and water. Col. French has crossed the border into Montana for news and to buy clothes and much needed supplies for us.

4 October

"D" and "E" divisions have left with Col. French on the return march to headquarters in Manitoba. God help them! The remainder of us are left in the West under the command of Col. Macleod.

5 October

Col. Macleod has hired an experienced Métis guide, Jerry Potts. Potts is the son of an Indian woman and a Scottish trader. He has spent his whole life on the plains and knows his way around! Potts is guiding us to the notorious Fort Whoop-Up! Heaven knows what we will find there!

9 October

What a disappointment Fort Whoop-Up turned out to be. The colonel was taking no chances. He had us surround the fort. Then Col. Macleod rode up boldly and hammered on the gate. We found the whiskey traders had gone. There was nobody there but a few Indians and one fur trader. We searched the fort top to bottom but no whiskey was found.

15 October

Hard at work building a police post. It is located on the banks of the Old Man's River near Fort Whoop-Up. There are good pastures here and tall cottonwood trees for log buildings.

17 October

One man died of typhoid fever. He became sick on the march. His body was the first we laid to rest in a little cemetery between the post and the river.

18 October

The fort will be in the form of a square, about seventy metres to a side. On the east side will be the men's quarters. Officers' quarters will be on the west. Hospital, stores and guard room on the south. Stables and blacksmith's shop on the north. All buildings will face inward. Their back walls will be the walls of the fort. There will be gates on two ends of the square.

30 October

The flag flies proudly over the barracks. We have named the post Fort Macleod after our commanding officer. The Mounties have arrived in Whoop-Up country!

THE BEGINNING OF POLICE WORK IN THE WEST

Now permanent police posts were established in the West. The real work of the Mounties could begin.

First, the liquor trade must be controlled and stopped. Dishonest whiskey traders were taking Indian furs and guns in exchange for a powerful drink called 'Whoop-Up Bug Juice'.

'Whoop-Up Bug Juice' was made by colouring a quart of alcohol with black chewing tobacco. It was then spiked with red pepper, Jamaica ginger and molasses. The mixture was watered down and boiled to become 'firewater'.

This horrible mixture was sold to the Indians. One buffalo robe bought twenty cupfuls. A rifle-high stack of robes would buy the gun.

Macleod was determined to bring that whiskey trade to an end. Shortly after the arrival of the Mounties an Indian came into Fort Macleod. He complained that traders had just given him two gallons of whiskey for two fine horses. The Mounties set out quickly. The traders were caught and fined. The whiskey was poured out on the snow. A first blow had been struck at the whiskey trade.

Within a short period of time most of the whiskey traders were run out of Whoop-Up country. 'Law and order' were being firmly established.

In addition to dealing with the whiskey traders, the Mounties had to win the respect of the Indians. Macleod sent invitations to the chiefs to meet with him. When they came, he treated them warmly and gave them gifts of tobacco.

He had not come to take away their lands, he told them. Queen Victoria, the Great White Mother, had heard that whiskey was bringing sadness to the Blackfoot tribes. The Great White Mother was sending the Redcoats to bring law and justice for both Indian and white man.

The Indians believed that the Mounties and Macleod had always treated them fairly. They grew to trust him and his promises to them.

The leading Chief of the Blackfoot was at this time a man named Crowfoot. He carried an eagle's wing, a badge of kingship among the Blackfoot tribes. In his younger days he led warriors in battle with great skill and success. Braves competed with one another for the right to join Crowfoot on each of his raids. He had become the most outstanding man of his race — a poet, speech-maker, and leader as well as warrior.

Crowfoot and Colonel Macleod became good friends. They liked and respected each other. Each trusted the other. Their friendship would be very important for the Indians as well as the Mounties in the future.

Crowfoot gave Macleod the name 'Stamix Otokan' (Bull's Head). Once Crowfoot said to Macleod, 'You are a brave man, Stamix Otokan. The law of the Great White Mother must be good when she has such a son as you. We will obey that law.'

Crowfoot, 1885.

The friendship between Crowfoot and the Mounties was tested in May, 1876. A messenger from Chief Sitting Bull was sent to the Blackfoot camp with tobacco. Sitting Bull was the chief of the American Sioux Indians. The Sioux had been on the warpath for some time. Eventually their uprising led to the killing of General Custer and members of the U.S. Cavalry.

Now Sitting Bull was inviting Crowfoot to join the Sioux in war. Together they would kill all the white men south of the Canadian-American border. Then the Sioux would come north and help the Blackfoot tribes kill all the whites on the Prairies. The Sioux bragged that they had destroyed strong, stone cavalry forts in the United States. They could easily demolish the small wooden forts of the Mounties.

Some young Blackfoot braves called for war. But Crowfoot reminded them of what the Police had done for them. The Mounties were friends of the Blackfoot people. They had driven out the whiskey traders and jailed the 'wolfers' who had killed Indians. Therefore Crowfoot would not smoke Sitting Bull's tobacco, which the messenger had brought.

Sitting Bull's messenger threw down the tobacco in anger. If that was Crowfoot's answer, then the Sioux would kill the Long Knives (the Americans) by themselves. Afterwards, they would come north and see if the Blackfoot tribes still knew how to fight.

The Sioux came during the winter of 1876. Thousands of Sioux men, women, and children under Sitting Bull crossed the border into Canada. Some warriors were wearing the scalps of Custer's men at their belts. They were being chased by the U.S. Cavalry which wanted revenge for the death of General Custer.

Their arrival in Canada created a tense situation for the Mounties. Inspector J.M. Walsh and a dozen Mounties had to ride into the Sioux camp and lay down the law to them. Sitting Bull told Walsh that he had buried his weapons on the American side of the border. He promised that he would do no wrong in the country of the Great White Mother.

For the next four years the Sioux stayed in Canada camped in the Cypress Hills. Eventually they returned to the United States. While they were in Canada, however, there were many occasions when the Mounties had to use great courage and firmness in dealing with them.

Once, some of Sitting Bull's men stole some horses from the Police. A dozen mounties rode into the Sioux camp and demanded that they give the horses back. Sitting Bull only laughed at the Mounties. With a sneer, the Chief said that the horse he was riding was stolen too. A policeman moved quickly. He hooked his arm around Sitting Bull and threw the Chief to the ground. The Sioux warriors looked on in disbelief. Shots were fired, but the Mounties did get their horses back!

Most Indians learned to admire the bravery of the Mounted Policemen. They knew that when they broke the law they would be treated strictly. However, if they kept the law the Police would deal justly and fairly with them.

Unfortunately there were some serious incidents of violence between the North-West Mounted Police and Indians. On the One Arrow Reserve near Batoche, in present-day Saskatchewan, a young Cree named Almighty Voice was arrested for killing a cow. While he was in jail, someone told him in a cruel joke that he would be hanged the next

Almighty Voice, 1892.

day. Believing the joke, Almighty Voice escaped from jail. He became the subject of a widespread manhunt. When he was discovered by Sergeant Colin Colebrook, Almighty Voice shot the Mounted Policeman.

For two years Almighty Voice managed to escape his hunters. He was finally cornered in 1897 with his companions in a small grove of trees. Almighty Voice was not going to be taken prisoner easily. The Mounted Police called in all their men from surrounding detachments and twenty-five constables from Regina. For two days Almighty Voice and his two companions held off over one hundred heavily armed Mounted Policemen and volunteers. Finally, when the Police advanced, the three Indians were found dead. This was one of the sad incidents in the otherwise friendly relationship between Mounties and Indians.

In the 1870s and 1880s the Canadian government decided to move the Indians onto reserves. In Canada this was achieved with almost no bloodshed and warfare. The friendship that the Mounties had built up with the Indians helped when it came time to make the treaties. The Mounties were trusted to explain what the Great White Mother's treaties were saying to her Indian sons and daughters.

PERSONALITIES OF THE NORTH-WEST MOUNTED POLICE

COLONEL GEORGE ARTHUR FRENCH

Colonel French was born in Ireland in 1841. He became the first Commissioner of the North-West Mounted Police. He believed that the new force should be well-trained and well-disciplined.

To toughen up the new recruits, he drilled them outside Fort Garry in −35°C weather. He issued salt to rub on their saddle sores until, as one Mountie said, 'We became so tough we could even sit on a cactus.'

For breaking the Commissioner's rules, Mounties were punished with severe fines. If they were caught swearing, they were fined $5. For falling asleep at their post, they lost their pay for two weeks.

Colonel French gave the Mounted Police an early reputation for discipline.

LIEUTENANT-COLONEL JAMES F. MACLEOD

Macleod had been a member of Colonel Wolseley's expedition to the Red River in 1870. He was promoted for his excellent service as a soldier.

He was appointed Assistant-Commissioner of the new North-West Mounted Police. He was trained as a lawyer as well as a policeman. All through his career he urged the Mounties always to be fair and just. He told his men that he did not like the American saying 'Wanted: Dead or Alive.' He demanded that all prisoners be brought back alive. Any Mountie who brought in a prisoner dead was sentenced to three months of hard labour in the cells.

Colonel Macleod gave the Mounted Police an early reputation for law and justice.

SUPERINTENDENT J.M. WALSH

In the summer of 1875, a Police fort was built in the Cypress Hills near the Canadian-American border. Many Indian tribes hunted in this area, which was infested with whiskey traders. The fort was under the command of James M. Walsh. It was named Fort Walsh after its commander.

Walsh had deep admiration for the Indians. When the Sioux came from the United States, Walsh encouraged them to stay in Canada. For this, he was removed from his command at Fort Walsh. The government preferred that the troublesome Sioux return to the United States.

Walsh was probably the only white man Sitting Bull ever really trusted. United States newspapers called Walsh 'Sitting Bull's Boss'. Once the Sioux Chief pulled a knife on Major Walsh. Walsh grabbed Sitting Bull by his shoulders and the seat of his pants, and threw him out of the tent. The Sioux warriors only stood by and watched.

Superintendent Walsh gave the Mounted Police an early reputation for courage.

JERRY POTTS

Jerry Potts was one of the real 'characters' of the Canadian West. He joined the Mounties as a guide and interpreter in 1874. He stayed with them until his death in 1896.

Jerry Potts.

Jerry was round-shouldered, bow-legged, and covered with the scars of many battles. He was one of the best guides the North-West Mounted Police ever had. No man had a better understanding of the Prairies. He could always find water when the Mounties were thirsty, and he could find a buffalo when food was scarce.

Even in snowstorms and on very dark nights, Potts never got lost. He knew all the prairie landmarks. Once he was looking for a pile of stones as a landmark. Colonel Macleod asked, 'Are you lost Jerry?' Potts answered, 'No, the stones are lost.'

Potts was a man of few words. The story is told of an Indian chief who gave a long speech to the Governor-General. The chief spoke for ninety minutes. When Jerry translated it, he summed it up in four words: 'The Chief wants grub.'

Early in his life, Jerry received a gun wound. A pellet lodged in his ear. He refused to have it taken out. Jerry called it his good luck charm. In 1896 the pellet worked itself out of his ear. Jerry was very upset. It was a bad sign. He was right! Jerry died the same year.

Jerry Potts was buried at Fort Macleod with full Mountie honours in recognition of his work.

THE ROYAL CANADIAN MOUNTED POLICE TODAY

The Mounted Police force in Canada is now over 100 years old. Many changes have taken place in that time. Twice the name has been changed. First in 1904 it became known as the Royal North-West Mounted Police, and in 1920 it took the name Royal Canadian Mounted Police. That same year headquarters moved to Ottawa from Regina.

Over the years the uniforms have also been altered. Today the Mounties only wear their scarlet jackets for special ceremonial events. The day-to-day dress is dark brown jackets with brown or blue pants. The trousers have a yellow stripe down the side of the leg.

The tiny little force of 300 men has now grown to 11 000. In all parts of Canada the RCMP enforces national laws. They investigate such crimes as dealing in narcotics, spying, counterfeiting, and smuggling. They still have responsibility for upholding the Indian Act. In all provinces except Ontario and Quebec they act as the provincial police as well.

You may still see Mounties on horseback on parade at the Parliament Buildings in Ottawa or in their famous Musical Ride. However, most of the Mountie's work today is done with cars, airplanes, ships, motorcycles or ski-doos. The most up-to-date methods of criminal investigations are being used by the force. These include finger-print analysis, ballistic tests on guns, and trained dogs.

The RCMP force has come a long way since its beginnings on the Prairies in 1873. From a few scattered police outposts, the force has grown to over 700 detachments (local squads).

ACTIVITIES

1.   What were the two main tasks which the North-West Mounted Police had been sent out West to do? Why were these tasks necessary in the 1870s?

2.   Describe the ways in which the NWMP built up a feeling of trust with the native peoples.

3.   Pretend that you are an interviewer for a newspaper. You have been sent out to talk with an old-timer who was a member of Col. Macleod's detachment at Fort Macleod. Write a story for your paper describing the early days in 'Whoop-Up Country'.

4.   It is 1880. The NWMP needs more recruits. Create posters to be used in Ontario to recruit new members to the force. Be sure your posters appeal to the kind of recruits you wish to attract.

5.   Discuss. 'The Mounted Police made the Canadian West a different kind of place than the American West.'

6.   Make a chart to compare the North-West Mounted Police in 1873 with the Royal Canadian Mounted Police today. Take into consideration such things as numbers of men and detachments, location, training, living conditions in barracks, rules and regulations, main duties, methods of transportation, salaries etc.

7.   Construct a model of the NWMP Fort MacLeod in 'Whoop-Up Country'. Use the description in the text, the photos, and the map to help you.

8.   Make a collage to illustrate the work of the NWMP. Include diagrams, pictures, descriptions of tours of duty, personalities and incidents in its early history.

20 Treaties with the Indians

Ninety-six kilometres south-east of Calgary a small marker stands beside the Trans-Canada Highway. It reminds travellers of a treaty signed by the Blackfoot Indians. By this treaty the Indians turned over 129 500 square kilometres of their land to the Canadian government.

In July 1977 the one-hundredth anniversary of the signing of this treaty was marked by a special celebration. It took place exactly where the treaty had been signed, 6.4 km from the highway, beside the Bow River. The original treaty was made between the Great White Mother, Queen Victoria, and the members of the Blackfoot tribes. In the 1977 ceremony Prince Charles represented his great-great-great grandmother. Direct descendants of the Indian chiefs who signed the original treaty were there too. Members of the Royal Canadian Mounted Police took part also.

Since the 17th century, both the French and British had made treaties with the Indians. Between the French and the Indians, treaties were not written down. Indians were not asked to give up any of their land. The treaties were made to gain friendship and help for the French in the fur trade.

When the British drew up treaties with the Indians, it was to obtain the surrender of Indian land. In the beginning the British paid the Indians money or goods (guns, blankets, or trinkets). When the money was spent, it was gone. Therefore, after 1818, the British started to pay treaty money as an annuity. An annuity is like a steady allowance. The Indians received a certain small amount of money every year.

Indians who made a treaty never lost all their land. They were always guaranteed reserves — some land that was set aside just for their use. These reservations were areas where the white men could not settle and where Indians would never have to pay land taxes to the government.

After Confederation, Canada made a series of treaties with the Indians called the Numbered Treaties. In all, there were eleven treaties signed from 1871 to 1921. On the map on page 197 you can see that huge areas, over two million square kilometres, were turned over to Canada by the terms of these treaties.

The Indians who signed these treaties received their reserves, money, and food in times of famine. The government agreed to build schools on the reservations. It would also provide Indians with tools for their new way of living as farmers. Axes, hoes, ploughs, spades, grindstones, oxen, and cattle were given for farming. Some Indian chiefs were presented with a horse and wagon as well as a medicine chest.

Does it seem strange to you that the Indians would give up most of their land? They had at least three important reasons for signing the treaties.

Old Fort Garry, Winnipeg, Manitoba.

Buffalo bones being gathered from the Prairie.

For centuries the Indian tribes of the Plains depended on the buffalo in order to live. In the 1870s the buffalo began to disappear from the Canadian Prairies. Buffalo had once roamed in vast herds all over the western plains of North America. A North-West Mounted Police officer on a march from Fort Macleod told that for days he was never out of sight of the buffalo. But in Canada and the United States the buffalo had many enemies. No longer were they just hunted for food. Buffalo hunting had become a sport, made much easier with the introduction of repeating rifles which did not have to be reloaded after every shot. The great demand for buffalo robes and buffalo tongues encouraged whites, Métis, and Indians to slaughter the beasts ruthlessly. It was not unusual to find hundreds of rotting bodies of dead buffalo lying on the Prairies. Only the tongue and hides had been taken.

Leather manufacturers in the East would pay $2 for each hide. Buffalo Bill Cody, hunting in the American West, killed 4280 buffalo in eighteen months. J.A. Gaff, a rancher in southwestern Saskatchewan, claimed a bigger record: 5200 in his best season in the 1870s. Thousands of hides were shipped from Fort Macleod and Fort Calgary to Fort Benton in Montana. The I.G. Baker Company of Fort Benton shipped 250 000 hides east in the single season of 1874. Other hides were collected at Saskatchewan River posts and freighted to Winnipeg.

Settlers were also anxious to be rid of the buffalo. Ranchers complained that the buffalo herds were destroying pastures that they needed for their cattle. They sometimes lost their cattle when they wandered off and joined the herds of buffalo. The farmers objected because the great beasts trampled the crops as they moved across their farms.

As railways were built across the continent in the United States, the herd was split. Many of the buffalo refused to cross the tracks. This meant that some never moved north to Canada again.

In less than ten years the buffalo were almost destroyed. In 1877 the government passed a law to try and protect the buffalo. The killing of buffalo cows between November and August and the killing of calves under two years was forbidden. However, the law came too late. By 1879, the buffalo had all but disappeared. Only white buffalo bones scattered across the Prairies reminded the Indians of the big herds of the past.

But the buffalo bones were not wasted. The bones could be sold for $5 or $6 a tonne. They were the first product the settlers could gather off their property and sell for cash. They were also the first cargo shipped out of the West when the new CPR railway was built. Thousands of tonnes of bones were loaded on freight cars and sent to Chicago to use in bleaching sugar or making fertilizer. Over 3000 railway carloads were shipped from Saskatoon alone.

It took years for the Indians and Métis to believe that the buffalo would not come again. Thousands of Canadian Indians crossed into the United States looking in vain for the herds. Métis in Saskatchewan followed rumours of buffalo herds for hundreds of kilometres. For a long time after the last hunt, Indian hunters would wake up suddenly in the night thinking they heard the thunder of approaching buffalo hooves. But it was only a dream. There were no more buffalo.

A second reason why the Indians were prepared to sign treaties was the increase of white settlement. Macdonald's policy was to fill up the West with settlers. As the railway moved farther west, more and more settlers appeared. Towns such as Calgary, Medicine Hat, Swift Current, Regina, and Moose Jaw grew up along the railway path. The presence of the North-West Mounted Police helped to make the land safer for settlement.

The Indians knew they could not stop this march of settlers into their territory. They had heard that in the United States their Indian brothers had fought a losing battle against the settlers. Indian lands had been taken, and Indians had been killed by American soldiers and settlers. Canadian Indians were afraid that without treaties, the same thing could happen to them.

A third disaster struck the Indians about this time. White man's diseases swept through many Indian tribes. Small-pox, measles, chicken pox, scarlet fever, diphtheria and tuberculosis claimed large numbers of lives. In the small-pox epidemic of 1870, between 600 to 800 of the Blackfoot population died. Even today, many of the patients in our tuberculosis hospitals are native people of the North.

The Indians felt helpless to do anything about the white man's diseases. They became more discouraged and their spirits fell lower. The treaties seemed to offer the food and care the Indians considered they needed at this time.

Facing starvation, increasing white settlement, and continuing ill health, the proud people of the Plains signed a series of treaties and moved onto reservations. In general the treaties were much the same. Treaty Number Seven between the Canadian government and the Blackfoot people is an example of how the treaties were made.

TREATY NUMBER SEVEN — THE BLACKFOOT TREATY

On the Bow River south of Calgary there is a place where the swift waters of the river are shallow. This spot, known as Blackfoot Crossing, had been for a very long time a favourite meeting place of the Blackfoot people.

It is October, 1877. Along the banks of the river teepees stretch for many kilometres. All the Indians of southern Alberta are meeting there. Chief Crowfoot and his Blackfoot Indians have arrived. Piegan Indians with Chief Eagle Tail, Stony Indians with Chief Bearspaw, Rainy Chief and the North Bloods, and the Sarcee Indians with Bull's Head have walked or ridden to the crossing. The last to arrive is Red Crow and his South Blood Indians. Now the talks can begin.

Opposite the teepees a large field tent is set up with a canopy in front of it. This is for Lieutenant-Governor Laird of the North-West Territories and Commissioner Macleod of the Mounted Police. The Indians think Lieutenant-Governor Laird is the Queen's father. His Honour Laird and Colonel Macleod are accompanied by one hundred and eight scarlet-coated Mounties on their well-groomed horses.

The Toronto *Globe* has a reporter there to observe the signing of this important treaty. From his accounts of the event, we have a good idea of what happens.

CANADIAN
Illustrated News

11. MONTREAL, SATURDAY, SEPTEMBER 9, 1871. { SINGLE COPIES, TEN C } $4 PER YEAR IN ADV

Half an hour before the opening ceremony is to begin, a gun is fired as a signal for the Indians to come together. The chiefs come forward and sit close to the Lieutenant-Governor's tent.

Lieutenant-Governor Laird welcomes the Indians and says that he has travelled a long distance from the Great White Mother (Queen Victoria) to make a treaty with them. In his reply, Crowfoot says, 'I am glad to see the Queen's Chief and Stamix Otokon (Colonel Macleod) who is a great chief and our friend.' Both sides appear friendly and respectful towards each other. Excitement grows now as they wait to hear what each side will say.

The day the talks begin all eyes are on the Lieutenant-Governor's tent where the Union Jack flies. Straight-backed Mounties are standing guard. A table and chairs are set up under the canopy of the tent. His Honour David Laird and Colonel Macleod come forward and take their seats. With them is their interpreter Jerry Potts. The Indian chiefs draw close and make a half-circle on the grass around the tent. Headmen and braves squat farther back. Women and children watch in the background.

Lieutenant-Governor Laird delivers the following to the Blackfoot tribes:

The Great Spirit has made all things. It is by the Great Spirit that the Queen rules over this great country and other great countries. The Great Spirit has made the white man and the red man brothers, and we should take each other by the hand. The Great Mother loves all her children, white man and red man alike; she wishes to do them all good. The bad white man and the bad Indian she alone does not love, and them she punishes for their wickedness. The good Indian has nothing to fear from the Queen or her officers. You Indians know this to be true. When bad white men brought you whiskey, robbed you, and through whiskey, caused you to quarrel amongst yourselves, she sent the Police to put an end to it. You know how they stopped this and punished the offenders, and how much good this has done. I have to tell you how much pleased the Queen is that you have taken the Police by the hands and helped them, and obeyed her laws since the arrival of the Police. The Great Mother heard that the buffalo were being killed very fast . . .

. . . In a few years the buffalo will probably be all destroyed and for this reason the Queen wishes to help you to live in the future in some other way. She wishes you to allow her white children to come and live on your land and raise cattle, and should you agree to this she will assist you to raise cattle and grain, and thus give you the means of living when the buffalo are no more. She will also pay you and your children money every year, which you can spend as you please.

I have already said we will give you money, I will now tell you how much. If you sign the treaty every man, woman, and child will get twelve dollars each; the money will be paid to the head of each family for himself, women and children. Every year, forever, you, your women and children will get five dollars each. Chiefs will get a suit of clothes, a silver medal, and flag, and every third year will get another suit. A reserve of land will be set apart for yourselves and your cattle, upon which none others will be permitted to encroach (trespass). For every five persons 2.59 square kilometres (one square mile) will be allotted on this reserve, on which they can cut the trees and brush for firewood and other purposes. The Queen's officers will permit no white man or Métis to build or cut the timber on your reserves. Cattle will be given to you, and potatoes, the same as are grown at Fort Macleod. The Commissioners would strongly advise the Indians to take cattle, as you understand cattle better than you will farming for some time, at least as long as you continue to move about.

Ammunition will be issued to you each year, and as soon as you sign the treaty one thousand five hundred dollars' worth will be distributed amongst the tribes. As soon as you settle, teachers will be sent to you to instruct your children to read books. I have now spoken. I have made you acquainted with the principal terms contained in the treaty which you are asked to sign . . . Go, therefore, to your councils, and I hope that you may be able to give me an answer tomorrow.

Many of the chiefs ask questions. Button Chief of the Blood tribe admits that the Police have been very good to the Indians. No longer is he afraid when he goes to sleep at night. But he still complains that whites and Police are cutting down large amounts of firewood. He thinks the government should pay for this wood and asks for still more money. He wants $50 for each of the chiefs and $30 for all others. Lieutenant-Governor Laird replies that Button Chief asks for too much. He suggests that the Indians should pay the Queen for sending the whiskey traders away and bringing in the Mounties. At this, Crowfoot and the other chiefs laugh heartily.

For a few days the chiefs and their councils talk over the terms of the treaty. During this time most chiefs allow their tribes to accept little gifts of tea, tobacco, sugar, and flour. With these rations, these Indians are eating better now than usual. However, Crowfoot does not allow any of his tribe to take any rations. Nobody will be able to say that he was bribed or influenced by gifts of any kind.

On Friday, 20 October 1877, the chiefs gather to talk about the treaty. Several of the chiefs make speeches. The first speaker is Crowfoot. He begins.

> The plains are large and wide. We are the children of the plains, it is our home, and the buffalo has been our food always. . . . If the Police had not come to the country, where would we all be now? Bad men and whiskey were killing us so fast that very few, indeed, of us would have been left today. The Police have protected us as the feathers of the bird protects it from the frosts of winter. I wish them all good, and trust that all our hearts will increase in goodness from this time forward. I am satisfied. I will sign the treaty.

Button Chief says,

> I must say what all the people say, and I agree with what they say. I cannot make new laws. I will sign.

Red Crow continues,

> Three years ago, when the Police first came to the country, I met and shook hands with Stamix Otokon (Col. Macleod). Since that time he made me many promises. He kept them all — not one of them was ever broken. Everything that the police have done has been good. I entirely trust Stamix Otokon, and will leave everything to him. I will sign with Crowfoot.

Old Sun, Head Chief of the North Blackfoot tribes, adds these comments,

> Crowfoot speaks well. We were gathered to meet the Great Mother's Chiefs here, and we would not disappoint them. We have come, and will sign the treaty. During the past Crowfoot has been called by us our Great Father. The Great Mother's Chief (Governor Laird) will now be our Great Father. Everything you say appears to me to be very good, and I hope that you will give us all we ask — cattle, money, tobacco, guns, and axes, and that

Paying the 'treaty money' to the Indians at St. Peter's, Red River.

you will not let the white man use poison on the prairies. It kills horses and buffalo as well as wolves, and it may kill men. We can ourselves kill the wolves, and set traps for them. We all agree with Crowfoot.

The following day Crowfoot comes forward and asks to be the first chief to sign the treaty. While the chiefs are making their marks on the treaty, a thirteen-gun salute is fired. In addition to the Indians, eight Mounted Policemen sign below Lieutenant-Governor Laird and Colonel Macleod.

The Indians choose as their reserve lands a stretch of 320 km on the Bow River. This strip of land is 6.4 km wide, running along the north bank only. It passes through some of the best game-hunting land, but the poorest farming land on the Prairies. In choosing this site, Crowfoot and the Indians are thinking more about hunting in the future than farming.

The Lieutenant-Governor distributes (to the chiefs) flags and uniforms, after the signing. He also presents them with medals. As he shakes hands with them in the name of the Great White Mother, the North-West Mounted Police band plays 'God Save the Queen'.

The next afternoon the Indians fight a make-believe battle on horseback for the visitors. They fire their rifles in all directions and send bullets whistling past the heads of the spectators. It is a spectacular display of horsemanship and shooting skills.

Three days are spent in paying the treaty money to the various tribes. The Indians are paid by members of the North-West Mounted

Police. It is hard work to find out the correct number in each family. Many Indians, after receiving their money, come back to say they made a wrong count. They have discovered another wife, a few more children, a blind mother or lame sisters.

The actual number who sign Treaty Number Seven is as follows:

10 Head Chiefs at $25	($250)
40 Minor Chiefs and head men at $15	($600)
4342 men, women and children at $12	($52 104)

The total cost now of this treaty is $52 954.

On the final day there is hand-shaking all around. Lieutenant-Governor Laird and his party ride off to Battleford with a great deal of ceremony. The Mounties give him three cheers as he leaves. Colonel Macleod and the Police are planning to return to their post on the Old Man's River.

SUMMARY OF TREATY NUMBER SEVEN

INDIAN PROMISES

- to give up about 129 500 square kilometres in southern Alberta
- to observe strictly the treaty
- to be loyal subjects to the Queen
- to obey the laws
- to keep the peace
- not to harm people or property
- to bring Indian law-breakers to justice

GOVERNMENT PROMISES

- hunting rights on the land as long as the Indians obey the laws and the treaty
- reserves (approximately 2.6 km² for each family of five people)
- treaty presents (money, tools, cattle, ammunition, clothing, yearly payments, salaries)

These questions have come up many times: Did the Blackfoot people understand the treaty they signed? Did they understand how completely changed their lives would be because of the treaty? Did the Indians know they were giving up 129 500 square kilometres of land forever? Most Indians say no. They say their people could not understand the idea of giving up the land forever. To an Indian, the sky, the water, the land, and the buffalo belonged to everybody. All they thought they were doing was allowing the white men to share the land and use it.

What did the Indians think they were doing in this treaty? They thought they were making a friendship agreement with the white man. In return for allowing the white man to share their land, the white man would give the Indians food, clothing, and money. The buffalo were disappearing. Settlers were coming into the area and Crowfoot knew that nothing could stop them. Crowfoot saw the treaty as a way of making sure of help and protection for his people in the future.

Only a year before, Crowfoot had refused to join Sitting Bull in a plan to wipe out the white people and be rid of them forever. Instead, he decided to stand by Colonel Macleod and the Mounted Police. Now he would trust Macleod again to look after his people. Since Macleod thought that this treaty was good for the Blackfoot, Crowfoot decided to sign it.

Within three years of the signing, the buffalo had disappeared from the plains. A terrible famine swept across the Prairies. The Indians had not yet learned how to farm, nor had they completely accepted the idea of living on the reservations. The once proud dwellers of the plains were reduced to killing their horses for food, eating gophers and mice, stewing their moccasins, and boiling rawhide for nourishment. The fact that some Indians under Chief Poundmaker and Big Bear became discontented and fierce is not surprising.

INDIAN LAND CLAIMS TODAY

In the July 1977 ceremony, Prince Charles presented silver medallions to the chiefs whose ancestors signed Treaty Number Seven. When it came time for the chiefs to speak, they told Prince Charles that all was not well among the Indian people. They asked him to help them in their struggle for justice for their people. One of the chiefs told the Prince: 'Our tribes still suffer from poverty, unemployment, alcoholism, poor health, and lack of good opportunities for education. We have become a forgotten people. We don't want it to take another hundred years before we can take our rightful place beside our fellow citizens of Canada.'

Today in newspapers and on television other Indians are speaking in much the same way. They believe that because their ancestors did not understand the language of the treaties or the importance white men would put on them, they were cheated. Their Indian grandfathers gave up hundreds of thousands of square kilometres of land in return for a few dollars, some animals, a small reserve, and perhaps a wagon for the chief. Giving up this land meant that their whole way of life was lost. The chiefs today would like to work out with the government a better treaty deal for their people.

About half the Indians of Canada are not covered by treaties. For example, Indians of Quebec and the North-West Territories never surrendered their lands by treaties to the government. As the first inhabitants of that land, they believe it still belongs to them even though they do not have legal documents to prove it. This is known as their aboriginal rights. They are demanding that the government settle their claim to the land and pay the Indians for the right to use it. Before hydroelectric plants or pipelines can be built, the Indians insist the government assure them that they will receive a large share of the benefits from the development of the land. The Indians, as original owners of the land, maintain these aboriginal claims are fair, just, and lawful. In some cases, Indians are going to the Supreme Court of Canada to prove it.

The Métis have been treated even worse. They have never made treaties with the government. They have received neither reserve land nor money at any time. Government neglect of the Métis was one of the chief reasons for the Métis uprising in Saskatchewan in 1885.

JAMES BAY HYDRO-ELECTRIC PROJECT

In 1971 the government of Quebec announced their plan to develop a huge hydro-electric project. This was to be located in the James Bay region of northwestern Quebec. When the Cree Indians heard about the project, they objected strongly. They said they had never signed treaties with the government. Therefore, the land still belonged to them.

For two years the project was halted until native land claims could be settled. In 1975 an agreement was reached with the Cree Indians. They were given $225 000 000 by the federal and Quebec governments. In return, the Indians handed over 1 061 900 square kilometres.

MACKENZIE VALLEY PIPELINE

Another project that has run into problems with native land claims is the Mackenzie Valley pipeline. This a plan to bring Arctic oil and gas through pipelines to southern Canada and the United States.
1. The building of a pipeline is complicated because the Indian and Inuit peoples of the North have never signed treaties with the government. The building of the pipeline along 4200 km of the Mackenzie

INDIAN TREATIES

-----Present Provincial boundaries

TREATY NO. 11
1921

HUDSON
BAY

TREATY NO. 8
1899

TREATY NO. 10
1906–1907

TREATY NO. 5
1875

TREATY NO. 9
1905

TREATY NO. 6
1876–1899

ROCKY MOUNTAINS

TREATY NO. 7
1877

TREATY NO. 4
1874

TREATY NO. 2
1871

TREATY NO. 3
1873

TREATY NO. 1 1871

MAP STUDY

1. Examine the location of the areas covered by each of the numbered treaties. Identify the parts of the present-day provinces surrendered by each treaty.

2. Examine the dates when the treaties were signed. What does this suggest to you about the signing of the treaties and the opening of the West?

3. Estimate what portion of the land was kept as reserves for the Indians.

River Valley could change life in the North forever. Inuit people living along the Arctic coast, and Indian people in the river valley, have been here for centuries, long before white men came. They hunted caribou, caught fish to eat, and trapped animals for fur. Many people still live off the land in the old way.

2. Before any pipelines are built, native people want their land claims settled. They also want to be sure that their land will not be destroyed through pollution. In addition, they want their share of jobs and improved living conditions that may come with the building of the pipelines. Building a pipeline would bring with it many changes. People from the South would come into the North to help build it. Roads and airstrips would have to be built; power lines would have to be put up; processing plants would have to be built to prepare the gas to move through the pipe. Perhaps even a railway would follow.

3. Justice Thomas Berger was asked by the government of Canada to talk to the people of the north to see how they felt about the building of the Mackenzie Valley Pipeline. He travelled to each of the thirty-two communities in the North-West Territories that might be affected by the pipeline. In 1977 he presented his report. In it he urged that native land claims be settled before any beginning was made on the pipeline.

ACTIVITIES

1. Re-read the promises Governor Laird made to the Indians in Treaty 7. Make a list of the treaty presents the Indians received. What does this list tell about the things the Indians valued? How did the Indians plan to use these goods in the future?

2. How do you think the Blackfoot tribes felt after signing Treaty No. 7? Imagine you are a descendant of an Indian who signed this treaty. How would you feel about the treaty your ancestor signed and why?

3. What would be the long-term effects of the numbered treaties on the Indian way of life?

4. Pretend you are Crowfoot. Write a story in which you describe your reasons for deciding to sign the treaty.

5. Explain: 'The rapid disappearance of the buffalo herds changed the Indian and Métis way of life.'

6. Describe the white man's killing of the buffalo. Do you consider this a sport as they did?

7. Collect newspaper and magazine clippings on aboriginal rights

The Mackenzie Valley pipeline.

and Indian land claims. (The Mackenzie Valley pipeline and the James Bay project are possible topics.) As a group project make a large scrapbook for all your clippings. You might like to write letters to the editor of local newspapers expressing your opinions about native land claims.

8.   Debate: Treaties signed by the Indians were fair.

9.   In western Canada, the Indians were settled onto reserves without the bloodshed that happened in the United States. Some people say that this was largely owing to the help and presence of the North-West Mounted Police. Explain what they mean.

10.   What effect will the building of the Mackenzie Valley pipeline have on the lives of the native people? Compare these to the effects on the native people of the building of the CPR.

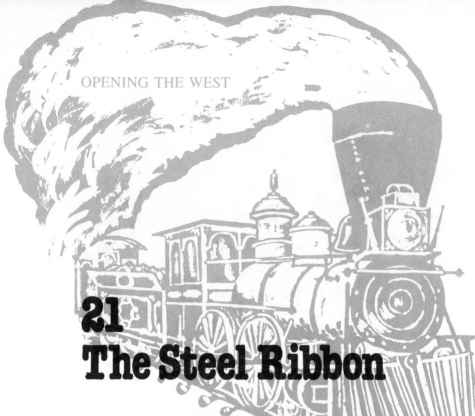

21
The Steel Ribbon

Suppose you were taking a trip from the east coast to the west coast. If you were in a hurry, you might decide to travel by air. But, if you really wanted to experience Canada and see the countryside, a good way to go would be by train.

You can depart for Vancouver from Saint John, New Brunswick, on Sunday night at 8:50. When you are ready for bed, the porter shows you to your berth. You probably think it is more fun to sleep in the top bunk. If you do, you climb up a short ladder. Your bed is already made up with sheets, blankets and pillows. In the morning you have your breakfast in the dining car, and at 8:50 a.m. you pull into the Montreal station.

There is a short stop-over in Montreal and then at 11:00 a.m. you board the luxury train 'The Canadian.' It is equipped with a scenic dome-car where you can get an excellent view of the countryside as it slips by. You are on your way to Vancouver — 4633 km away. By 1:25 p.m. you are in the capital city of Ottawa. The afternoon and evening take you through the mining regions of northern Ontario. At night as you sleep the train roars past the lakes, rocks, and forests around Lake Superior. Tuesday night at 9:15 you arrive in Winnipeg, the 'Gateway to the Prairies'.

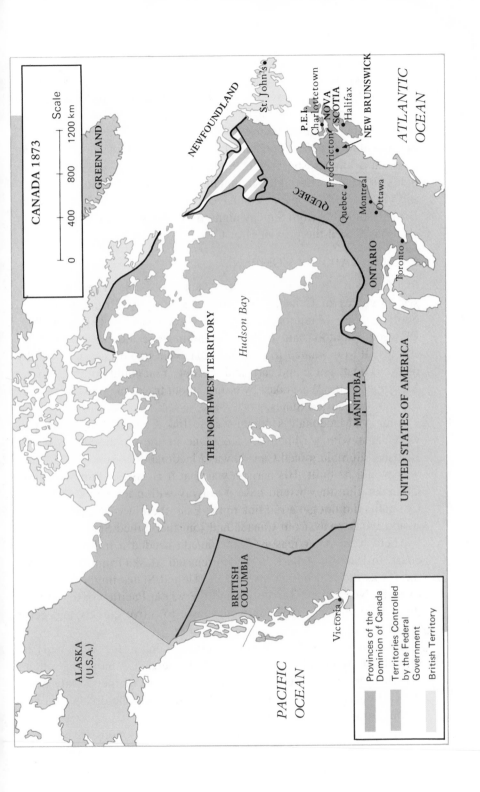

CANADA 1873

Scale

0   400   800   1200 km

GREENLAND

NEWFOUNDLAND

St. John's

P.E.I.
Charlottetown
NOVA
SCOTIA
Halifax
Fredericton
NEW BRUNSWICK

ATLANTIC
OCEAN

QUEBEC

Quebec
Montreal
Ottawa

ONTARIO

Toronto

Hudson Bay

THE NORTHWEST TERRITORY

MANITOBA

UNITED STATES OF AMERICA

BRITISH
COLUMBIA

ALASKA
(U.S.A.)

Victoria

PACIFIC
OCEAN

Provinces of the
Dominion of Canada

Territories Controlled
by the Federal
Government

British Territory

The next day you travel across the flat Prairies through Regina and Calgary, where you arrive at 12:20 p.m. Wednesday afternoon. Now the train begins its climb through the mountains. This is when you want to be in the dome-car to see the majestic mountain sights. The scenery is really breath-taking. At times the train is hugging the side of the mountains. A few moments later you are crossing over a roaring river on a high trestle bridge. Suddenly everything outside becomes black as you roar through a mountain tunnel. At 8:25 Thursday morning you reach Vancouver. You have travelled from New Brunswick to British Columbia from Sunday night to Thursday morning. The road of steel has linked the provinces of Canada together.

PACIFIC RAILWAY COMPANY

In 1871 such a journey would have been impossible. There were only six provinces in Canada: Ontario, Quebec, New Brunswick, Nova Scotia, a tiny Manitoba, and on the west coast, British Columbia. Between Manitoba and British Columbia were the North-West Territories. If you wanted to cross Canada, you would have to travel by railway, boat, horse and cart, and on foot. You could not go from the Maritimes to the West coast by train without travelling most of the way through the United States.

John A. Macdonald's dream was to link Canada's east coast and west coast with a ribbon of steel. One of the conditions on which British Columbia joined Canada was Macdonald's promise that a railway would be built. His bargain was that if British Columbia entered Confederation they would have a railway within ten years. If British Columbia did not get a rail link to the East, there was a good chance it would break away from Canada and join the United States.

There were other reasons why Canada needed a railroad coast to coast. In 1867 the Americans had purchased Alaska from Russia. Now there was the real possibility that the United States might try to take over the North-West Territories and the whole Pacific coast. To hold those western lands, Canada would have to move quickly and get a railway built.

Sir John A. saw that the empty fertile plains in the West must be settled. But to do this, a railway would be needed to move the settlers West and to bring their farm products to eastern markets. Only when the east coast was linked to the west coast would the dream of a real union 'from sea to sea' come true.

After the election of 1872, Macdonald and the Conservatives turned

Surveyors on the Prairie.

their attention to railway building. The 'Intercolonial Railway' linking Ontario and Quebec to New Brunswick and Nova Scotia still had to be finished. This had been decided on at the time of Confederation and was begun by the first Canadian parliament. Now Macdonald was looking for a group of private businessmen to take on the task of building the railway to the West.

And what a task that would be! Surveyors would be needed to find the best route through swamps, forests, mountains, and prairies. It would take expert engineers to build bridges and blast tunnels. Thousands of workers would be needed to put down the track. Above all else, it would cost a lot of money.

A group of businessmen under Sir Hugh Allan formed the Canadian Pacific Railway Company to do this job. Allan was rumoured to be the richest man in Canada.

A man named Sandford Fleming had been hired as chief engineer to make the surveys and select the best route for the railroad. However, before much work was actually done, the whole project came crashing down.

THE PACIFIC SCANDAL

Some secret papers were stolen from Sir Hugh Allan by a former employee. These were turned over to the Liberal Party. People said that these secret papers proved that Allan and his friends had given large amounts of money to Macdonald. The Liberals charged that $350 000 had been turned over to Macdonald's government. It looked as if Allan was buying the right for his company to build the railway.

The Conservatives admitted that Allan had given their party $350 000 during the election campaign of 1872. However, they claimed that it was a custom for all political parties to get gifts of money from their friends. The Liberals called the gift of money a bribe. Many Canadians agreed and named the event the 'Pacific Scandal'. The scandal forced the Conservatives to resign. For the time being, it ruined the hopes of the railway company.

It appeared that the railway to the west coast would never be built. It also looked as if Sir John A. Macdonald, the Father of Confederation, would end his career in disgrace.

For the next five years Alexander Mackenzie was the Prime Minister. The Liberal Party was the government in Canada. Sir John A. was the Leader of the Opposition. The Liberals had never been very enthusiastic about the building of a railway. They called it one of Sir John A.'s wild schemes. Liberals thought it was far too expensive for such a young country as Canada to undertake. Their government decided not to spend large amounts of money. They planned to build the railway bit by bit when the country could afford it.

During the Mackenzie years a great depression set in. The hard times were not only found in Canada, but throughout the world. Crops

Sandford Fleming, 1895.

were attacked by insects like weevils, grasshoppers, and potato bugs. Many new small Canadian businesses ran out of money. They could not compete with cheaper goods brought in from the United States. This depression was not the fault of the Liberal government. But when people are unhappy because crops and businesses are poor, they often blame the government.

In the election of 1878, Macdonald said he had a 'National Policy' that would solve the country's problems. His plan was this. Keep cheaper American goods out of Canada. Encourage Canadians to buy goods made by other Canadians. Fill the rich prairie lands with settlers. Let them buy manufactured goods made in eastern Canada. Let them sell their agricultural products to eastern Canadians. Encourage them to do all this by building an east-west railway.

The people of Canada liked the idea of the National Policy. In 1878 Macdonald was back in power. The railway project was on again! In 1880 George Stephen and Donald A. Smith formed a company to build the railroad. This new company was also called the Canadian Pacific Railway Company.

Stephen and Smith worked out a deal with the Conservative government. In return for building a railway line, the company would own and operate it. In addition, the government would give the company 10 000 000 ha of land. This land would be sold later to settlers to raise money for the company. Also, the 1100 km of railway lines that had already been finished were transferred to the Canadian Pacific Railway Company.

The Conservative government granted the company a twenty-year monopoly. Having a monopoly meant that for twenty years no railway could be built south of the Canadian Pacific Railway lines. This monopoly was very important to the railway company. It meant that no other competing railroad that might connect with American lines would be permitted. Thus the Canadian Pacific would have complete control of all east-west rail traffic in the southern part of the Prairies for twenty years.

Another term of the contract made with the Canadian Pacific was that all materials, such as steel tracks and spikes, could be brought into Canada free of taxes. In addition, Canadian Pacific stations, sidings and land on which the lines were built were to be tax-free forever.

In return, the railway company promised to complete the line to the west coast within ten years. About 3040 km were yet to be built.

THREE REMARKABLE MEN

GEORGE STEPHEN

The President of the Canadian Pacific was the remarkable man, George Stephen. He was a Scot who came to Canada when he was twenty-one. He began to earn his own living in the cloth business at age ten.

Some people called him a genius at making money. He soon built up a small fortune until he was one of the richest men in Montreal. He was President of the Bank of Montreal by the time he was fifty. He lived in a fine house, wore elegant clothes, and moved in the highest society.

More important still, Stephen knew most of the big businessmen of Europe and North America. He hoped to use his rich contacts to raise the money to finance the railway.

DONALD A. SMITH

Donald Smith was Stephen's cousin and business partner. Unlike Stephen, he appeared shaggy and weather-worn. He looked like an outdoor man; in fact, he had spent most of his life in Canada working for the Hudson's Bay Company.

His first job with the Hudson's Bay Company was counting muskrat skins. For a while he was teased as the 'gloveless greenhorn' from Scotland because he tried to handle the skins without wearing gloves. He did not know that the rough muskrat hides would tear his hands badly. However, he did go on to learn this and all he could about the fur trade. For more than twenty years Smith was isolated in the wilderness of Labrador. While there, he saved and invested his money. By the time he moved to Montreal he had become a very rich man.

Smith was sent to the West by Macdonald in 1870 to help work out a settlement with Louis Riel over the Red River Rebellion. Later, between 1871 and 1873, he became a member of parliament for the new province of Manitoba.

With his cousin, George Stephen, he made a fortune by buying an American railway at a bargain price. Now these two Scots were ready to risk their money again in the building of a railway to British Columbia.

WILLIAM CORNELIUS VAN HORNE

The Canadian Pacific Railway brought in a third remarkable man. He was William Van Horne, who was given the gigantic job of supervis-

George Stephen, 1871.

W. C. Van Horne.

ing the whole construction process. He was certainly the right man for the job.

Van Horne was an American born in Illinois. He began his railway career at age fourteen as an office boy. Within a year he had mastered Morse Code and become a telegraph operator. At twenty-one he was a ticket agent; at twenty-four a train dispatcher; at twenty-five, a superintendent of telegraphs; and at twenty-eight, the general superintendent of the railway. He achieved his success more by ambition, hard work, and ability than by good luck.

When Van Horne was eighteen the general superintendent of the railway visited the little town where he was working. At that moment Van Horne made up his mind that someday he himself would be superintendent:

I found myself wondering if even I might not somehow become a General Superintendent and travel in a private car. The glories of it, the pride of it, the salary pertaining to it, and all that moved me deeply, and I made up my mind then and there that I would reach it. And I did ten years later, at the age of twenty-eight.

The goal I had promised myself was never out of my mind, and

I avoided every path, however attractive, that did not lead in its direction. I imagined that a General Superintendent must know everything about a railway — every detail in every department — and my working hours were no longer governed by the clock. I took no holidays, but gladly took up the work of others who did, and I worked nights and Sundays to keep it all going without neglecting my own tasks. So I became acquainted with all sorts of things I could not otherwise have known. I found time to haunt the repairshops and to become familiar with materials and tools and machinery and methods — familiar with locomotives and cars and all pertaining to them — and to learn line repairs from the roadmaster and the section-hands — something of bridges from the engineer, and so on. And there were opportunities to drive locomotives and conduct trains. And not any of this could be called work for it was a constant source of pleasure.

No wonder people said that Van Horne knew more about railroading than any other man in America.

When Van Horne arrived in Winnipeg, he boasted that they would put down 800 km of track in the first season. People laughed at him, but soon changed their minds. Despite spring floods that first year, 671 km of main track and 161 km of branch lines had been laid!

Laying the track.

Van Horne's idea was to start work at three different places. One team started to build the railway in northern Ontario and worked towards Winnipeg. Other gangs started building from the Pacific coast, and from Winnipeg towards the mountains. In the mountains teams were building both eastward and westward.

ACTIVITIES

1. Make a trip to a railway track to see exactly how the tracks are laid. Notice how the steel plates, spikes and ties fit together. Make a large drawing to illustrate this. Use extreme caution on this field trip and do not stand on the tracks at any time.
2. Compare the railroad policies of Canada's first two prime ministers.
3. Do some library research to find out what other achievements Sir Sandford Fleming is famous for.
4. Make a large class mural to record the building of the CPR. The following might be included:
    - the process of laying track
    - the political and company personalities
    - the workers
    - problems faced
    - the route
5. Why did Macdonald introduce the National Policy? What did he claim it would do? What were the three elements of the National Policy? How was each part supposed to contribute to the overall plan of growth and prosperity for Canada? How did Canadians react to the National Policy?

22
An Almost
Impossible Task

ACROSS THE PRAIRIES

In the summer of 1882 Van Horne was everywhere on the Prairies. From the end of the track, he would ride ahead on horseback or in a buckboard supervising everything. The pace was frantic. Van Horne was always urging the men on and firing anyone who said something could not be done.

The railroad building operation was run like an army. As soon as the workmen laid a bit of track, a train was sent over it carrying up supplies to end-of-steel. Each work train carried the materials required for 0.8 km of railway. It dumped off the exact number of rails, ties, spikes, metal plates, and telegraph poles. The train then moved back to the nearest siding where it was immediately reloaded. No time was lost.

Stations also sprang up along the route. The first gang put up the frame of the building. They were followed by a second gang which added the floor, sides and roof. A third gang did the plastering and the painting. The station gangs began work 200 km behind the track-layers, but caught up to them by the end of the season.

Most of the supplies were brought to the Prairies by American railways. Not only steel and lumber, but tonnes of food were required every week. This was moved up to the end-of-steel where camps for the workers were located. These workers were referred to as 'navvies'.

The navvies usually lived in boarding cars two storeys high. In the upper storey the men slept, and in the lower storey they ate their meals.

Eighty navvies slept in each car. There were also office cars, cooking cars, freight cars, shops-on-wheels, and sometimes the private car of Van Horne himself. Stephen Pardoe, who worked on the construction gang, left an eyewitness account of the workers' camps.

The camp of each outfit presented an almost military appearance. One or two large dining-tents, with the cooks' quarters and the office tent were generally in the centre. All around stood orderly lines of small two-man tents, and at one side the big horse tents, and the rows of wagons. The food prepared by the cook and his 'cookees' was, though rough, generally good and plentiful. Beef and pork, beans and potatoes, bread and hot biscuits, syrup, tea and coffee, were heartily consumed three times a day. Early dawn brought the cry of 'Roll out,' and by the time the men had shaken themselves out of their blankets the horses had been driven in ready to be caught and given their feed of oats and water. Then breakfast, followed by the cry of 'Hook up' from the foreman, and the whole force would commence its first five-hour stretch of work. 'Unhook,' at noon, and dinner; another five hours' work before supper; and then the blankets, till the morning of a new day. . . .

In places the track was laid so rapidly that there was not time to set up camps. Large two-storey boarding cars were built for the use

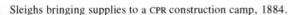

Sleighs bringing supplies to a CPR construction camp, 1884.

CPR construction train.

of the men. In the upper storey the men slept, and in the lower they had their meals. Each car held sleeping accommodation for eighty men. The construction train consisted of twenty-one flat cars (or trucks), and was backed up by the engine, which never had to go more than 13 km for supplies. The ties were packed thirty-three to a car, and the rails were thirty pairs to a car, together with five boxes of spikes, sixty pairs of fish-plates, and one box of bolts. The ties were loaded onto carts and taken ahead, distributed, spaced, and lined well ahead of the track-layers. In order to unload the rails the train was backed up to the end of the track, and the rails then thrown off the cars. The engine then drew off, and the rails were loaded onto a trolley drawn by horses. A gang followed to affix the fish-plates, and was in turn succeeded by the spikers.

The speed with which the work was done is illustrated in the building of the stations. The station buildings were erected by a series of gangs of workmen following each other. The first gang put up the framing, and rafters; the second put on the sheeting, flooring, and roofing; and they were followed by the plasterers, and painters. As each gang finished its particular class of work it moved westward. There were no delays or hitches in the work.

From *Engineering Wonders of the World* by J. M. Gibbon and Stephen Pardoe.

No liquor was allowed in the camps. However, the men thought up all sorts of clever inventions for sneaking in liquor. Imitation Bibles, made of tin, were filled with alcohol and sold to the men. Metal kegs of alcohol were hidden in the centre of barrels of lamp oil. Another clever fellow shipped an organ to end-of-steel for the use of the navvies during church services. It was actually a hollow shell filled with liquor. A whiskey peddlar walked along the track with what looked like cans of explosives. He carried a red flag which kept the Mounties away. But the men knew that he carried alcohol over his shoulders and not explosives.

The Mounties kept a sharp eye open to prevent whiskey smuggling. The result was that drunkenness was not a big problem. The Canadian Pacific was able to keep its own men on the job and 1450 km of steel were laid on the Prairies in fifteen months.

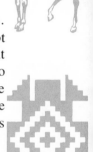

More than once the railroaders ran into problems with Indian tribes. The most serious incident arose with Crowfoot and his Blackfoot people. When they signed treaties, the Indians had been promised that the reserve lands belonged to them forever. They were told that no white man could trespass on the reserves without the permission of the Indians. Now the railway started to move onto the corner of the Blackfoot reservation. The government had planned to pay the Indians for this land, but had neglected to tell the Indians about it.

Now the young Blackfoot warriors were furious. They were urging Crowfoot to organize war parties to drive the invaders out. Crowfoot himself felt angry and insulted that he had not been warned of the railway's plans. It was possible that the aging Chief would not be able to control his warriors.

Father Lacombe hurried south from Calgary to the Bow River. He was a close friend of Crowfoot. He had lived and travelled with the Indians for many years. During the small-pox epidemic of 1870, Lacombe had nursed the Indian victims with so much pity that hundreds of Indians afterwards became Christians. The missionary well understood the emergency that existed. He brought with him a large supply of tea and tobacco and called the Indians to council.

There was much drinking of tea and ceremonial pipe-smoking. Father Lacombe reminded his Indian friends that he had never given them bad advice. He persuaded them to allow the railway to use a small piece of their land. Although he did not have the power to do so, he promised that in return the government would give them extra land. The Indians listened to Lacombe and the crisis passed.

Van Horne was so delighted that he sent Crowfoot a life-time pass on all lines of the Canadian Pacific Railway. Crowfoot was so proud of his gift that he wore it for the rest of his life on a chain around his neck.

He even wrote a poem to Van Horne to thank him for the life-time pass:

> Great Chief of the Railway:
> I salute you O Chief, O Great.
> I am pleased with railway key,
> Opening road free to me.
> The chains and rich covering of your name,
> its wonderful power to open the road,
> show the greatness of your Chiefness.
> I have done.

As the railway stretched across the Prairies a lot of people hoped to get rich quickly. All along the rail line, stations would be built. Towns and cities would spring up around the stations. The men who owned land around the towns could become very rich.

People began to go crazy buying land — wherever they thought the railway might build a station. Prices of land could double overnight. Land bought one day for $25 a hectare could be sold the next week for $250 a hectare. They hoped that perhaps the next year it could be worth $2500 a hectare. Stories of fortunes being made overnight encouraged more people to get into the buying and selling of land. This was called the Manitoba 'land boom'.

An old man owned 22 ha on the outskirts of Winnipeg. In 1880 he had been unable to sell it for $700. Discouraged, he moved back to Ontario. In 1881, strangers knocked on his door and offered him $40 000. The old man went to his lawyer with tears in his eyes. He thought that someone was trying to play a trick on him. By the time he decided to sell, the price of the land had risen to $45 000.

But the land boom ended as quickly as it began. Sometimes the railway decided to build its stations in another place. Quite often land bought without being seen turned out to be swamp or waste land. One Friday, people were buying lots at very high prices as far west as Edmonton. On Saturday, the buyers were trying frantically to get rid of this land at any price. Prices fell back down. Men who had made fortunes in land deals woke up to find they had lost everything.

BUILDING PROBLEMS

Canadian geography created gigantic problems for railroad builders. On the flat open Prairies it was fairly easy to lay the track. But in northern Ontario and in the mountains it was quite a different matter!

Two freight trains meet head-on between Ottawa and Montreal.

When Van Horne first saw the region north of Lake Superior he called it 'two hundred miles of engineering impossibility.' But since there was no such word as 'can't' in his vocabulary, he set to work. His men had to cut down hills, fill in swamps, blast through very hard granite, and lower lake levels. Day and night they were driven mad by mosquitoes. These insects were so large that they reminded one worker of a cross between a bulldog and a horsefly.

Muskeg and rock were the two biggest problems. Muskeg is an odd substance. It looks like solid ground, but it is really a thick layer of moss and dead plants hiding a lake of black water. In winter, when it is frozen and covered with snow, muskeg is passable. But step on it in summer and you sink out of sight. Tonnes of gravel which the railroaders poured into it just disappeared. One of these lakes of muskeg swallowed the track seven times and sucked in three locomotives!

However, Van Horne was determined that the muskeg would be bridged. Finally after much work, the men drained the muskegs and filled them with tonnes of earth. They drove down wooden supports hundreds of metres into the earth until they touched solid rock. Then on this secure foundation track could be stretched and trains could run.

Northern Ontario rock was the other major challenge to be overcome. It took seven and a half million dollars worth of dynamite to move the Ontario granite. But the cost in men's lives was even higher. One man tried to pack a dynamite cartridge tighter by tapping it down with an iron crowbar. He was blown to pieces. Another explosive, nitroglycerine, was even more dangerous. This chemical exploded with the slightest movement. Therefore it could not be safely transported by wagon. Men had to carry it in bottles strapped to their backs. A stumble or a fall meant certain death for the carrier and those around him.

North of Lake Superior nitroglycerine was used daily to blast some of the hardest rock in the world. In one stretch of 80 km of railroad more than thirty men lost their lives because of it! They were killed by explosions or falling rocks. This was the price men paid to build a transcontinental railway.

MEET THREE NAVVIES

Navvies came from all over the world to build the CPR. Irishmen, Englishmen, Scots, Italians, Americans, Swedes, Chinese, and Canadians had a part to play in the project. One of the camp songs the navvies sang in the evenings told their story:

> For some of us are tramps, for whom work has no charms,
> And some of us are Farmers, aworking for our farms,
> But all are jolly fellows who came from here and far,
> To work up in the Rockies on the CPR.

WASYL HRYHOLCZUK

Wasyl Hryholczuk had come to Canada from the Ukraine. He had $50 in his pocket when he reached Halifax with his young family. By the time he travelled to his new farm on the Prairies his cash was almost gone. He built a one-room shack, and then left his homestead in the care of his wife and children. He set off to look for a job on the railroad.

Wasyl earned $1.50 a day as a unskilled labourer. He had to take the roughest jobs, which were usually given to immigrant workers who could not speak English. But Wasyl was thrifty, and saved almost every penny he earned. In three or four months he hoped to have saved enough to go back to his homestead and his family. He would walk back the 160 km because it would cost too much to hire a wagon. With the money he had saved, he could buy a cow, two windows for his crude hut, and hinges for the door.

Like many settlers, he was thankful for the chance to make a few extra dollars railroad building. With the cash earned he could buy a few things for his farm and his family.

LARS PETERSEN

Lars was a Finnish railway worker. He was a giant of a man and as rough and tough as they come. He had worked on every major railway construction gang across America. The railway was in his blood.

He was one of the best 'spikers' in the business. When Van Horne had a contest to see which team could put down the most tracks in one day, Lars was chosen to be a member of one of the teams. His crew showed great teamwork. They broke all records. In one day they laid 10.3 km of track — 8400 hammer blows per man in a ten-hour day!

Some day Lars would retire and live in southern Manitoba. There were already a number of Finnish railway workers living on farms there. But for now, Lars loved the adventure of seeing the ribbon of steel leap ahead of them towards the Pacific. He was content to enjoy the fun and friendship of the camp and let the future take care of itself.

HARRY NASH

Harry Nash was one of the most important men in the camp. He was a cook. He was known to everyone by the nickname 'Montana Pete'. Since the work gangs had little to look forward to, meals were a big event. Montana Pete was a good cook. He could rustle up a huge meal in no time flat. There was not much variety in the menus. Ham or beef stew, pork and beans, fresh baked bread or biscuits covered with maple syrup were served three times a day. All this was washed down with gallons of strong tea or black coffee.

Sometimes the navvies would go out onto the prairie in their free time to shoot wild partridge. Others would hunt for wild duck eggs or berries. When they brought these treasures back to the camp, Montana Pete could fix a feast fit for a king.

BRITISH COLUMBIA

The British Columbia section of the line was the most difficult and dangerous. Three mountain ranges had to be crossed: the Rocky Mountains, the Selkirk Mountains, and the Gold Mountains. Wooden trestles had to be built over deep river canyons. The Mountain Creek trestle alone was 50 m high and 331 m long. The trestle looked so high and so fragile that one engineer refused to drive his engine over it. Van

CPR tracks through the Selkirk Mountains.

Horne threatened to take over the controls of the engine himself. Then the red-faced engineer replied, 'If you ain't afraid of getting killed Mr. Van Horne, with all your money, I ain't afraid either.' Van Horne answered, 'We'll have a double funeral — at my expense of course.' The engine passed over the trestle safely.

In places the railway was forced to creep along the edges of cliffs. Below, torrents and rapids roared. One of the most terrifying stretches of trail was christened the 'Golden Stairs'. Here, a narrow ledge, less than 60 cm wide, had been cut into the cliffs very high above the foaming river. All supplies had to be brought along that trail. It was so frightening that men used to hang onto the tails of their pack horses to get across. They kept their eyes shut until they passed the most dangerous places. One worker had a horrible moment when his horse ran into a nest of hornets. On another occasion, he met two men on the trail with a pack horse coming from the opposite direction. Since it was impossible to turn around, they simply pushed one of the poor animals over the cliff.

In many places workers had to blast a way for the tracks through the rocks of the canyons. Men had to be lowered on ropes down the slippery canyon walls. They were bare-foot so they could keep their balance better. They drilled holes into the rock for the dynamite charges. Then they were hauled back up to the surface and everyone ran for cover.

Many men died or were injured by pieces of flying rock. One construction worker, nicknamed 'Texas', said that he never felt safe on the job. Every minute or so he could hear the cry 'look out below' and heavy rock or stones would come thundering down on them. The work was so dangerous that some claimed that 'every kilometre of tunnel and track was stained with blood along the British Columbia section of the line.'

Andrew Onderdonk was the contractor in charge of building the British Columbia stretch of railroad. To keep costs down, Onderdonk brought in several thousand Chinese workers. A few came from California where they had worked during the Gold Rush of 1849. Thousands, however, were packed like cattle in sailing ships and brought from southern China. Only the men came to Canada. They had to leave their wives and children behind in China. For men who were used to living with all their relatives in close family groups, it was an especially lonely life.

The Chinese workers had only one goal. It was to save enough money to be able to return someday to China and buy a small plot of land. They were willing to work hard for half as much as workers of other nationalities expected.

Separate camps were set up for the Chinese workers, and they kept largely to themselves. Rice, salmon and tea were the main items in their diets. Many became sick from scurvy, a disease caused by the lack of fresh vegetables. Since there were no doctors to help them, some died. Almost two hundred Chinese were buried in the little graveyard at Yale, British Columbia.

Unfortunately, the Chinese were never popular in British Columbia and they were often badly treated. Even though the Chinese were not wanted, they were needed. Without them, British Columbia would not have had a railway. It was said that they took jobs away from Canadians. But Onderdonk could never find enough Canadians who were willing to do the back-breaking railway work for such low wages. Some white people objected to the Chinese because they appeared different. Their clothing, language, queue hair style (which whites called 'pigtails'), customs, and skin colour set them apart.

White railroad officials and citizens of British Columbia often treated the Chinese harshly. It was not a proud chapter in Canadian history.

Once a white foreman, named Miller, failed to warn his Chinese gang of a dynamite explosion. A piece of rock was thrown up by the blast and a Chinese worker was killed. The dead man's friends took off after the foreman with shovels. Miller plunged into the river to save himself. A near-riot followed. Miller would surely have been killed by an angry mob if the company had not come to his rescue.

On other occasions it seemed that Chinese workers were given the most dangerous jobs. Sometimes hundreds of Chinese pulled on cables to move supplies up the treacherous Fraser River. Many men fell to their deaths; others lost their lives in blasting accidents and rock slides. When Chinese were killed on railway construction, British Columbia newspapers did not even bother to report their deaths. However, Canadian newspapers did write articles about the Chinese. They referred to them as 'coolies'. They wrote violent and discriminating stories about them. They even published cartoons making fun of the Chinese, and they urged the government to send all the workers back to China.

Few of the Chinese workers ever saved enough to return to wives and families in China. Though each Chinese worker was paid about $25.00 a month on the railway, expenses were taken from that amount. The company insisted that he buy his work clothes, tools and other necessary items from the company store. Here the prices were usually higher than anywhere else. Also he was charged $4.50 a week for room and meals. During three winter months there was no work and no wages. Added to his debts was money he had borrowed to pay his passage to Canada. This sum, $40, had to be paid back to an agent in China.

When construction jobs on the Canadian Pacific Railway ended, most Chinese had no choice but to stay in Canada. They faced a grim future in a country which did not seem to want them. They took low-paying jobs which most white people found disagreeable. They worked as servants, in canning factories, and in laundries.

Over the years Chinese people have contributed to Canada's growth. As well as their work on the railway, they started a market garden industry in British Columbia and have started thousands of businesses all across the country. Many Chinese Canadians have become important members of the community. In 1972, Dr. George Pon of Toronto, the grandson of one of those early railway workers, became Vice-President of Atomic Energy of Canada.

Canadians must not forget the part the Chinese railway workers played in our history. With picks and shovels and with their bare hands they helped to build the British Columbia section of the Canadian Pacific Railway.

Originally the Canadian Pacific Railway planned to cross the Rockies through the Yellowhead Pass. This route had been chosen by Sandford Fleming and would have taken the track north close to Edmonton. However, in 1881, the Company decided to take a route farther south. They would cross the Rocky Mountains through the Kicking Horse Pass. This would shorten the route to the Pacific by 127 km. It would also help keep out American railroads from the south.

Chinese camp, Kamloops, B.C.

But there was a serious problem with the Kicking Horse Pass. The track would have to go through the Selkirk Mountains. The Selkirks rise over 3350 m just west of the Rockies. Nobody knew a way through this mountain range! Some said it could not be crossed. In 1882 the steel was racing westward across the Prairies towards Kicking Horse Pass. Onderdonk and his crew were building eastward from the coast towards the same pass. Somebody would have to find a way through the Selkirks, and quickly!

The man chosen for this apparently impossible task was Major A.B. Rogers. He was a tough little American surveyor and engineer. He was past fifty years of age when he set out in the summer of 1881 searching for a way through the Selkirks. That summer turned out to be a terrible ordeal for Rogers and his men. The Selkirk Mountains were a wall of rock, glacier and forest. Not until 24 July 1882, the next year, did he find a difficult but acceptable pass through them. It was later given the name 'Rogers Pass' after the person who discovered it.

Major A. B. Rogers.

MAJOR A.B. ROGERS

Because he cursed from sun-up to sundown, Rogers was known as 'Hell's Bells Rogers'. He was thoroughly disliked by his men. He fed them nothing but beans and bacon. He drove them mercilessly and insulted them continually.

Major Rogers looked as frightening as he acted. Piercing blue eyes and unbelievable foot-long white side whiskers made him look like the crotchety man that he was.

The major was ambitious, not for money, but for fame. More than anything else in the world he wanted to leave the name 'Rogers' on the map. When he found his pass through the Selkirks, the Canadian Pacific Railway gave him a cheque for $5000. He refused to cash the cheque, and had it framed. He said he wouldn't take $100 000 for it. It would stand forever as the reminder of what he had accomplished.

One of his few friends said of him: 'His driving ambition was to have his name handed down in history; for that he faced unknown dangers and suffered unbelievable hardships.'

SUPERINTENDENT SAM STEELE

Superintendent Steele was in charge of all North-West Mounted Police detachments along the Canadian Pacific line. He had served with Wolseley at the Red River in 1870. He was so strong that he could carry 135 kg barrels of flour on his massive shoulders over the portages.

He joined the North-West Mounted Police in 1873 and became its first sergeant-major. Steele took part in the Great March West, bargained with Sitting Bull, and served in the Yukon during the Klondike Gold Rush.

PROBLEMS — MONEY

By 1885, the Canadian Pacific Railway was facing some serious problems. Sections of track still had to be completed in northern Ontario and British Columbia. But more important was the shortage of money. Costs of laying the track through these very difficult areas had skyrocketed. People with money to invest in the project did not want to risk pouring more of their money into it. The Opposition members of Parliament were against the government lending any more money to the Canadian Pacific. They said it would be as useless as pouring gold into the canyons of British Columbia. They doubted that the railway would even earn enough money to pay for its axle grease.

By March 1885, there was no money left to pay the construction crews. The men at the Beaver River camp of British Columbia refused to work any more until they were paid. Three hundred armed strikers brought all work to a halt. They attacked railway property, and forced the calling in of the North-West Mounted Police. Superintendent Sam Steele, ill with fever, left his sick-bed to deal with the dangerous situation. The crowd was in a very ugly mood. Steele and eight Mounties held off the crowd with the warning, 'I will shoot the first man of you who makes a hostile movement.' Steele stood his ground and the grumbling mob slowly broke up and went back to work.

In the meantime, George Stephen and Donald Smith had to turn their attention to the problem of money. They were able to gather together one million dollars of their own personal fortune. Both were prepared to sell their family possessions in order to raise the necessary amount. This would keep the railway going for another three weeks, but after that they did not know where to turn for any more money.

Things seemed very bleak for the Canadian Pacific. Stephen wired to Donald Smith, 'Stand fast, Craigellachie.' This was a saying both men understood from their days in Scotland. It was a battle-cry of one of the old Scottish clans. The saying was used as a call in the Scottish Highlands to bring the clan to its meeting place at Craigellachie Rock. Stephen was really telling his cousin, 'Stand fast! Don't give up! We'll win yet!'

At the crucial moment Macdonald acted. He reminded Parliament that the railway had already proved its value. In the Red River Rebellion of 1870, the troops took three months to get to the West from Ottawa. Just that spring in 1885, trouble had arisen again with Louis Riel. This time it had only taken nine days to get the necessary troops to the West. In fifteen years this was the difference that the railway made. For this reason the railway did get one more government loan. This was enough to finish the line of steel.

BUILDING A RAILROAD

MAPPING THE ROUTE

In April 1871, Sandford Fleming was put in charge of planning a route for the railway. He was asked to find the best route from the Ottawa Valley to the Pacific coast, a distance of over 4000 km across the country. He set out with a crew of surveyors. They travelled by wagon, canoe, mule, or on foot. The surveyors had to be physically strong because the work was quite exhausting. They would have to

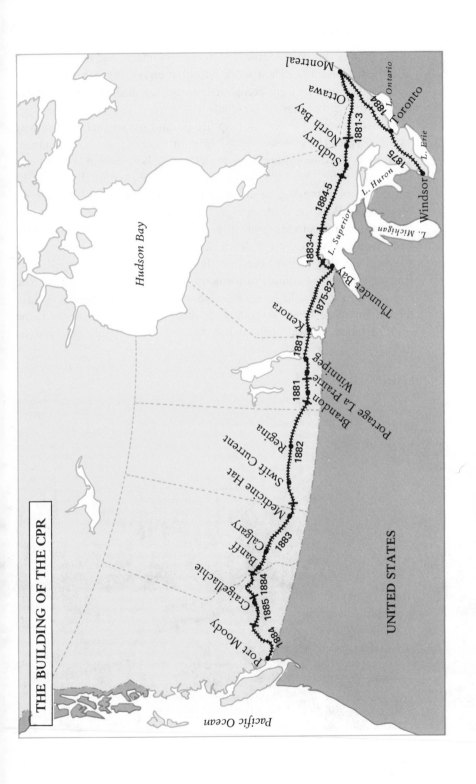

THE BUILDING OF THE CPR

Pacific Ocean

Port Moody
1886
1885 1884
Craigellachie
Banff
Calgary
1893
Medicine Hat
Swift Current
1882
Regina
Brandon
Portage La Prairie
Winnipeg
1881
1881
Kenora
1875-82
1883-4
1884-5
Sudbury
North Bay
1881-3
Ottawa
Montreal
1884
Toronto
L. Ontario
L. Erie
1875
Windsor

Hudson Bay

L. Superior

Thunder Bay

L. Huron

L. Michigan

UNITED STATES

spend months in the wilderness of northern Ontario and the mountains of British Columbia. Their work was also physically dangerous. Before all the surveys were completed, forty men had lost their lives in forest fires, drownings or accidents.

The surveyor's job was to map the ground over which the railway would travel. He picked a possible path covering a short distance. Then he walked along the route to determine how easy it would be to lay tracks there. Was the land rocky? If so, rock would have to be moved. Was it muskeg or swamp? If so, land fill would have to be brought in. Was the route straight? The fewer the curves, the easier and cheaper it was to lay track. Was the path through open land? If not, trees would have to be cut down and a passage opened. Were there river valleys that would have to be bridged? Were there steep slopes? Railways move by contact of a smooth wheel on a smooth track. The rise in elevation could be no more than one metre up for every fifty metres forward. When these and all other factors were checked, the route decided on was marked with an axe by chipping off bark on trees.

Laying the track.

PREPARING THE ROADBED AND LAYING THE TRACK

Before rails could be put down, a roadbed had to be prepared. Rails could not be put directly on top of the soil. They needed a much stronger foundation. Crushed stones were brought in by mules and wagons as a base. Then men with picks and shovels spread the stones in a layer about a metre deep. Horses pulled a giant scraper along the roadbed to flatten it. The weight of trains running over the roadbed further packed it down.

Wooden planks about two metres long, called ties, were then placed on the level roadbed. The ties were set exactly 61 cm apart. Steel rails were placed on top of the ties. The rails were anchored to the ties with steel plates and spikes. Lengths of rail, 9.14 m long, were then bolted together.

The whole operation was carried out by well-organized groups of workers. One group laid the ties. Another distributed the spikes and bolts. A third gang adjusted the rails to make sure they were in the exact place. This gang was followed by a group called 'spikers' who hammered in the steel spikes.

ACTIVITIES

1. Why were Chinese workers paid less money than workmen of other nationalities?
2. How did each of the following factors affect the building of the railroad in Canada?
    a) climate
    b) physical features of the land
    c) money
    d) personalities (Van Horne, Stephen, Macdonald)
    e) labourers.
3. Imagine that in your attic you have discovered the diary of an ancestor who worked as a navvy on the CPR. Write up several daily records of the kind of thing you might read in such a diary.

23
The Task Completed

THE LAST SPIKE—CRAIGELLACHIE

The last railway spike was driven at 9:22 a.m. on 7 November 1885. At last Montreal and the Pacific were linked by a ribbon of steel. The brief ceremony took place high in the Eagle Pass at Craigellachie, British Columbia. It was a misty, dull morning. A group of railway officials arrived in overcoats and silk hats. Among them were Van Horne, Smith, Fleming, and Rogers. George Stephen was 13 000 km away in London, England, where he was still trying to raise more money. At the ceremony marking the completion of the railway, a group of workmen gathered behind the officials. There were no politicians present.

Van Horne had decided that the last spike would be an ordinary iron spike like any of the millions that had already been used along the way. Major Rogers, known for his discovery of the Rogers Pass, held the spike in place. Donald Smith, whose every penny had gone into the railway, lifted the hammer to drive it into the ground. The first time Smith hit the spike, he bent it. Another had to be put in its place. Smith drove in the new spike with careful taps. There was a moment's silence, and then the workmen gave a rousing cheer.

When Van Horne was asked to make a speech, he replied, 'All I can say is that the work has been well done in every way.' The contract had allowed the company ten years to build the railway. It had been completed in five years.

The Canadian Pacific conductor then called 'All aboard for the Pacific', and the officials climbed on the train. After they departed, the workmen had a 'last spike' ceremony of their own.

The first train from the Atlantic to the Pacific arriving at Port Arthur, 30 June 1886.

Although the ceremony at Craigellachie marked the joining of track from the East and West, it was several months before regular passenger service could begin. Some water tanks, stations, and rail sidings still had to be built. More sleeping cars, freight cars, dining cars and passenger cars had to be purchased.

The twenty-eighth of June 1886 was the 'red letter' day. At 8:00 p.m. the Pacific Express Number One steamed out of Montreal station on the way to the Pacific. It was the first scheduled through passenger train. After a long trip of 139 hours, it chugged into Port Moody, British Columbia, on 4 July 1886. The Pacific Express was only one minute late. Eventually, the western end of the railway was moved from Port Moody to Vancouver where there was an excellent deep-sea harbour.

The first trains consisted of a baggage car, a luxurious first-class day car and sleeper, the dining car, and the colonist car. The colonist car was a much cheaper way to travel. The colonist cars would be the most important to the future development and settlement of Canada. They would bring almost a million settlers from all over the world to western Canada.

From the windows of the colonist car, the settlers got their first look at their new homeland. The car was set up with pairs of seats facing one another, which pulled out into hard wooden beds. Above the seats another hard wooden bed, the upper berth, swung down from the wall like a shelf. Every car had a cooking area as well as washbasins and drinking water. However, the colonist did have to supply his own pots and pans and to bring all the food the family would eat during the

Inside a colonist car.

journey. There were no toilets in the cars, but the train did make regular stops at stations along the way.

In most cases the settlers brought all their possessions with them on the train. These included horses and oxen. These animals and the heavy possessions were packed in the freight cars. Often the man of the family rode in the freight car to look after his possessions while his family rode in the colonist coach.

As more and more people travelled across Canada on the trains, the Mounties showed that their concern for law and order also applied to the new railway. Once, when the trio of bandits, Bill Minor, 'Shorty' Coloquhous, and Billy Dunn, stopped the train at gun point near Kamloops, Commissioner Perry quickly formed a posse and set out on horseback after them. After almost two days, the Mounties spotted the gang. A short gun fight took place and all the robbers were captured. This incident was a strict warning to others who may have considered holding up Canadian Pacific trains.

In the next few years after passenger service was established, Van Horne worked hard to promote the railway. He advertised the comforts and pleasure of travel by train.

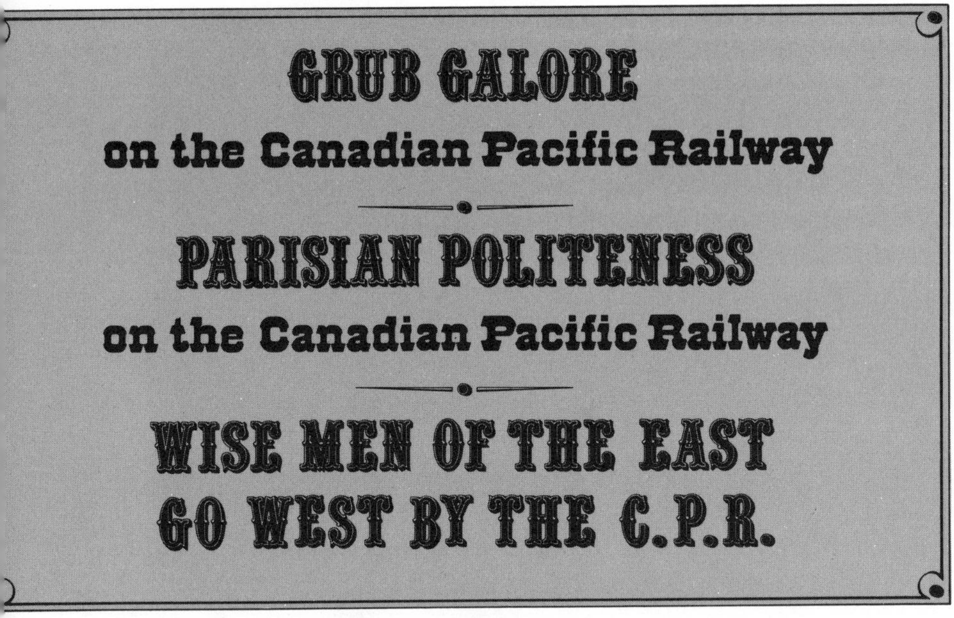

GRUB GALORE
on the Canadian Pacific Railway

———•———

PARISIAN POLITENESS
on the Canadian Pacific Railway

———•———

WISE MEN OF THE EAST
GO WEST BY THE C.P.R.

CPR hotels, such as the Chateau Frontenac in Quebec City, were built in major cities close to the stations. A luxury resort hotel was built at Banff, Alberta, so that tourists could enjoy the breath-taking views of the mountains. Artists were invited to paint pictures of the glorious scenery, and their paintings were sent around the world as Canadian Pacific advertising.

George Stephen's dream was to have a fleet of steam ships crossing the Pacific Ocean to China and Japan. Seven chartered ships left Japan 19 June 1886 with a load of tea bound for Britain. The tea left Vancouver on trains on 30 July and reached Montreal on 7 August. This was the quickest delivery of goods from Japan on record. From Montreal, the cargo was hurried on to its destination in Britain. During the 1890s, 156 American railways failed. The CPR was able to keep going because of the valuable trade it had built up with the Orient.

What happened to the three remarkable men after the completion of the Canadian Pacific? George Stephen was honoured by Queen Victoria for his work. He was given the title 'Baron Mount Stephen'.

The CPR placed a bronze statue of Stephen in its Windsor Station in Montreal. Near Field, British Columbia, a mountain — Mount Stephen — bears his name forever.

Donald Smith was honoured by the Queen with the title 'Lord Strathcona'. He was later sent to Britain to be Canada's official representative in that country. In London he spent most of his time encouraging British families to move to Canada and settle in the Canadian West. The mountain peak named in his honour, Mount Sir Donald, looks down on the Rogers Pass.

In 1894 Van Horne became Sir William Van Horne in recognition of his part in the building of the Canadian Pacific. In his later days he built a railway in Cuba and was involved in business ventures in Mexico, Brazil and Guatemala. A range of mountains west of Field, British Columbia, was named the Van Horne Range. Since boyhood Van Horne had been interested in geology. Through his hobby, he discovered nine new fossil specimens which were named 'van hornei' in his honour. When Sir William Van Horne died in 1915, the Canadian Pacific Railway suspended all operations for a short period of time as a tribute to the man who did so much to build their railway.

ACTIVITIES

1. You have been hired by a newspaper to send a detailed report on the last spike ceremony at Craigellachie. Write the report based on information found in the text and in the photograph.
2. What sort of man was Van Horne? How important was he in building the CPR?
3. Gather some facts and figures on the CPR today. Show how the company has grown and what services it provides.
4. 'If there had been no railroads, there would not have been a Canada from sea to sea.' Discuss. (From *Canada's Railways* by R.J. Phillips.)
5. Van Horne sent the following telegram to Sir John A. Macdonald when the railroad was finished. Was what Van Horne said true? Why? 'Thanks to your far-seeing policy and unwavering support, the Canadian Pacific Railway is completed. The last rail was laid this morning.'
6. Debate: 'The completion of the CPR was as important an event in Canadian history as Confederation.'

The last spike.

PICTURE STUDY OF THE LAST SPIKE CEREMONY

The white-haired old gentleman driving the last spike is Donald A. Smith. Directly behind Smith, standing with his hands in his pockets' is William Van Horne. Next to Van Horne is Sandford Fleming (squared white beard and top hat), who surveyed the original route. The young boy next to Fleming is Edward Mallandaine, a water boy. Also present at the ceremony were Major Rogers and Superintendent Sam Steele.

VALUES EXERCISES

1. List some of the difficulties that the Chinese railroad workers faced in Canada. Why do you think Chinese workers were not treated as well as workers who came from other countries?

2. Between 1895 and 1947 laws were passed in Canada to keep Chinese people out. These were brought about largely by pressure from unions of workers. The workers were afraid the Chinese might take away their jobs.

A tax of $50.00 had to be paid by each Chinese person wishing to enter Canada. In 1900 this tax was raised to $100.00 and in 1903 to $500.00.

The Chinese Immigration Act of 1923 said that no Chinese people were allowed to enter Canada unless they were merchants or students. Between 1923 and 1947, only forty-four Chinese were allowed into Canada.

a)   What do you think were the reasons for not admitting Chinese to Canada? Do you think that these reasons were always fair? Why or why not?

b)   How effective would the tax be in keeping Chinese out? Explain your answer.

c)   How would these laws be enforced?

d)   Explain whether or not you think the Chinese Immigration Act was an example of racial discrimination.

24
The Rebellion
of 1885

It is the summer of 1885. The small court room in Regina is jammed with curious spectators. Louis Riel is charged with treason for leading an armed rebellion against the Queen and her Canadian government. If he is found guilty the punishment is death by hanging. All Canada is watching to see what the outcome of the trial will be!

What had happened over the last fifteen years to bring Louis Riel to this moment? This was the same Louis Riel who led the rebellion in the Red River area in 1869-1870. Now he was back in Canada.

Following the Red River rebellion, Riel had fled from Fort Garry to the United States before Colonel Wolseley could arrest him. He did return to Canada, and in 1874 he was elected by Manitoba to the House of Commons in Ottawa. Although he went to Ottawa, he was not allowed to sit as a member of the House of Commons. In Ontario there was a warrant out for his arrest for the murder of Thomas Scott. Many people threatened to shoot him if he appeared in the House of Commons. Riel was sent from Canada in 1875 and was not allowed to return for five years. He went back to Montana in the United States. It was there in 1884 that Riel was living with his family and teaching school.

In that year, Gabriel Dumont and three other Métis rode almost 1100 km from the Saskatchewan River Valley to Montana. Although Gabriel Dumont was a well-respected hunter and military leader, he was not the educated, fiery spokesman the Métis needed. Dumont's mission in Montana was to persuade Riel to return to Canada to fight again for the Métis cause.

They told Riel a very sad story. After Manitoba joined Confederation in 1870, many Métis had moved farther west into present-day Saskatchewan and Alberta. They were looking for open spaces of land and freedom to live in the traditional Métis ways. Now Canadian surveyors had suddenly appeared in the North West and started to divide the land for settlement. The railway was coming through, and it would be only a matter of time before white settlers would flood into their homeland. Their hopes appeared to be threatened again. It was the same old problem for the Métis.

When Riel first returned to the North West, he seemed to have no thought of an armed rebellion. He wanted to try the peaceful way first. Riel dreamed of bringing the Indians, the Métis, and the white settlers together to speak to Ottawa with one voice. They drew up a petition to the government. For the Métis, this petition demanded legal proof that they owned the small spaces of land where they lived. They also wanted a voice in their own government. The Indians were close to starvation because the great herds of buffalo were almost wiped out. Therefore, for the Indians it asked for food and more money to help set up farms on the reserves. For the white settlers, it protested the high prices of farm machinery made in eastern Canada, the high costs of moving goods on the railroad, and the low prices received for their wheat. These settlers also wanted a larger voice for the North West in Ottawa. Although the government promised to look into these problems, Ottawa did nothing until it was too late.

By March 1885, Riel had decided to act. He would use the same methods in Saskatchewan that had been used successfully earlier in Manitoba. He would set up his own government and arm his followers. Then he could force the Canadian government to arrive at a better deal for the citizens of the North West.

It was a desperate gamble. Riel failed to realize that conditions had changed since 1870. Now there was the North-West Mounted Police to support the Canadian government. There was also a railroad to bring troops and arms quickly from eastern Canada.

Riel's call to take up arms lost him the support of the white settlers. They wanted to see changes come in a lawful way. Riel had also lost the support of the Roman Catholic Church when he broke with the church and set up his own religion. Only the French-speaking Métis and some Indians continued to support him.

Among the Cree Indians, it was only chiefs Big Bear and Poundmaker and their followers who joined Riel in the rebellion. These

Louis Riel.

tribes had refused to give up their way of life and move quietly onto the reserves. During the early years of the 1880s, they had become increasingly hostile. As food became more and more scarce, there were instances of Indians breaking into food warehouses. On several occasions these Indians challenged the authority of the North-West Mounted Police.

In 1883, a band of Cree Indians pitched their camp on CPR land. Corporal Wilde and a constable were sent to investigate. The Indians refused to move. They tried to cause a fight by pushing the police and firing some shots. This was a direct challenge to police authority. Wilde took out his pocket watch. He announced he would give the Indians fifteen minutes to move. When the time was up, he dismounted, walked over to the chief's lodge and started to take it down. Faced with Wilde's bold action, the Indians backed down. But Big Bear and the Crees were getting the reputation among the Mounties of being troublemakers.

When Poundmaker and Big Bear heard about the early success of Riel and the Métis, they began to swing into action. Indians in the

United States had often taken up arms to fight with their government. However, 1885 was the only time in Canadian history that Indians rebelled against the government.

What chance will Riel, the Métis and the few Indians have against the Canadian government?

BLOODSHED

26 March 1885. Seventeen North-West Mounted Policemen set out from Fort Carlton to pick up food and ammunition stored at Duck Lake. About three miles from Duck Lake they found the road blocked by an angry and excited force of Métis. Refusing to be drawn into a fight where they were greatly outnumbered, the Mounties returned to Fort Carlton.

Superintendent Crozier of the North-West Mounted Police decided to lead a force of fifty police and fifty volunteers back to Duck Lake to secure their provisions. On the way they met Gabriel Dumont and his men. A forty-minute fight followed. From the top of a ridge the Métis could see the Mounties as they advanced along the trail. The Mounties became easy targets for the Métis. Ten Mounties were killed and eleven were injured in the attack. Four Métis and one Indian were also killed. The North-West Mounted Police were forced to abandon Fort Carlton and retreat to Prince Albert. The rebellion had begun.

News of the defeat of the Mounties swept across the Prairies like wildfire. Encouraged by this Métis success, *some* Indians decided to strike. One group of Indians broke into the Hudson's Bay Company store in Battleford and stole needed supplies.

At Frog Lake, Chief Big Bear was unable to control his warriors. They killed the Indian agent (a government worker), two priests, and five other white men. Then his warriors headed towards Fort Pitt. Big Bear, who had been a friend of the white man, warned the police to retreat. 'My young men are wild. I can no longer control them,' he said. Other Indians under Chief Poundmaker attacked Battleford.

Chief Crowfoot and his Blackfoot tribe and most of the Indians on the Prairies, however, refused to become involved in these battles. The government had rushed extra supplies of food and blankets to them. Hundreds of carloads of flour and sides of bacon as well as extra amounts of tea and tobacco were distributed to half-starving Indians. By doing this, the government hoped to keep these nearby tribes neutral during the trouble on the Prairies. Trouble had often been prevented in the past when the Mounties or the Hudson's Bay Company

Government troops heading through Touchwood Hills.

men had handed out extra allowances of food to the hungry natives.

Ottawa was alarmed at the news of Mountie deaths at Duck Lake. The government decided to send troops immediately to help put down the rebellion. The problem they faced was how to get the troops quickly to the West. The CPR had not yet been completed. Sections of track, 138 km in total, still had to be laid.

William Van Horne, vice-president of the CPR, was struggling to get the railroad completed. He still needed more money to finish the job. He saw this problem as a chance for the CPR to get another loan of money from the government. He promised to have the troops in Qu'Appelle in ten days in return for another loan. Van Horne would use one method or another to get the troops to the West over those incompleted sections of the track!

The first forces, under General Middleton, left Toronto on 28 March 1885. Ahead of them was a journey of approximately 2200 km.

Four times the troops had to leave the train in freezing wind and weather to cross the gaps in the railroad. Over the ice and snow of the two shortest gaps, the soldiers marched. They also had to drag their guns and horses through deep snow in temperatures well below 0°C. It was a very rough introduction to the life of a soldier. Most of these men were volunteers who only a few days before had been shopkeepers and clerks in eastern Canada.

The capture of Batoche.

Over the two longer gaps, the troops rode in sleighs provided by the railway company. On the stretches of track between gaps they were carried in open flatcars. The horses suffered even more than the men because there was no way of sheltering them from the wind and rain on these flatcars. One soldier, George Beauregard, recalled the misery of being packed into flatcars sheltered only by a scrap of canvas.

There were fifty of us to a car, piled one on top of another, drenched by the rain which fell on our backs in torrents. For the first time, we really knew what misery was. Without any way of warming ourselves, we could scarcely find the courage to revive our spirits by singing.

Eight days later, the first troops arrived in the West. An eyewitness who saw the troops getting off the train in Winnipeg said they looked as if they had already gone through a war. Many of them were frost-bitten and half-blind with the glare of the snow.

Van Horne had kept his promise. The troops were in Qu'Appelle in nine days. The government was happy and the CPR had earned the loan to complete the railroad.

About 5000 armed troops were now in the West. Added to these were 500 North-West Mounted Police and 50 surveyors. These surveyors claimed to be rough, tough, and dirty, but knew the country well.

One force advanced under General Middleton from Qu'Appelle to Riel's headquarters at Batoche. A second column of men, under Colonel Otter, headed north from Swift Current towards Battleford. Otter's job was to relieve Battleford which had been surrounded by Poundmaker and his Indians. A third force, under General Strange, left the train at Calgary. They set out for Edmonton and the North Saskatchewan River to track down Big Bear.

General Middleton marched slowly with 850 men towards Batoche. A large group of men were left behind at Qu'Appelle as reinforcements. Middleton had with him cannons and a large wagon train of supplies.

Métis scouts brought to Riel daily reports of the progress of Middleton and his troops as they marched towards Batoche. Riel and Gabriel Dumont could not agree on what should be done. Dumont, a skilled buffalo hunter, wanted to act at once. He knew that Middleton's troops outnumbered the Métis and were also much better equipped for fighting. Dumont's plan was to annoy the troops, worry them and slow them down by means of ambush. On the other hand, Riel thought that it would be better to wait until the soldiers attacked Batoche. Riel said that he had prayed about it, and God told him that if the Métis waited, they would win. Eventually, Dumont got his way and the Métis proceeded with the plan to ambush Middleton.

Middleton had his first skirmish with the Métis at Fish Creek. Here Dumont trapped the army in a coulee, a shallow ravine, in the same way the Métis often trapped the buffalo. Middleton's troops fought back, but the Métis managed to kill 50 of them. Dumont himself lost four men. He considered it a Métis victory because he had slowed Middleton down, which allowed him more time to gather a larger force of Métis and Indians.

During the Battle of Fish Creek, Riel was at his headquarters in Batoche. He could hear the boom of Middleton's cannons 13 km to the south of him. All day long Riel stood praying for success with his arms stretched out to form a cross. When his arms tired and seemed about to drop, his Métis friends came forward and held them up.

Middleton's attack on Batoche came on 9 May 1885. His plan was to use the steamer *Northcote*. The *Northcote* was used normally on the Saskatchewan River to supply the Hudson's Bay Company posts. The

Northcote had been ordered down from Medicine Hat to ferry Otter's troops across the river. Then it was to sail farther down the river to assist in the raid on Batoche. The steamer had been fitted out as a gun-boat. Its sides were barricaded with planks, boxes and mattresses. Troops could take cover on the ship and fire on Batoche.

As the *Northcote* approached Batoche, it was to blow its whistle as a signal for the attack to begin. As the steamer fired from the river, the General and his men would attack on the shore. However, the first naval battle on the Prairies was a disaster! The *Northcote* arrived too early at Batoche. Métis scouts discovered the plan and set a trap for the *Northcote*. They stretched a steel wire across the river. As it approached, the *Northcote* struck the wire and the smoke funnels were ripped down. The whistle came down with the smoke stacks and was not able to blow!

But on land, things eventually went better for General Middleton. Batoche was a small village on the east side of the South Saskatchewan River. It consisted of a few houses near the ferry crossing. Also, there was a Roman Catholic church, priest's house and a cemetery. The Indian camp was located nearby. Dumont's idea was to get his men to dig several rifle pits in the ground around Batoche. Métis riflemen could hide in these pits and fire at any approaching troops. These pits were carefully hidden in the bush and shrub.

For three days Dumont's plan worked. When Middleton's troops attacked the high ground near the church, they were in full view of the Métis in their protected pits. As seen from below, Middleton's troops stood out against the brightness of the sky. It was a clever scheme.

The Métis fought bravely. Riel moved among his people unarmed. He was encouraging his fighters. The story is told of José Ouellette, Dumont's ninety-three-year-old father-in-law. Several times he was encouraged by Dumont to retreat to safety. Each time the old fellow replied, 'Wait a minute! I want to kill another soldier!' Such was the courage of the Métis who were fighting for their homeland!

For three days the cautious General Middleton refused to allow his army to attack the Métis rifle pits. Finally, the troops charged the pits without orders. The Métis by now were running out of ammunition and were only firing small stones and nails.

On 15 May 1885, Riel gave himself up. He had written a letter to Middleton offering to surrender himself if Middleton would allow the Métis to go free. On the outside of the envelope, Riel had scribbled the words 'I do not like war.'

Gabriel Dumont tried to persuade Riel to flee with him to the United States. Riel felt he could not bear the hardships of trying to escape through the woods. Sadly Dumont left without his leader. The old buffalo hunter slipped through Middleton's military patrols and entered the United States.

In the meantime, at Battleford, frightened citizens had taken shelter from Poundmaker's Indians in the North-West Mounted Police barracks. Colonel Otter and his troops were making the 300 km trip north from Swift Current to relieve Battleford. Two hundred loaded wagons, 600 horses, and 500 men made the long journey.

For many of the volunteers from eastern Canada, it was the first time they experienced the open spaces and the bitterly cold April winds of the wide Prairies. At night the freezing temperature made sleeping on the frozen ground a torture for the men. They had nothing to eat but salt pork and hardtack. This hardtack was like a thick, stale biscuit that the men said was often full of maggots. To drink there was only unsweetened tea made from the bitter, salty water of the prairie ponds. During the day the weather became very hot and both men and beasts were nearly driven crazy by northern mosquitoes. It meant constant swatting of the insects with branches cut from prairie bushes.

Asleep in the trenches during the Rebellion.

At last, however, tired and footsore, Otter's column arrived at Battleford. Imagine the surprise and relief felt by the people of Battleford when they heard the sound of the approaching military band. For almost a month, Battleford had lived in constant fear of attack. Now outside help had arrived.

Colonel Otter decided to pursue Poundmaker and his Indians. Otter thought that it would be wise to destroy Poundmaker before he and Big Bear could join forces and go on to help Riel at Batoche. Otter met Poundmaker in a bloody battle at Cut Knife Hill, about 65 km west of Battleford. Otter had secret weapons, two cannons and a Gatling gun with which he expected to be able to frighten or blast the Indians into flight.

Otter's plan was to move forward under the cover of night to attack the Indians on the morning of 2 May 1885. Because an Indian village never sleeps, Poundmaker and the Crees were ready for the attack at daybreak.

The government troops took up position on the high Cut Knife Hill overlooking Poundmaker's camp. From there they could fire the cannons down on the teepees of the rebels. But the Indians took positions in the shelter of wooded valleys below. It suited their way of fighting. They would gladly leave the exposed positions to Otter's men.

Although their guns were old, Indian marksmanship was good. Snipers were able to pick off Colonel Otter's troops one by one. Gradually the Indians were able to encircle the base of the hill. They crept through the bush until Otter's men were almost completely surrounded. The troops in the meantime were firing down on the Indians with their Gatling gun. At first the Indians were alarmed with the noise of its rattle, but soon they realized that the bullets were passing harmlessly over their heads. One band of Indians even tried to rush the hill to seize the guns, but were forced back with rifle fire. At the crucial moment in the battle, the two cannons refused to fire. They were old and not in good working condition.

By late morning Otter's troops were in serious trouble. The list of wounded soldiers was growing in number. The war cries of the Indians were coming closer. Colonel Otter knew that the Indians would soon surround him and cut off his only line of retreat across Cut Knife Creek. Otter gave the order to withdraw to Battleford. It was a humiliating defeat.

Surprisingly the Indians did not pursue. Colonel Otter himself admitted that the Indians could have cut his retreating troops to pieces. It

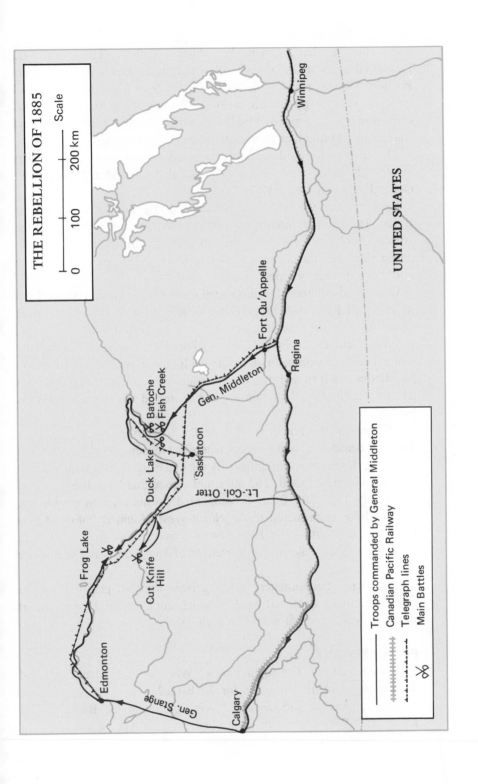

THE REBELLION OF 1885

Scale

0   100   200 km

United States

Winnipeg
Fort Qu'Appelle
Regina
Gen. Middleton
Batoche
Fish Creek
Duck Lake
Saskatoon
Lt.-Col. Otter
Frog Lake
Cut Knife Hill
Edmonton
Gen. Strange
Calgary

——— Troops commanded by General Middleton
░░░░ Canadian Pacific Railway
┼┼┼┼ Telegraph lines
✄ Main Battles

seems that at that moment Poundmaker called off his warriors. Poundmaker insisted that his Indians fight only in self-defence. Thus Poundmaker was responsible for saving the lives of Colonel Otter and his men. In calling back his warriors, Poundmaker brought about his own downfall. General Middleton now joined Colonel Otter at Battleford and together they outnumbered Poundmaker.

The news of Riel's defeat at Batoche convinced the great chief that to struggle alone was useless. Poundmaker surrendered himself to General Middleton on 23 May 1885.

Farther west, General Strange attacked Big Bear at Frenchman's Butte. Though the Indians fought fiercely, Strange's men had the advantage of having heavy guns. Big Bear's troops now began to desert him. He and a few of his warriors evaded arrest by heading north into the heavy woods and lake country.

General Middleton himself headed one of three groups who set out in search of Big Bear. Finding Big Bear was all the more important to the military because Big Bear's Crees had taken white prisoners, including women, at Frog Lake and Fort Pitt. The thought of white women being prisoners in an Indian camp was especially horrifying to Middleton. As it turned out, the prisoners were released unharmed on 21 June 1885. Big Bear himself had protected the women from his braves.

All through the hot days of June the soldiers pursued Big Bear. Through dense bush and swamps where the mosquitoes drive men and horses mad, the chase continued. By the end of June, Big Bear was out of ammunition and food. The old Chief sensed that his cause was lost. On 2 July 1885 Big Bear, accompanied by his eight-year-old son, Horse Child, surrendered to the North-West Mounted Police at Fort Carlton. The North-West Rebellion was over. From the outbreak of fighting at Duck Lake to the surrender of Big Bear was exactly one hundred days.

Louis Riel, Poundmaker, and Big Bear were all prisoners of the Canadian government. All would now be brought to trial for their part in the Rebellion. What would be their fate?

PICTURE STUDY
1.   Where are the Canadian troops? What are the advantages and disadvantages of their position for the battle?
2.   Where are the Indians and Métis fighting in the Battle of Cut Knife Hill? Why is their position ideal for their type of warfare?

The battle of Cut Knife Creek.

3. Compare the equipment and weapons used by both sides in the Battle according to the picture.

4. Where would you place Col. Otter's 'secret weapon' in the battle? Why?

5. Pretend you are a soldier fighting with Col. Otter. Write a letter to your parents in eastern Canada giving an 'on-the-spot' description of the Battle of Cut Knife Hill.

PERSONALITIES OF THE LEADERS

POUNDMAKER

How did he get the name 'Poundmaker'? It seems that he had a special ability to attract buffalo into pounds. A pound resembled a huge corral. Sometimes a herd of buffalo were stampeded into this trap. On other occasions, the buffalo were drawn in quietly by a person like Poundmaker. He would dress in a buffalo robe and use a bell to capture the herd's curiosity. One time Poundmaker lured 500 buffalo into his pound.

Poundmaker was a handsome, tall Indian, standing about 2 m. His shiny black hair hung down in two braids almost to his waist. He was very proud of his hair. One of his worries in prison was the thought of having his long hair cut short.

GABRIEL DUMONT

This Métis buffalo hunter was one of the most colourful figures of the Riel Rebellion of 1885. He was a crack shot. When he was only ten years old he could put a bullet through a duck's head at one hundred metres. He was also an excellent horseman who caught and tamed his own wild horses.

After the Rebellion, Dumont worked in the United States as a sharpshooter in Buffalo Bill's travelling Wild West Show.

Dumont and his friends plotted to rescue Riel from his Regina prison. The rescue attempt never took place. The Mounties kept Riel under constant guard. They used a force of three hundred men. Not even the clever and courageous Dumont could get his friend out of that prison!

In July 1886 the Canadian government pardoned those who had taken part in the North-West Rebellion. Dumont did not go back to the South Saskatchewan River until 1890. During the last years of his life he would sit at his cabin door and tell neighbourhood children tales of the Rebellion. He would show them the scar from the wound in the head he received at Duck Lake. Then the old buffalo hunter would say 'You see, my skull was too thick for my enemies to kill me!'

GENERAL FREDERICK MIDDLETON

Middleton was a British general who had spent his whole life in the army. He was placed in charge of all troops sent to put down the Riel Rebellion. Why was a British general in command of Canadian troops? Because Canada at this time was still a colony of Britain. It was the Mother Country's right to appoint an experienced British soldier to command the Canadian militia. The militia were citizens trained to defend the country and fight as an army. However, they were only called into service in times of emergency.

Middleton was something of a snob. He would have preferred to have British regular soldiers to fight in his army. He put down the Canadian militia as 'Sunday soldiers', and he did not trust the North-West Mounted Police.

He was also rather stubborn and was unwilling to follow advice.

Poundmaker.

Gabriel Dumont.

Big Bear.

General Middleton.

Therefore, he did not listen to his officers who were much more familiar with the Canadian countryside than he was. He also underestimated the fighting skills of the Métis and Indians.

BIG BEAR

The Mounties called Big Bear 'the most troublesome Indian on the Prairies'. He was of stocky build with hard muscles and little eyes. He was considered a fierce warrior and an excellent horseman. In battle he could cling to the side of a galloping horse and use it as a shield. He would then shoot at the enemy from the underside of the horse's neck.

ACTIVITIES

Mapwork

1. On an outline map of western Canada locate the following places:

North Saskatchewan River	Qu'appelle
South Saskatchewan River	Prince Albert
CPR	Duck Lake
Batoche	Winnipeg
Battleford	Fort Carlton
Fort Pitt	Swift Current
Medicine Hat	Regina
Cut Knife	Frog Lake

Devise symbols to mark each battle site and to indicate who was fighting whom at each location.

2. The CPR played an important role in getting troops to the West to put down the Rebellion. People sometimes say that the CPR should build a statue to Riel. Why would they say this? What did the railroad owe Riel?

3. In chart form make a list of the similarities and differences of the forces of Middleton and Dumont under the headings:

    a) experience and qualifications of the military leader;

    b) available military equipment;

    c) skills of the fighting men;

    d) importance of the railroad in the campaign.

4. Gabriel Dumont and his Métis followers made a long trip to Montana to see Riel. Pretend you are a member of this Métis group.

    a) What qualities would you consider important for your leader?

    b) Make a list of the arguments you would use to persuade Riel to come back to Canada to lead his Métis people.

5.   Act out a pow-wow of Indian chiefs who are trying to decide whether or not to join Riel in his fight. Include Big Bear, Poundmaker, and Crowfoot. Be sure you consider the following:
  a)   the problems in deciding which side will win;
  b)   the role of the NWMP;
  c)   the Indians' respect for the white man's military strength;
  d)   feelings among the tribes;
  e)   problems facing the Indian people.

6.   Do you think that the Métis should have fought against the government? Can you think of anything else they could have done instead?

7.   Pretend you are Louis Riel. Write a speech to persuade the Métis to follow you into battle against the Canadian government. Be sure you explain why they should take up arms.

8.   Why did the Métis choose Riel as their leader at Red River? How would you evaluate Riel's leadership during the Red River Rebellion? Pay particular attention to his responsibilities, his qualities of leadership and the willingness of others to follow him.

Why did the Métis choose Riel to lead them again in the North-West Rebellion?

Evaluate Riel's leadership in the North-West Rebellion.

HOW TO WRITE A BIOGRAPHICAL OUTLINE

A *BIOGRAPHICAL OUTLINE* is a brief outline of the main events in the life of a person. Here are the steps you should follow:

1.   Find out as much about the person as you can. Try your school and local library.

2.   Make a point-form summary of the information you collect.

3.   From the information you collect, pick out the important details and the events in which the person played a leading part.

4.   Use the point-form summary and write out the biographical outline in paragraph form.

Write a biographical outline of Louis Riel's life.

25
The Rebels on Trial

The formal charge of treason was laid against Louis Riel, Poundmaker and Big Bear.

The Indians had difficulty understanding this charge against them. When Poundmaker surrendered and was brought before General Middleton at Battleford, he offered to shake hands. Middleton refused. The General sat on a chair with his interpreter nearby and his officers in a half circle behind him. Poundmaker and his chiefs sat on the grass before him. The General said, 'Poundmaker, you are accused of high treason.' However, there was no phrase for 'high treason' in the Cree language. The interpreter tried to make the charge clear to Poundmaker. 'You are accused of throwing sticks at the Queen and trying to knock off her bonnet' was the explanation of the charge.

Poundmaker insisted at his trial that he had not fired first at Cut Knife Hill. He also replied that he was only trying to improve the living conditions for his people. He pointed out that he actually saved the lives of white people by holding back his warriors when Otter and his men were retreating at Cut Knife Hill. The jury ruled that Poundmaker was guilty. He was sentenced to three years in Stoney Mountain Penitentiary.

Big Bear was also tried for treason at Regina. People generally thought that Big Bear was a 'bad Indian', probably because of the deaths of white people at Frog Lake and the taking of the white prisoners. However, some witnesses did tell the court that Big Bear cried out against the killing of the whites at Frog Lake. He personally protected the prisoners that his warriors captured.

The proud old chief delivered a speech in his Cree tongue to the court. He pleaded more for his people than he did for himself.

I ruled my country for long. Now I am in chains and will be sent to prison. . . . Now I am as dead to my people. Many of them are hiding in the woods paralyzed with fear. Can this court not send them a pardon? My own children may be starving and afraid to come out of hiding. I plead to you Chiefs of the white man's laws for pity and help for the people of my band.

The country belonged to me. I may not live to see it again . . . I am old and ugly but I have tried to do good. . . . Because Big Bear has always been a friend to the white man, you should now send a pardon to my people and give them help.

Big Bear was found guilty and also sentenced to three years in the Stoney Mountain Penitentiary.

Poundmaker and Big Bear were released from prison after two years. Both Indians returned to reservations, but died within a few

The surrender of Poundmaker.

months of their release. It was thought that the shock of imprisonment was too much for these proud, free men of the plains.

Poundmaker was buried on the Blackfoot Reserve. But, eighty-one years later — in Canada's Centennial year — the Cree Indians moved his bones back to the Cut Knife Reserve. Here, a plaque to honour the great chief was erected.

In all, 44 Indians were convicted of various crimes. Eight Indians were hanged. In addition, 18 Métis were eventually sent to prison for their part in the rebellion.

The trial that aroused the greatest interest and excitement all across Canada was the trial of Louis Riel. This trial in Regina has been called the most important one in Canadian history. The outcome of it would be felt in Canada for many years to come.

Six white settlers were chosen to act as Riel's jury. All six were English-speaking and of the Protestant religion. Because Riel was French-speaking and of the Roman Catholic religion, his friends feared that he would not get a fair trial.

Excellent lawyers were hired to defend Riel. Money had been raised in Quebec by the Riel Defence Committee to pay for all the expenses of his defence.

His lawyers saw at once that the only hope of saving their client was to prove him insane. They pointed out to the jury that twice he had been in insane asylums. They described some of Riel's strange behaviour. While General Middleton's troops were marching towards Batoche, Riel had been considering new names for the days of the week. On other occasions, he had suggested that the Pope, leader of the Roman Catholic church, be replaced by a Canadian churchman. In his diary, Riel had often talked of seeing religious visions and hearing voices from heaven which told him what to do.

Riel himself would not accept this excuse of insanity. In two long speeches to his jury he argued that he was sane. For Riel, to plead insanity would be a disgrace. It would also make his Métis followers look foolish for following an insane man.

At the trial, General Middleton repeated what he had felt when he first met Riel following his surrender. Middleton decided after two days of conversation with him that Riel was perfectly sound in mind. The General did find that Riel was a proud and vain man very much haunted by religious thoughts.

The lawyers for the Canadian government argued that Riel was sane. They pointed out that doctors at the trial had said so. They asked,

Riel addressing the jury.

'How could an insane person lead 700 men into a rebellion unless they were all insane?' 'How could the Métis have lived with Riel and not noticed his insanity?' 'No, Riel was sane!' 'He had taken up arms against the government. He had stirred up the Indians. He was guilty of treason!'

What was the jury to do with Louis Riel? People in Ontario saw him as a rebel and said, 'Hang him!' They remembered that he had shot Thomas Scott and led the Métis and Indians in a rebellion. People in Quebec saw him as a patriot who loved his country and said, 'Pardon Riel!' They remembered that he was a French Roman Catholic who had tried to get the Métis their rights.

Riel's jury took only one hour and twenty minutes to reach a decision. They declared him guilty. Then, Mr. Justice Richardson, the trial judge, addressed the following to Riel:

It is now my painful duty to pass the sentence of the court upon you, and that is, you shall be taken now from here to the police guard-room at Regina jail . . . and that you be kept there till the 18th of September, that on the 18th of September you be taken to the place appointed for your execution, and there be hanged by the neck till you are dead, and may God have mercy on your soul.

A RIEL UGLY POSITION.

Letters from all provinces and many parts of the world poured into Ottawa. 'Hang Riel', said some; 'Free Riel', said others. Twice the execution was delayed. Sir John A. Macdonald and his Conservative government were in a tricky position. Sir John A. himself had no sympathy for Riel. If Riel was not hanged, Ontario would be enraged. The Conservatives would lose votes in Ontario in the next election. If

Riel was punished then Quebec would be angry with the Conservative Party and vote against them.

Finally, Macdonald decided he would have to take his chances with losing support in Quebec. 'Riel shall hang,' he is reported to have said, 'though every dog in Quebec shall bark.'

On the bright but cold day of 16 November 1885 the execution was carried out in the Regina jail. Riel was dressed in a black coat, a woolen shirt, grey trousers and moccasins. Two priests, two guards and the deputy sheriff walked with him from his cell to the scaffold. Riel said, 'I thank God for having given me the strength to die well . . . I die at peace with God and man, and I thank all those who helped me in my misfortunes.' Riel showed no signs of weakness. During the Lord's Prayer the trap door opened. Riel was hanged.

On the day of the execution, crowds gathered quietly in English-speaking Canada to hear the news. They seemed impressed when they read how bravely Riel had died.

In French-speaking Canada, however, the reaction was quite different. Flags flew at half-mast. Black-framed pictures of Riel appeared in store windows. Hundreds of students in Montreal shouted 'Glory to Riel!' Likenesses of Sir John A. Macdonald were burned openly in the streets.

In the newspapers and in Parliament, French-speaking Canadians blamed the death of Riel on Macdonald and English Canada. They said that he had been murdered because he was French. They began to ask, 'Could Confederation, which had joined English and French together, manage to survive?'

THE LONG-LASTING RESULTS OF THE 1885 REBELLION

FOR THE INDIANS

1. The only Indian rebellion in Canadian history had been put down by force. From now on there was no longer a strong core of rebellious Indians anywhere in the North West.
2. The Indians realized that the government was going to enforce the treaties. They had no other choice than to move onto the reserves.
3. The rebellious Indians lost their annual government payments. Their horses and ammunition were seized.

FOR THE MÉTIS

1. Many Métis fled to the few areas of wilderness in northern Alberta that still remained.

2.   Others took scrip worth $160-$240. They remembered how they had been unable to keep their land after 1870. When this money was gone, the Métis had nothing.

3.   The proud 'Métis Nation' was broken up. Not until recently have Métis organizations been formed again to improve conditions for their people.

FOR FRENCH-ENGLISH RELATIONS IN CANADA

1.   The bitter split between English-speaking and French-speaking people in Canada would take a long time to heal. Neither side would forgive the other for its view of Riel.

2.   Hard feelings between Protestants (Ontario) and Roman Catholics (Quebec) would last for a long time after Riel's execution.

FOR POLITICAL PARTIES

1.   The people of Quebec who had always voted for the Conservative Party stopped voting for them. They would not support the Party which had hanged Riel.

2.   The people of Quebec began to vote in large numbers for the Liberal Party. This was especially true after the Liberals chose a French-Canadian leader, Wilfrid Laurier.

FOR WESTERN CANADA

1.   The CPR railroad had been completed to bring the troops west.

2.   Now that the rebellions had been put down, settlers felt secure in moving to the West.

3.   Many soldiers who fought in the Rebellion stayed in the West to live and farm. East and West did not seem so far apart any more.

4.   With the Indians settled on the reserves, the land could be opened up for agriculture.

ACTIVITIES

1.   Role Play: Divide your class into groups and put Riel on trial. You will need a judge, a prosecuting lawyer, a defending lawyer, Riel, a six-man jury, witnesses, reporters, and spectators. If you decide not to hang Rield, what else can you do with him? Did Riel get a fair trail in your class? in Regina in 1885? Explain your answer.

2.   a) Why would Riel be considered a hero in Quebec?
b) How did the Riel situation create problems for Sir. John A.

Macdonald? c) How would the people of Ontario react to Quebec's opinion of Riel? Why?

3. Dumont, Riel's commander, was eventually pardoned for his part in the Rebellion. Riel was hanged. Debate in your class the fairness of this. Research the part played by each man to support your side in the debate.

4. Many people in Ontario thought Riel was a 'traitor'. People in Quebec called him a 'hero'. Use a dictionary to define these words. Then explain why you think Riel was a 'hero' or a 'traitor'.

5. One of the members of the jury at Louis Riel's trial later said: 'We tried Riel for treason and hanged him for the murder of Scott.' What do you think the juror meant? Was it a fair summary of what happened? Why?

6. Some people say that Louis Riel was a courageous fighter for the rights of Indian and Métis people. Others say Riel was hungry for power and betrayed the trust his Indian and Métis followers put in him. Which point of view is closest to your own? There is probably no right or wrong answer to this question. What you should do is try to gather as much evidence as possible to support your point of view.

7. See if you can define the word 'rebellion'. A dictionary may help. Should anyone ever fight against the government of his or her country? Why or why not? Can you think of situations in your own lifetime where people have fought against the government? In what ways were these fights similar to the North-West Rebellion? In what ways were they different?

8. Arrange the following events in the history of the Canadian West in the order in which they occurred:

a) The Manitoba Act;
b) The Riel Rebellion in the Red River Colony;
c) The Last Spike Ceremony at Craigellachie;
d) Treaty Number Seven is signed with the Indians;
e) Louis Riel hanged;
f) The Long March of the North-West Mounted Police;
g) Gabriel Dumont summons Louis Riel to return to Saskatchewan;
h) British North American Act;
i) Pacific Scandal;
j) John A. Macdonald outlines his National Policy.

Compare the four rebellions you have studied this year under the following headings:

	Upper Canada 1837	Lower Canada 1837	Riel 1870	Riel 1885
What were the causes of discontent?				
Who were the leaders?				
What changes were proposed for change?				
What alternatives to rebellion were tried?				
What event marked the outbreak of rebellion?				
Who were those opposed to the ideas of the rebellion?				
How successful was the rebellion?				
What were the outcomes of the rebellion?				

26
The Sod House
Frontier

The April of 1883 was still bitterly cold when General Willoughby and his family unloaded all their possessions from the colonist train at Moose Jaw. They had gone west early in the spring so that there would be time to get a crop planted that year.

Next day at dawn the wagons were loaded and they set out on the trail to find their new homestead. They had to move slowly because the horses, which they had brought with them from eastern Canada, were not used to western trails. A few of the settlers had oxen. Though slower, the oxen were stronger. Oxen could also be used later to pull a plough to break through the tough prairie sod. As a last resort, if all else failed, oxen could be eaten.

After a few days on the trail, a terrible spring blizzard struck. The travellers were trapped in tents for three days. Some of their horses died during the storm. A few of the settlers gave up then and there and headed back to Moose Jaw.

The others struggled on. They left some of their possessions on the Prairie in order to lighten the loads for the surviving horses. The prairie wind cut their faces like razors. Wagons had to be floated across icy rivers and streams. As the weather cleared, spring mud buried wagon wheels to the axles. Sometimes the men had to unload the wagons, push them out of the mud, and then re-load.

Only a few kilometres could be covered each day. Every night there was the added task of setting up camp, gathering fuel, and cooking meals. But finally the journey ended. Guided by rough maps, the settlers began to search in brush and prairie grass for the stakes the

A rough road in the West.

surveyors had left that marked their quarter sections. The search could take days. A stake driven by a surveyor into a low spot in summer might be completely covered with water in the spring. Finally they could unload their wagons for the last time. The homesteaders were home.

But home was really just a spot on the Prairie. A house still had to be built and the ground broken. In every direction was prairie. No sign of another human life could be seen. To the new homesteader there was the feeling of being completely alone in a new land.

SURVEYING THE LAND

On 1 December 1869, the Hudson's Bay Company lands were turned over to Canada. The Canadian government wanted to open these lands for settlement as quickly as possible. As early as the summer of 1869, the government had sent out surveyors. The surveyor's job was to measure and map the land. Once the land had been surveyed, it could be divided into farms and sold to settlers. All the land west of Fort Garry to the Rocky Mountains was going to be surveyed.

There were three steps in the division of the land:

1.   The land was divided into *townships*. Each township was a square whose sides were nearly 10 km in length.

2. Each township was subdivided into 36 *sections*. A section was a perfect square with each side measuring 1.6 km. In each township the sections were numbered 1 through 36, starting in the south-east corner. Section 8 and part of section 26 were kept by the Hudson's Bay Company. The other even-numbered sections belonged to the Canadian government. These would be free homestead lands for settlers. Sections 11 and 29 would be school lands. The other odd-numbered sections were set aside as railway lands. The CPR could sell these sections to raise money for the construction of the railway.

This illustration shows what a prairie township looked like when it was divided into sections.

A PRAIRIE TOWNSHIP

LEGEND

Free homestead lands

School lands

Hudson's Bay Co. lands

Railway lands

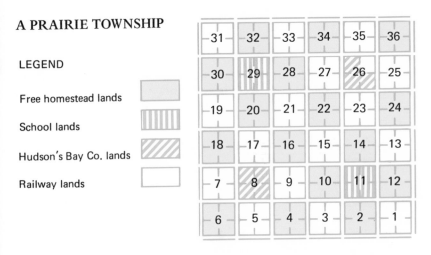

3. Each section was then divided into quarters. A *quarter-section* contained 65 ha. Each quarter was marked out by direction, as follows:

NW	NE
SW	SE

DOMINION LAND ACT 1872 (also called The Homestead Act)

The Dominion Land Act said that any adult, or head of a family, could claim a quarter-section of land. He could only choose from the free homestead land. All he had to pay was a $10.00 registration fee. He was required to live on the land for six months each year, to build a house, and cultivate 16.2 ha. This must be done within three years. If the settler carried out these conditions in three years, full ownership would be turned over to him.

Later, if the homesteader wanted, he could add another quarter-section of land next to his homestead. He could buy this cheaply for about $5.00 a hectare.

ACTIVITY

PICKING OUT A HOMESTEAD

You have applied for a homestead in this prairie township. You are about to select the quarter-section you wish for your farm. The map will provide some information to help you make a good choice.

PICKING OUT A HOMESTEAD

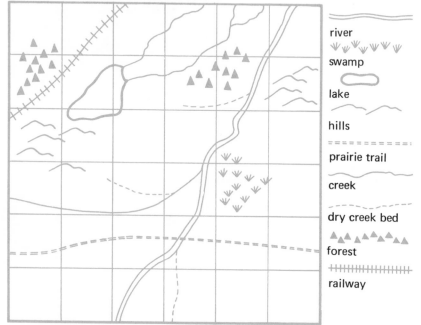

river

swamp

lake

hills

prairie trail

creek

dry creek bed

forest

railway

1. Number the sections in the township. Cross out the sections which are not available for homesteads.
2. Examine the map and note the features of the land.
3. List the advantages and disadvantages of each of these features from the point of view of a homesteader.
4. Decide which quarter-section you would select as your homestead. Remember you may wish to add adjoining land in the future. Give reasons for your choice.

When settlers arrived on their new homestead, the first thing they had to do was build a shelter. Tents would do for the summer but not for the very cold prairie winter.

In the wooded areas of eastern Canada pioneers built their first shelter of logs. They also used the plentiful supply of wood for fuel. However, over much of the Prairie there were no large trees and few bushes grew due to the recurring prairie fires. The settlers fell back on the only material available — prairie sod. The sod house and the sod barn became the mark of the prairie frontier. For fuel there was dried buffalo manure.

The greatest appeal of sod buildings was that they were cheap. Almost all the material that went into them was free. The total cash cost of one sod house was $2.97. That was for one window, roof jack, door hinges, and a door latch. The most primitive style of sod shelter was a dug-out. A hole was dug in a hillside and piles of sod built up around it. A dug-out was a safe place in a wind storm or tornado. But one disadvantage of a dug-out was that animals or even people sometimes dropped through the roof at night!

To construct a sod house trenches were ploughed for the bottom of the walls. Then sod was chosen from a dry, grassy creek bed. The sod had to be thick with plenty of roots.

The sods were cut into strips 71cm long, 36 cm wide and 10 cm deep. They were hauled to the building site on wagons. They were placed grass-side down and piled like bricks but no mortar was used. Sometimes the walls were made 71 cm wide with double thickness of sod.

If it was possible to get light poplar poles, they were placed from the tops of the walls to a central pole to form a roof. Hay was spread on the poles, and sods placed on top. Most sod houses had a dirt floor and a dirt roof. If it rained all day outside, the roof of a sod house became so full of water that it rained for two days inside. A lady who was born on a rainy day in a sod shack with a dirt roof told this story. The roof was leaking so badly that they had to hold an umbrella over her mother while she was being born. Another disadvantage could be mice and insects which sometimes came with the sods!

Thousands of these sod houses were built all across the Prairies. A pioneer sod house 4 m × 6 m contained about 35 t of sod. The thick walls kept the buildings warm in winter and cool in summer. Even in the middle of winter, water in a kettle would not freeze in a sod house if the fire went out at night. By contrast, in a fragile lumber building water in a kettle froze during the Saskatchewan winter nights.

There were very few windows in a sod building because the holes would weaken the walls. When people later moved into frame buildings with many windows, they found it difficult at first to sleep in the early morning sunlight.

Besides being cheap to build, another advantage of a sod house was that it was almost completely fireproof against the dreaded prairie fires. You just could not burn down a sod house.

Neighbours would gather around to help the newcomers put up a sod house and barn. This was called a 'sodding bee'. The whole neighbourhood came and a sod house could be built in a day. The women provided plenty of pies, cakes, roasts, fresh bread, and other good things to eat. There was always some food left over, so at night a fiddle would be brought out, and an open-air dance held to welcome the new family into the community.

Sod houses have all but disappeared today. But in the early days they provided the settlers with a first home and a good shelter from the cold blasts of winter and the heat of summer.

THE ICELANDERS

One of the first groups of people to take up homesteads were the Icelanders. Four hundred people from Iceland docked at Quebec in 1874 on their way to make new homes in the United States. They were fleeing volcanic eruptions in their own country. They were invited by the Canadian government to stay in Canada. They agreed to do so when they were promised three things:

1. freedom and Canadian citizenship;
2. a large tract of land where they could farm and fish together;
3. their own language and customs.

So the Icelanders stayed in Canada. A man named Sigtryggur Jonasson, their leader, set out to find a site where they could settle. He selected a place on the west shore of Lake Winnipeg where they started

A sod hut.

their settlement of 'New Iceland'. They named the place Gimli, or paradise, after the home of the Norse gods. An Icelandic community still exists there today. Jonasson is remembered as the Father of Icelandic settlement in Canada.

Their first winter in New Iceland was anything but paradise. Winter set in very early and the settlers had no time to build houses. Some were forced to live in buffalo tents belonging to the Hudson's Bay Company. Most of the tents were old and torn. In one of them, on a bitterly cold day in November, with the snow blowing across the mother's bed, the first Icelandic Canadian was born. There were many deaths from starvation that winter. They were without cows, and so there was no milk for the children. The fishing nets they brought from Iceland were too large-meshed to catch lake fish. Wild game was scarce. Many settlers, young and old, died of scurvy.

The following year, 1876, a small-pox epidemic struck the colony. Again, many more of the Icelanders died. As often happened in the early epidemics, the neighbouring Indian tribes also suffered. The Indians had no resistance to the European diseases. The Indian village across the lake from New Iceland was wiped out. The Icelanders who lived burned down their cabins to destroy the germs.

Those who survived carried on with courage. One example was Hjalmar Hjalmarsson, whose feet were so badly frozen that they had to be amputated at the ankles. He spent five months in bed, and for the next three years he did his homesteading on his knees.

Fortunately, the little colony survived. The Icelanders went on to develop the inland fishing industry in the lakes and rivers of Manitoba. They caught Winnipeg goldeye and sturgeon and sent them to the markets of Winnipeg and eastern Canada.

Icelanders have always enjoyed books and reading. Even in the midst of the terrible conditions of those early days, the settlers taught their children to read and write. One of the men, Jon Gudmundson, regularly published a small newspaper that first winter. He wrote it in his own handwriting and read it aloud to groups as he travelled from house to house.

An important explorer, Vilhjalmur Stefansson, was born in the Icelandic community in Manitoba in 1879. He moved to the United States, but participated in many Arctic expeditions. He was the first white man to come in contact with a group of Inuit known as the Copper Eskimos. When an Arctic expedition was planned for 1914, Stefansson persuaded the Prime Minister, Sir Robert Borden, to provide the money to make it a purely Canadian expedition. On many occasions Stefansson risked his life travelling on moving ice floes. He discovered five Arctic islands, the last unknown land masses of North America. In 1952, a large island north of Victoria Island was named in his honour. Stefansson, born an Icelandic-Canadian, was one of the greatest explorers and students of the Arctic.

Arrival of the first Mennonites at Winnipeg.

Many Icelandic women also made special contributions to the history of Canada. One was Margret Benedictsson. In the early 1900s she and some women in the Icelandic community campaigned with other women in Manitoba for the right to vote. By January 1916, their efforts met with success. Manitoba was the first province in Canada to let its women citizens vote.

Today, there are 27 000 Icelandic Canadians. Many are the descendants of these early settlers in Canada. Winnipeg has one of the largest Icelandic populations of any city outside Iceland.

THE MENNONITES

Another early group of settlers, the Mennonites, came to Canada for a different reason. They came to find religious freedom. They were members of a Protestant religious group that had been formed in 1537 under the leadership of Menno Simons. Their faith demanded that they should never go to war. In 1874 they left their homeland in Russia when the Russian government ordered them to serve in the army.

When they came to Canada between the years 1874 and 1876 the Mennonites settled west of the Red River. They were already experienced in farming the prairies of Russia. They were the first Western settlers to farm the open prairie. Before, new settlers had always feared the empty plains and even the Icelanders huddled near rivers, lakes, and creeks. But the Mennonites knew about farming open spaces. They knew that the prairie soil would be good for growing grain because it looked like the rich farmland they had left.

The Mennonites lived in villages rather than on individual farms. Each family owned the land on which its house and buildings stood. However, the farmland was divided among all the families of the village. Each family was given some of the best land and some of the worst land to farm. This ensured each family an equal opportunity for success.

The Mennonites were peace-loving, hard-working Christian people. But above all, they were very successful grain farmers and excellent gardeners. Within two or three years, they had turned the Prairie into outstanding farms.

In 1876, J.C. McLagan wrote:

Seldom have I beheld any spectacle more full of promise of a successful future than the Mennonite settlement. When I visited these people, they had only been in the province two years. Yet, in a long ride I took across many miles of prairies, which but yesterday were absolutely bare — the home of the wolf, the gopher, and the eagle — I passed village after village, homestead after homestead, furnished with all the conveniences of European comfort and up-to-date farming methods. On either side of the road cornfields were already ripe for harvest, and pastures were full of herds of cattle.

From *Extraordinary Tales from Manitoba History*
by J.W. Chafe.

The biggest contribution the Mennonites made to Canada was that they were the first to prove the open prairie could be farmed successfully.

COLONIZATION COMPANIES — CANNINGTON MANOR

Sometimes the Canadian government sold large amounts of land to individuals or colonization companies. The person or company would find and bring out groups of settlers to fill up the land. If the land was not settled, it would be returned to the government. One of the most unusual experiments involved Captain Pierce and Cannington Manor.

Captain Pierce was a cultured English gentleman. His dream was to set up a colony of well-to-do English families near Moose Mountain in southeastern Saskatchewan. He managed to attract several upper class English men and women to the settlement. They arrived in the wilder-

A tennis party at Cannington Manor.

ness loaded with dinner jackets and evening gowns, cricket bats and tennis rackets. They had little or no experience with farming. They brought servants or hired Canadians to be servants for them.

The Cannington people passed their time in dances, sports, and boating on Cannington Lake. They built a racetrack and raced thoroughbred horses. One family, the Bectons, imported fox hounds from England and started the Cannington Manor Hunt Club. The hunts were conducted in correct hunting gear — red jackets and riding boots. The women also participated in the hunt, riding side-saddled. The thoroughbred dogs, however, were frequently 'out-foxed' by the local prairie coyotes! It must have been a strange sight to stumble on the village of Cannington Manor in Saskatchewan in the 1880s.

The mill that was built brought honour to the Manor when its flour won a gold medal at the world's fair held in Paris in 1885. Horses raised at the Manor also won an international reputation by winning many racing awards.

But the experiment gradually began to die. Many of the prominent English families moved away. Some of the young men went off to fight in the British Army or to look for gold in the far Canadian West. Only a few families remained to farm. Captain Pierce had dreamed of transporting an upper-class English way of life to the prairie frontier. He had wanted to create 'a little bit of England' in the wilderness. By the 1890s the golden days of Cannington Manor had ended.

Cannington Manor was not like any other settlement before or after it. It certainly was not what one would expect to find west of the Manitoba border in the 1880s!

ACTIVITIES

1. An Icelandic name exercise: In Iceland, last names are formed from the first name of the father with the addition 'sson' for boys, and 'sdottir' for girls. If Erik Jonsson has a son named Stefan, Stefan becomes Stefan Eriksson. His daughter, Ingrid, would become Ingrid Erkisdottir. When Ingrid marries, she does not take her husband's last name, but is called Mrs. Eriksdottir.

Try to make the last name of this boy and girl:
Leifr, son of Karl Gunnarsson,
Margaret, daughter of Frederik Thomasson.

Can you figure out the first name of: Erik Jonsson's father? What would your name be if you had the same method of giving names to children? Can you guess why Margret Benedictsson's last name does not fit the rule given in this question?

2. Brainstorm these questions:

Why would people leave their homelands and set out for Canada in the 1880s? Why do people move to Canada from other countries to-day? Compare and contrast reasons why people came to Canada 'then' and 'now.'

Ground Rules for Brainstorming:

1. Write down as many reasons as you can think of to answer the questions. All answers are acceptable.

2. Don't stop to discuss the answers at this time.

3. Get as many people suggesting ideas as possible.

4. One person's suggestion may trigger an idea in some other person's mind.

27
Come West

By the 1880s the Canadian Prairies were ready to produce large amounts of wheat. All that was needed were people to grow it. Government from Ottawa had replaced the rule of the Hudson's Bay Company. The buffalo had disappeared from the Plains. Treaties had been made with the Indians and most of their lands had been surrendered for settlement. Riel's last rebellion against advancing settlement on the frontier had been crushed. The North-West Mounted Police had established law and order. Most important, a railway had been built to bring in settlers and to carry their harvests to the markets of the world. Though the Dominion Land Act had provided free homesteads since 1872, not very many settlers had yet arrived.

From 1881 to 1896 settlers took up only 56 000 homesteads in the West, and abandoned 16 000 of these. In 1896, only 16 835 immigrants came to Canada, the lowest number since 1868. In fact, during the previous fifteen years, the number of Canadians going to the United States was greater than the number of immigrants coming to Canada. Then everything happened at once. A new Prime Minister, Laurier, and a new Immigration Minister, Sifton, took office in Canada. The Canadian Pacific Railway joined the government in the country's biggest advertising campaign. It was to sell 'the Golden North-West' to people in Britain, United States, Europe, and eastern Canada.

Clifford Sifton thought of himself as a 'Westerner', although he had been born near the village of Arva, Ontario. When he was only thirteen his family moved to Brandon, Manitoba. During his childhood, he became sick with a fever that affected his hearing and left him partially

Canadian advertising for immigrants from Great Britain.

deaf. As he grew older, his deafness became gradually worse, until he feared that he might lose his hearing altogether. Despite his handicap, Sifton had an outstanding record at school. He graduated in law at the University of Toronto, and opened a law office at Brandon. He entered politics and served first in the Manitoba provincial government. Because of his impressive service in Manitoba politics, Laurier invited Sifton to join the federal government as a cabinet minister.

As Minister of the Interior, one of Sifton's duties was to fill up the Prairies with settlers. Sifton believed that the British were the most desirable settlers for Canada and so he started an advertising campaign to attract British settlers to Canada.

ADVERTISING IN BRITAIN FOR SETTLERS

The Canadian government and the railroads wanted to promote the West in Britain. One of the best ways to do this was through pamphlets. You could not walk down the main streets of Glasgow, London, Leeds, Manchester, or any other city or town in Britain without someone handing you a pamphlet or booklet about the glorious Canadian West. The pamphlets were full of pictures of wheat fields and new homesteads. They described the great opportunities available in Canada, how you could get free land, and how you could make a fortune.

Many of these pamphlets were given to schools in Britain. Where books were not too plentiful, teachers used the booklets and pamphlets as prizes at the end of the school term. Sometimes they were even used as readers. Many boys and girls read the booklets and dreamed of adventures some day in Canada.

Then there were 'movies'. Not movies as we know them today, but magic lanterns shows, which projected slide pictures of life in Canada. Pictures of men threshing unusually large crops, herds of cattle, and trainloads of settlers were shown in every British village. Following the lantern show a lecturer explained how the Canadian government offered 65 ha of free land. He answered the many questions that the excited British had to ask about Canada.

Another way of promoting Canada was the exhibition van. This wagon travelled the length and breadth of Britain showing samples of wheat, vegetables, soil, Canadian animals and birds, and pictures of western life. In 1893, the exhibition van visited 513 different villages, travelled 2900 km and was inspected by almost 2 000 000 visitors.

British newspapers helped to spread the word about Canada. There were full-page advertisements which the Canadian government and railroads paid for, and editorials that described Canada to their readers. The Canadian government also brought English newspapermen to Canada on free trips to see for themselves what Canada was like. They were lavishly entertained, and dazzled by Niagara Falls, the Rocky Mountains, the growing towns and cities, and the natural resources of the Prairies. As a result they returned to England and wrote enthusiastic reports about Canada in their newspapers. They encouraged British farmers and workers, who were thinking about moving to the United States, to set their sights on Canada instead.

Sifton kept the name of Canada constantly before the British people. It was impossible to miss the signs and posters advertising the 'Garden West'. They were in British post offices, stations, hotel lobbies, and on street signboards. During the Coronation of King Edward VII in 1902, a tall arch of Canada wheat was built on an important London street, the Strand. Canada's name was constantly before the millions of visitors who poured into London for the Coronation.

Some people complained that all this advertising was overdone. One pamphlet said that in Saskatchewan, in three years, a farmer could have his own peach orchard. One old-timer who spent his whole life in Saskatchewan said that he never did see a peach orchard in Saskatchewan, and never heard of one either. Gradually though, the advertising became more realistic. It did not paint the West in rosy colours only, but told the truth about the bad as well as the good side of life there.

British settlers in Canada were asked a series of questions about climate, storms, soil, water, and winter in their districts. Their answers were published in British papers together with their names and addresses. This helped to provide an honest picture of what life was really like homesteading in the West.

As a result of Sifton's advertising campaign in Britain, settlers from England, Scotland, Wales, and Ireland poured into the free land.

NUMBER OF IMMIGRANT ARRIVALS FROM BRITAIN 1897-1905

1897	11,383
1898	11,173
1899	10,660
1900 (Jan. to June)	5,141
1901	11,810
1902	17,259
1903	41,792
1904	50,374
1905	65,359

ADVERTISING IN THE UNITED STATES FOR SETTLERS

Sifton was also anxious to recruit American farmers to settle the West. He realized that American farmers had one special advantage. They had experience. They were used to farming the dry, wide plains, and they knew how to grow crops where there was limited rainfall.

Sifton opened immigration agencies in the United States in Chicago, Kansas City, St. Paul, and other large western cities. Between 200 and 300 agents were hired on commission to spread facts about the Canadian West. At first, progress was very slow. Sifton later described in a speech how the agents worked in the United States.

We had a young man working as an immigration agent in the United States who gave up and came back to Ottawa. When he came into my office, he told me there was no use in his continuing, that the Americans did not even know where Canada was. I told him to go home for a holiday, and then go back to his post. Six months later he sent a telegram saying that he could make no impression, and that he was again coming home. When he came to Ottawa, I sent for him and told him I did not want to get any more telegrams of that kind. In six months time, I got another telegram from him. This time, he said that he had got one Ameri-

can family, and thought he could get another. In the last five years
(1898-1903) that man has sent to Canada 5 000 of the best people
we have in the West.

Eventually the advertising paid off, and the Americans began to
come north to Canada. One reason for this was that land was selling in
the United States at $250 or more per hectare. An established Ameri-
can farmer could sell his farm at a good price. Then he could come to
Canada where he would receive 65 ha free, and buy good land from the
railroad or Hudson's Bay Company for a few dollars per hectare. This
way he could buy machinery and horses, and still have lots of money
left over! To many American farmers it seemed like a very good deal.

American newspapermen were also invited to take a free trip
through the West at harvest time. They saw the fields of golden wheat
waving in the breeze. They talked to farmers, merchants, and bankers,
and then went home to write glowing reports about how prosperous the
Canadian West appeared.

Most of the settlers who came to Canada from the American West
had a fair amount of cash, machinery, and experience. They often
bought large farms and quickly became successful. Since all the good
farm land in the United States had been taken up, many Americans saw
Canada as the new frontier. Thousands began to head northwards.

Colorado settlers arriving by special train.

NUMBER OF IMMIGRANT ARRIVALS FROM THE
UNITED STATES 1897-1905

1897	2,412
1898	9,119
1899	11,945
1900 (Jan. to June)	8,543
1901	17,987
1902	26,388
1903	49,473
1904	45,171
1905	43,543

ADVERTISING IN EASTERN CANADA FOR SETTLERS

The idea of the 'excursion' worked so well that it was an important method of advertising in eastern Canada too. In early spring and late fall, the CPR ran excursion trains for farmers in Ontario, Quebec, and the Maritimes. Workers were needed to help with threshing in the West, so thousands of easterners headed there. It was a free trip to the West as well as a chance to make some extra cash as a farm hand. Many young men who had never been far away from home jumped at the chance to visit the Prairies. Many who came out to work with the threshing gangs stayed on, or returned later to take up homesteads.

As more and more of the young men of Eastern Canada set out for homesteads, the girls they left behind complained that the West was stealing away their boyfriends and future husbands. Some put their complaints into verse, and it was sung in many parts of Ontario to the tune 'Little Brown Jug' or 'Yankee Doodle'.

The Poor Little Girls of Ontario

1. I'll sing you a song of that plaguey pest,
   It goes by the name of the Great North-West.
   I cannot have a beau at all,
   They all skip out there in the fall.

CHORUS One by one they all clear out,
   Thinking to better themselves, no doubt,
   Caring little how far they go
   From the poor little girls of Ontario.

2. First I got mashed on Charlie Brown,
   The nicest fellow in all the town.
   He tipped his hat and sailed away,
   And now he's settled in Manitobay.

3. Then Henry Mayner with his white cravat,
   His high stiff collar and his new plug hat,
   He said if he stayed he'd have to beg,
   And now he's settled in Winnipeg.

4. Then my long-legged druggist with his specs on his nose,
   I really thought he would propose.
   But he's sold his bottle-shop and he's gone,
   Clear out to little Saskatchewan.

5. I'll pack my clothes in a carpet sack,
   I'll go out there and I'll never come back.
   I'll find me a husband and a good one too,
   If I have to go through to Cariboo.

LAST   One by one we'll all clear out,
CHORUS Thinking to better ourselves, no doubt,
        Caring little how far we go.
        From the old, old folks of Ontario.

(1885)

ADVERTISING IN EUROPE FOR SETTLERS

Sifton's advertising campaign was also extended to the crowded rural areas of central and eastern Europe. He wanted people like the Ukrainians, Doukhobors from southern Russia, Poles, and Germans because they were solid peasant farmers who could survive the tough prairie environment. They had been farmers for generations, and Sifton hoped that their children and grandchildren would continue to farm. He arranged for agents of shipping companies to direct good settlers to Canada. He paid them a commission for each settler they sent, $2 for each person, and $5 for the head of each family.

Most European countries were not pleased that Canada was taking away large numbers of their people. Although it was illegal in most European countries for Canada to promote immigration, European peasants continued to leave. The Canadian government set aside large areas or blocks of land where immigrants from one country could settle. This helped to overcome the loneliness and isolation that many settlers in a new country would feel. Such blocks of land were set aside for Ukrainians and Doukhobors.

NUMBER OF IMMIGRANT ARRIVALS IN CANADA FROM OTHER COUNTRIES 1897-1905	
1897	7,921
1898	11,608
1899	21,938
1900 (Jan. to June)	10,211
1901	19,352
1902	23,732
1903	37,099
1904	34,786
1905	37,364

European immigrants were not always warmly welcomed into Canada. For one thing, people could not pronounce their names or understand their languages. Newcomers' customs were strange and their religions different. Many people thought they were inferior because they were not British. In many places non-English speaking settlers were shunned and ridiculed, and suffered forms of discrimination. In time, however, when they proved they were good neighbours and excellent farmers, the Europeans were gradually more accepted in their districts.

The policy of the Canadian government at this time showed signs of discrimination too. Orientals, Blacks, Jews, Italians, and city-dwellers were not encouraged to come to Canada because Sifton believed they would not make successful prairie farmers. This policy was known as selective immigration. It meant that some groups were encouraged to come to Canada, while others were discouraged, or at least ignored. Like most Canadians of his day, Sifton wanted to keep Canada Anglo-Saxon (British). Some other people would be allowed to come to Canada if he thought they would make good farmers.

WHY THE IMMIGRATION POLICY WAS SUCCESSFUL

Between the building of the Canadian Pacific Railway and the outbreak of war in Europe in 1914, more than two million people came to settle in the Canadian West. Sifton's advertising campaign played a large part in persuading them to come to Canada. A number of additional factors were at work as well.

1.   About the time Clifford Sifton took office, the world-wide depres-

sion began to end. In hard times, few families could afford to move. Now, as things got better, families could think about taking up homesteads.

2. By 1900, there was little good farm land left in the United States. There was, however, a great deal of good free land available in Canada. People all over the world began to think about moving to Canada to fill up the open land.

3. The countries of Europe at this time were becoming more and more industrialized. People were leaving the farms to go into the cities to work in factories. Since all these people had to be fed, and fewer farmers were producing food in Europe, these countries needed to buy food from Canada and the United States.

4. In Europe the demand for Canadian wheat, which could be made into bread, increased. The price of wheat almost doubled. Growing wheat became more profitable for the Canadian farmer.

5. Canada now had a transcontinental railroad by which grain could be shipped to markets. Steam-powered ocean vessels transported the wheat to Europe cheaply and quickly.

6. New farm machinery, such as ploughs and reapers, were being developed. These helped to make the farmers' work easier and more efficient.

7. Most important of all, millions of Europeans left their native lands between 1900 and 1914. Some were fleeing cruel treatment, compulsory military service in the army, or economic hardships and overcrowding. They were looking for new homes and better opportunities all over the world. Fortunately, many chose Canada.

Because of all these factors, Canada experienced the greatest wave of immigration in its history. Not only did the number of people grow rapidly, but the make-up of the population changed as well. By 1912, almost one-fifth of the population was not of British or French origin.

Because of the inrush of settlers, the West advanced rapidly. Roads and railway branch lines were built, and towns and villages sprang up. Regina, Edmonton, Calgary, and Saskatoon, which had been small, isolated outposts on the Prairies, became large and thriving trading centres. Almost overnight, the plains changed from a wilderness life of trapping to the business of growing wheat to feed the world.

As the population of the West grew, two new provinces were created. In 1905, Alberta and Saskatchewan became the newest members of Confederation. In thirty-eight years, Confederation had grown from the joining of four provinces in eastern Canada to the union of nine provinces coast to coast.

GROWTH OF CANADIAN POPULATION 1851-1971

1851	2 437 000
1861	3 330 000
1871	3 690 000
1881	4 325 000
1891	4 833 000
1901	5 371 000
1911	7 207 000
1921	8 788 000
1931	10 376 000
1941	11 507 000
1951	14 009 000
1961	18 238 000
1971	21 568 000

ACTIVITIES

1. Using the table 'Growth of Canadian Population 1851-1971', answer the following question. Which decade showed the greatest increase in the total Canadian population? Give possible reasons for this increase.
2. Use the charts in the chapter to discover the total numbers of immigrants who came to Canada during each year from 1897 to 1905. On large sheets of paper plot a graph to show these yearly totals.
3. Pretend you are government agents attempting to encourage settlement in the Canadian West. Divide into three groups — the first to work in Britain, the second in Europe, and the third in the United States. Develop an advertising campaign including posters, newspaper advertisements, etc., to attract settlers from your area of the world.
4. Examine a road map of Saskatchewan, Alberta, or Manitoba. Look carefully at the names of the towns and villages. Do they give you any clues about the nationality of the people who first settled there? Example: around Stockholm, Saskatchewan the people were Swedish.

28
Life on a Homestead

NEW TYPES OF WHEAT

If David Fife's cow had taken one more bite, Canada might never have become a great wheat-producing country. It happened like this. David Fife was a Scotsman who came to Canada in 1820 and settled near Peterborough, Ontario. Fife spent a lot of time experimenting with wheat. He was trying to develop a kind of wheat that would grow well in Canada. Though his neighbours laughed at him, Fife continued to mix different types of wheat, hoping to develop a stronger and more healthy strain.

In 1843, Fife sowed a few wheat seeds that he had received in the mail from a friend in Glasgow. The seeds had originally come from somewhere in Europe. David Fife planted them behind his house. Many of the stalks grew up, but they were disappointing, because they were small and thin. Only one plant had healthy stalks with good, fat heads. He decided to save the seeds from that plant.

Shortly before the wheat was ripe, Fife's cow broke into the garden. It was just about to munch the heads of the experimental wheat when Jane Fife looked out her kitchen window. She ran from the house waving her apron and shooing the cow out of the yard. The precious wheat had been saved.

From the seeds of that one plant, there came a new type of wheat known as Red Fife. Red Fife was a very hardy strain that did not come down with diseases that often destroyed wheat. It produced a high yield and was of excellent quality for bread-making. Most important, Red Fife matured ten days earlier than other kinds of wheat. This was a crucial factor on the Prairies where the frost-free growing season is short. Soon farmers across the Prairies were growing and harvesting Red Fife wheat.

At the turn of the twentieth century, Red Fife fathered another remarkable type of wheat. It was called 'Marquis', and was developed by Charles E. Saunders. Charles Saunders was the quiet, studious man in charge of grain research at the government's experimental farm in Ottawa. Saunders successfully crossed Red Fife wheat and a variety from India called Hard Red Calcutta. It grew into the healthy strain that Dr. Saunders named Marquis. Saunder's strain was even better for the Canadian season because it took just one hundred days to ripen for harvest. Marquis wheat was called 'the discovery of the century'. Now farmers could be sure that they had a type of wheat that could withstand the cold and would be certain to ripen before the frost. The more northern areas of the Prairies could be opened up for settlement, and Canada could become one of the great grain producing nations of the world.

OTHER NEW INVENTIONS

Several new tools were invented that made wheat farming more efficient and enabled the farmer to do the work more quickly. The American settlers introduced to the Canadian West the 'chilled steel' plough. This was able to cut through the tough prairie sod which had been baked by the hot sun. Steel discs were then pulled across the turned sod after ploughing to chop up the lumps.

Clearing and breaking new soil.

Grain elevators were soon built in every town on the Prairies. Here the farmers' wheat could be stored until it could be shipped out by rail. The railway boxcar was developed so that large amounts of grain could be moved in bulk to the Great Lakes or ocean ports. From there the wheat could be sent to Canadian or world-wide markets by steamers.

New machinery was also used at harvest time. Reapers were pulled through the fields to cut down the grain. These were followed by binding machines that could tie rope or wire around a sheaf of wheat. Then the sheaves of wheat were carried by wagon to the threshing machine that separated the wheat from the straw.

At first, all the machines were driven by horses or oxen. But by the 1890s the steam engine brought great changes to farm machinery. Now tractors, threshing machines, and binders could be propelled by steam power. Threshing machines were very expensive, so farmers did not often own them. Instead, they hired a man with threshing equipment and a gang of harvesters. The harvesting gang moved from farm to farm threshing grain for each farmer, and charging him for the job. Many of the young men from eastern Canada who went west on the harvest excursions worked on these threshing gangs.

It was an exciting day when the threshers moved their equipment into the farmyard. While the farmer worked hard with the gang harvesting his crop, the women of the farm kept the whole operation going by feeding this hungry gang of twenty extra men.

What would a typical woman's day be like at harvest time?

4:30 a.m.	Rise, go to the barn and milk the cows.
5:30 a.m.	Start preparing breakfast. Cook 150 pancakes, fry 10 dozen eggs, and 4 kg of bacon. Make enough coffee to fill a washtub. Serve all this food at long tables that had been set up in the kitchen.
7:00 a.m.	Wash all the breakfast dishes.
8:00 a.m.	Bake 40 loaves of bread. Start preparing the mid-day meal. Peel and boil 60 potatoes. Scrape piles of carrots and mash loads of turnip. Roast several slabs of beef. Bake rice puddings well-filled with raisins. Make a batch of 6 dozen doughnuts. Brew more coffee or strong tea.
12:00 p.m.	Serve the meal to the hungry gang.
1:00 p.m.	Clean up the house, tend to the children, and prepare for supper. Wash the lunch dishes. Bake two

Threshing outfit.

	dozen apple or pumpkin pies and a batch of cookies. Prepare vegetables and fry 70 pork chops.
5:00 p.m.	Return to the barn for evening milking.
6:30 p.m.	Serve supper to the weary men.
7:30 p.m.	After the men leave, remain in the kitchen cleaning up, and preparing food for the next day. Slice 4 kg of bacon for breakfast. Fill containers with syrup. Tuck the children into bed.
11:00 p.m.	Fall exhausted into bed.

With any luck, if the weather stayed good and the threshing machine did not break down, the threshing gang was usually finished in a week or so. However, if problems did arise, a threshing gang could almost eat the farmer out of house and home! Women and girls who cooked for the early threshing gangs will never forget the long hours and the hard work.

MEMORIES OF HOMESTEADING

Thousands of families took up homesteads on the Prairies between 1880 and 1914. Some of them wrote letters home to friends and relatives in which they described their new lives. A few kept diaries of day-to-day happenings. Still other pioneers later wrote down, or recorded on tape, their memories of those early days. Here are some of the things they remembered.

MOSQUITOES

You could just not believe what the mosquitoes were like. My mother would send me to the slough for a pail of water. The way was through very thick and long grass. This is where the hundreds of thousands of mosquitoes lived. You'd be wearing a long skirt and long stockings, so it was your face and your neck and your hands you had to hide. Imagine going out in June in the warm morning wearing mittens to get a pail of water.

That first summer when my father was plowing, I had to walk on one side of the horses and my smaller sister on the other waving cloths. Bits of cloth were tied to sticks to keep the horses calm enough to work. The mosquitoes were simply driving them out of their minds! It was a common sight to see a team with three people around it, one man plowing and the others brushing them off.

From *The Pioneer Years* by Barry Broadfoot.

A HAILSTORM BEYOND BELIEF

During dinner, the sky darkened and the storm clouds rolled up and there were flashes of lightning everywhere. Tremendous rolls of thunder warned us we were in for a storm. We took shelter when the storm rolled over us, and when we came out ten minutes later, our beautiful waving fields of wheat were a blackened, battered mess of mud and straw. Hail and terrible rain, but mostly hail. Huge hailstones could be seen everywhere.

Our farmyard was strewn with the dead bodies of mother's chickens, and the swollen river had swept away the geese and ducks that had been feeding on it. In our pasture were the bodies of our young cattle and calves that had been pounded to death by hailstones the size of walnuts.

All in ten minutes, without knowing what was going on as we huddled in the shelter, all the work of a year had gone for nothing. Looking out our window, we could see just blackened, battered crops in the mud, good for nothing at all.

From *The Pioneer Years* by Barry Broadfoot.

WALLPAPER

Wallpaper was out of the question, so old newspapers were saved and pasted on the walls to cover the cracks and keep out the cold. Pictures, from magazines that had literally been read to pieces, were used too. . .

By Kate Johnson, from the Provincial Archives of Manitoba.

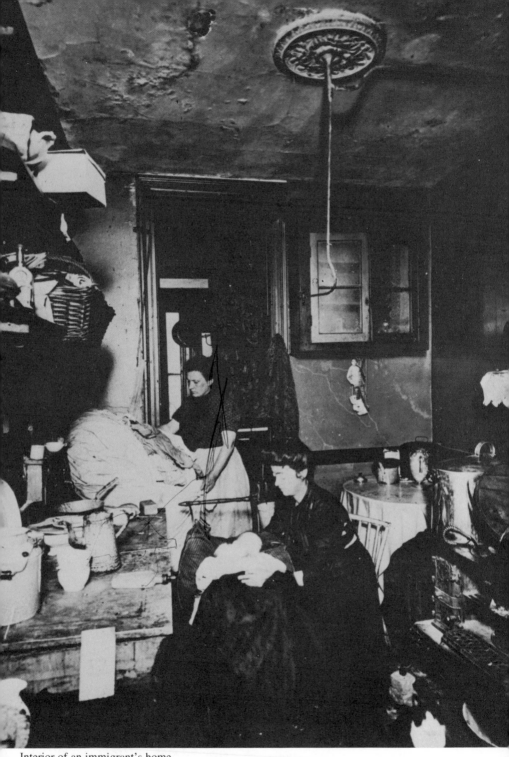

Interior of an immigrant's home.

GAMES

Chess and checkers had been brought from the Old Country, and many a long winter evening they kept the family occupied, father joining in the games and acting as instructor. On the back of the checker-board was another game, called fox-and-hounds, in which a red button was relentlessly pursued by three of another colour, usually brown or gray. The object of the chase being, of course, to corner the 'fox'.

When these games failed to fascinate, the youngsters turned to playing farmyard and spent the time trading horses, cows and pigs. Shoeboxes made stables and barns, and around them were grouped pens containing the livestock. The animals in these enclosures were paper cut-outs, sent from Denmark by grandma, and had been patiently pasted on cardboard by mother. Buttons from mother's button-bag served the purpose too, and were sorted according to size and colour, large white ones being used for sheep, while little ones of various colours became calves, colts or poultry.

By Kate Johnson, from the Provincial Archives of Manitoba.

CHORES

Kids were limited to certain things, sawing the wood, feeding the pigs, and taking the swill from the house to the pigs, cleaning up the yard . . . and of course as you grew older, you took on heavier responsibilities, such as getting in the cows and milking and helping around the general way. When you weren't in school you could tramp a load of hay in the hay rack and there were lots of odd jobs to be done.

By Edric Lloyd, from the archives of the Glenbow-Alberta Institute.

FOOD

I remember what my mother used to serve us in the winter, about the time of my twelfth birthday (1885):

Breakfast — Porridge or mush, milk and brown sugar, sometimes hash or cold meat, warmed potatoes, bread, butter if we had any, stewed or canned fruit.

Dinner — Stewed rabbit with dumplings, potatoes and another vegetable, sometimes plain pudding or pie.

Supper — Variable — a hot soup, pancakes, Johnny cake with syrup, sometimes a steamed pudding, fruit, hot biscuits, perhaps potatoes cooked some tasty way, often raw onions.

FACTS AND FIGURES ABOUT WHEAT TODAY

1. Wheat farming is one of Canada's most important industries. Farm cash receipts for wheat in 1975 were $2463 million in Canada.
2. There are over 11 million hectares of wheat fields in Canada.
3. In a record year, 1966, over 22 000 000 t were produced.
4. One kilogram of flour makes two loaves of bread.
5. Canada's best customers for large quantities of wheat and flour are Britain, Japan, the U.S.S.R., China, Germany, Belgium, the Netherlands, and Switzerland.
6. The world's largest producer of wheat is the U.S.S.R. Other leading producers are the United States, China, India, France, Canada, and Australia.
7. In the 1975 crop year, the largest Canadian production was in Saskatchewan, and the second largest was in Alberta.
8. Flour from wheat grown in dry climates makes the best bread because of its high protein content.
9. In 1975, 10 740 000 t of wheat were exported from Canada (75% of Canada's total crop).

ACTIVITIES

1. Prepare a short skit about David and Jane Fife to show how Red Fife wheat was developed.
2. Find out how a grain elevator works. Why are grain elevators built alongside railway tracks?
3. Pretend you are a member of a harvest threshing gang. You have come to Saskatchewan from Ontario to work on the harvest. Write a diary of your experiences and observations during the harvest season.
4. Compare the ways in which the opening of the Canadian North today is similar to the opening of the West in the last century. Make a bulletin-board display to illustrate the comparison.

29
The Ukrainians

Between 1897 and 1912, 594 000 people crossed to Canada from Europe. Of these, 170 000 — one of the largest groups of 'new' Canadians — were from the Ukraine. They were nicknamed 'the men in sheepskin coats' because of the kind of garments they wore.

Clifford Sifton once described the kind of immigrant Canada was looking for in Europe.

> The peasants, the men in sheepskin coats, are the ones that are wanted here in Canada. When I speak of quality, I have in mind something that is quite different from what is in the mind of the average person. I think that a stalwart peasant in a sheepskin coat, born on the soil, whose forefeathers have been farmers for ten generations, with a stout wife, and a half dozen children, is good quality, as an immigrant. I do not care whether or not he is British-born. It does not matter what his nationality is.

QUESTIONS:

1. What does the remark 'born on the soil' suggest about the immigrant's past?
2. Why was there a need for many children at this time in the development of the West?
3. Why would a 'stout wife' be more useful than a frail one?
4. Why would Sifton want this type of immigrant?

In the southeast corner of Europe, in an area known as the Ukraine, people began to hear that Canada wanted immigrants. The boundaries of the Ukraine extended to the Don River on the east, the Black Sea on the south, Romania and Poland on the west, and Russia on the north.

Ukrainian families on board a ship to Canada.

Kiev was the ancient capital of the Ukraine. Some of the features of the landscape were similar to parts of the Canadian Prairies. For example, the broad plains or steppes of the Ukraine resembled the Prairies. Both landscapes were cut by deep rivers and winding creeks. An immigrant from the mountain region of the Ukraine could not look at the Canadian Rockies without experiencing memories of the beautiful Carpathian and Caucasus Mountains at home. Soil of the Ukraine was fertile and good for growing wheat. The climate of the Ukraine was also similar to the Canadian Prairies. Much of both regions was buried with deep snow in winter, with many frosty days and nights. The crunch of hard-packed snow was one of the few familiar sounds for the Ukrainian immigrant in western Canada. Yet winter in the Ukraine was at least two months shorter; it waited for Christmas. Spring came early, so that work in the fields was in full swing by mid-March. The climate was good for fruit-growing. Travellers in the Ukraine were always impressed with the white-washed cottages in the villages surrounded by fruit trees and flowers.

QUESTIONS:

1. Map study. Locate in an atlas the area of the Ukraine outlined above. Compare the Ukraine and the Canadian Prairies under the headings:
    a) surface features
    b) climate
    c) crops produced
Use the following climatic data to help.

KIEV AND WINNIPEG COMPARED				
	Temperature (°C)		*Rainfall* (mm)	
	Kiev	Winnipeg	Kiev	Winnipeg
January	−6.0	−17.7	43	26
February	−5.3	−15.5	39	21
March	−0.6	−7.9	35	27
April	7.2	3.3	46	30
May	14.5	11.3	56	50
June	17.6	16.5	66	81
July	19.5	20.2	70	69
August	18.5	18.9	72	70
September	13.8	12.8	47	55
October	7.5	6.2	47	37
November	1.0	−4.8	53	29
December	−3.9	−12.9	41	22

2. Discuss the possible connections between the geography of the Canadian Prairies and its attraction for the Ukrainians. How well do you think the Ukrainians will adapt to life in Canada?

WHY LEAVE THE UKRAINE? WHY GO TO CANADA?

At the same time that Canada was looking for immigrants in Europe, many Ukrainians were thinking of leaving their homeland. As the population increased, land had become very scarce. This meant that the peasant farmer could never produce enough on his small plot of land to make a decent living. He would always be poor. There were few opportunities for education and self-advancement. The people were given no voice in the running of the country. The Ukrainians longed for freedom and the chance for a better life for their children. For many Ukrainians, Canada promised a new life.

They asked one of their most educated men, Dr. Joseph Oleskow, to investigate for them the possibilities available in Canada. Dr. Oleskow wrote this letter to the Canadian government on 16 March 1895:

Dear Sir,

A great number of Ukrainians desire to leave their native country due to overpopulation, shortage of land as it has to be subdivided by a father for his sons, heavy taxation, and unfavourable political conditions.

The question therefore arises to find a country with ample good, free land for settlement, willing to accept thousands of farmers, — who although possessed of modest means, are diligent and thrifty — and to offer them the opportunity to attain a decent living.

The representatives of the Brazilian government are conducting intensive propaganda with the aim of directing the flow of emigration towards Brazil,. . .

The Committee of the prospective emigrant farmers has decided to make enquiries about the possibilities offered to farmers wishing to settle in Canada. . . .

The writer would come to Canada in order to survey places suitable for mass-settlement of emigrants.

Begging to be excused for not having the courage to use my inadequate knowledge of English to be able to write this letter,

I remain,

Very truly yours,

[Signed] J. Oleskow

QUESTIONS:

1. In one column make a list of reasons why Ukrainians wished to leave their own country. In a second column beside each reason, show why the Canadian West might attract them.

2. From Dr. Oleskow's letter find out what other country Ukrainians were going to at that time. Explain why Canada would be a better choice.

Later in 1895 Dr. Oleskow actually visited Canada. He also wrote a pamphlet in which he described what Canada was like. The pamphlet was called *About Free Lands* and it played an important part in encouraging Ukrainians to choose Canada. Part of what Dr. Oleskow wrote is included here:

If someone finishes public school in Canada, he is an educated person and may be elected to public office. . . .

The climate varies in different parts of Canada. In the provinces where the free land is available, the country is very much like that of our country, only that the winters are more severe. . . . Railways are everywhere where settlements are situated. This is simply because railways are built first and people settle along the rail lines afterwards. . . .

The whole country is divided into squares called sections and a family can obtain a quarter of such a section. Each section has a number . . . . Even-numbered sections belong to the government and are given away as homesteads. . . . The settler receives ownership papers after three years, provided he can prove that he was residing on the land at least six months each year, that he built a house, and that he has brought under cultivation a certain amount of land. . . .

The crossing of the ocean lasts one week, and travel by rail in Europe and Canada takes about five days. . . . It is best to travel in groups under the guidance of an experienced person who knows the language. . . .

In order to make a living, one should have enough money to be able to live after arrival until the next crop is gathered, to be able to buy a pair of oxen for ploughing as well as tools for farming. . . . The best time to emigrate to Canada is in the early spring, because this will enable the settler to put in some potatoes and sow some grain on his ploughed acres. . . . Nobody should venture to Canada in the autumn because he will have difficulty in finding work and will have to spend his money, perhaps his last cent, to live through the winter. . . .

QUESTIONS:

1. Dr. Oleskow wrote the pamphlet *About Free Lands* before he actually visited Canada. How accurately did he describe the country that he had not seen?

2. Suppose you were a Ukrainian farmer considering moving to a

Immigrants on the *SS Empress of Britain*.

new country. How would Dr. Oleskow's pamphlet encourage or discourage you from choosing Canada?

CROSSING TO CANADA

In order to get to Canada from the Ukraine the emigrant had to buy steamship and railroad tickets. Those would cost about $85.00 for the grownups and about half that price for the children. To scrape together a sum of nearly $300 for a family of four was quite an undertaking for a poor Ukrainian peasant. In addition he had to have at least $25.00 to show the Canadian officials at the port of entry. There was also food to be paid for during the ocean and land voyage.

Very often, when the immigrant reached Canada, he had hardly a cent left to his name. One of the first men to arrive from the Ukraine used to show a penny to his children and grandchildren. 'This penny,' he would say, 'was all I had left to start a new life when I arrived in Canada in 1897! In Hamburg I was cheated out of my money by a land agent. This penny is an expensive souvenir. I will pass it on to my grandchildren as being all I have to show for my years of hard work in the Ukraine. It is all the money I had to start with in this wonderful new land of Canada!'

The ocean voyage to Canada was often filled with bitter experiences. Many Ukrainians travelled to Canada on freight and cattle steamers from Hamburg. The same ships that carried Canadian grain and cattle to Europe were used to bring a return load of people. For up to three weeks these poor human beings were packed together in horrible conditions of filth and over-crowding until they reached Quebec City.

The boat trip was not the end of it. Several days of railroad travel still lay ahead. The trains ran special Colonist cars. No soft seats here — just bare boards. No eating facilities were available. The passengers had to bring their own food or buy it at the larger stations along the way. When these new settlers finally arrived at their destination after a long journey, they were dirty, unshaven, and half-starved. But they had hope in their hearts. Now the long harsh journey was over and the new life on the Prairies could begin.

In Winnipeg the immigrants stayed over for two weeks in the immigration building. Here the immigration papers were signed and the homesteads decided on. The settler usually took the homestead the agent offered him, but the Ukrainians claimed the right to choose who their neighbours would be — usually friends or relatives from their native village. When that was completed, they started out for the newly chosen homestead.

Often they had to travel 30 or 40 km from the railway stop to their homestead in an ox-drawn wagon. There were few roads, and trails had to be cut and cleared. Men and women too would arm themselves with axes to hack through trees and brush before the wagon could make its way. Having arrived at their new home, the newcomers would pitch a tent and prepare to homestead. The long journey was over, but the hard work was about to begin!

QUESTIONS:

1.   Make a list of the stages in the crossing of Ukrainians to Canada and the difficulties encountered.

2. Imagine you are thirteen or fourteen years old. You have just arrived in Canada with your parents from the Ukraine. Write a letter to one of your best friends back home describing the ocean crossing and the trip to the homestead.

3. Draw a map to show a possible route that Ukrainians might follow from the Ukraine to the Canadian Prairies.

STARTING TO FARM ON THE PRAIRIES

Wasyl Melnyk was only twelve years old when he arrived with his family from the Ukraine in 1894. They took up a homestead near Edna, Alberta. It was a dry, pleasant summer. Raspberries ripened at the edge of the bush. Wild cranberries were turning red and delicious Saskatoons hung in handfuls. Partridges stalked near the trail and ducks covered the sloughs. But Wasyl had little time to investigate. There was work to be done.

The first duty of every homesteader was to slap-bang together some kind of shelter with a roof over it. For the Melnyk family, it was a dugout, framed over with rafters, and covered with sod. Inside the hut ledges in the sod were cut to serve as seats, beds, and tables. In dry weather, such a dugout could be surprisingly comfortable. But on wet days, the inside of the hut would be turned into a mud-hole!

Now, as the summer passed, Wasyl's family was hard at work building a more substantial home for the winter. The men cut young poplar trees, and, with the oxen, dragged them towards the building site. While the men put up the logs the women and children dug clay which they mixed with water and dried grass. The mud and grass were applied to the walls of the house and plastered into holes between the logs.

Mosquitoes were the worst problem they faced. The insects nearly drove them mad. Slapping at the mosquitoes or burning smudges only seemed to increase their fiendish attacks. Nothing but the patient endurance of the Ukrainian peasants made them carry on! In later years, less hardy settlers actually returned to their native land because of these fierce little insects.

When the thatched roof was finally put in place, the little house was snug and ready for the cold blasts of winter. Now Wasyl's mother put up the holy pictures and brought out little treasures to remind them of their former home in the Ukraine.

Wasyl's father and uncles then had to leave the family and go out and earn money to buy doors and windows for the house, or perhaps a

Ukrainian family harvesting.

cow or a team of oxen to help break the land. They found jobs working in the harvest fields or on the railway, but it was lonely for the family with the men away.

Meanwhile, the women and children picked berries, and Wasyl walked to the nearest town to sell them. The biggest profit was to be made from digging and selling seneca roots, or snake roots, used for medicines. All the children pitched in to dig the roots, dry them in the sun, and carry them to market. Many Ukrainian families were able to buy sugar and flour, and pieces of cloth for clothing, through the sale of this humble root.

The first winter on the farm was the hardest. Canadian winters were much harder than those in the Ukraine, but what was worse was the terrible loneliness and isolation. Finally, when they could stand the home-sickness no longer, the Melynk family set out to walk 24 km to visit their friend Yurkiw. They had known the Yurkiw family back home in their village in the Ukraine. When at last they knocked on the door, both Mrs. Yurkiw and Wasyl's mother burst into tears. For a few minutes, the women just sat down and cried. The loneliness and the need to talk to someone from home kept them chatting well past midnight. Then what a feast they had! Mrs. Yurkiw made 'pyrohi' (dumplings) and fresh white bread, and they had jugs of warm milk to drink. Wasyl ate until he was stuffed.

At last when spring came, Wasyl and his father managed to break and plough a little more than a hectare of land. This they seeded with wheat, oats, barley and potatoes. The Melnyk family had made a proud beginning at being farmers in Canada.

QUESTIONS:

1. Make a list of the problems to be overcome by the early Ukrainian pioneers. Tell how they solved those challenges. How do you think the pioneers would feel in the new land?
2. Sketch one of the early Ukrainian homes described above.

PROSPERITY IN THE PROMISED LAND

At the beginning of this century C.W. Speers sent the following report to the Commissioner of Immigration. He was reporting on the immigrants' settlements and their rapidly improving social conditions: 'I proceeded to inspect the large colony of Ukrainians in the Edna district of Alberta. There is every evidence of prosperity among them. They are in good comfortable houses and are doing remarkably well.

'Their social conditions are improving rapidly now; they are fast adapting to our customs; their homes are comfortable and very clean. They have built two large churches in this colony. The Church of the Russian Orthodox faith is 10.7 m × 22.6 m and will cost $1 200.00 while the Greek Catholic church is 10.7 m × 16.5 m and will cost $1 000.00. There are two schools already established in the colony which are open for eight months of the year. These Ukrainians are very anxious to learn our language, and are keeping their children in school when they have the opportunity. In all cases the teachers speak highly of the progress of the pupils — they are quick, bright, and attentive. There are 360 families in this colony.'

Another visitor to the colony was a reporter for the Toronto *Globe*. He told the readers in a newspaper article: 'At first, I was very much opposed to these Ukrainians, but after seeing for myself the progress they are making I changed my mind. They are good settlers.'

Similar admiration and approval of the Ukrainians appeared in the Toronto *Globe*, written by Frank Yeigh, a traveller and journalist who visited their colony in 1902:

Farther along I saw the house of a settler who has been here for five years. He is now a prosperous market gardener, raising potatoes and hens, onions and garlic, cabbages and beets for the Winnipeg market. He drives to market each week with his team of oxen. If the weather is too hot for his beasts, he will mercifully make the journey by night, even though his own rest is sacrificed.

The cattle in the grove nearby are his too and the butter and the milk they produce add to his savings. I tell you these Ukrainians could give pointers to Scotsmen in thrift and economy.

Hardworking are these simple peasants, rising before sunrise and labouring until darkness. The women labour as hard as the men in the fields. Only the babies are immune from work, and there were enough of them to give promise of thickly populating the colony in the future.

Everywhere their welcome to the stranger was cordial. 'We are pleased to have you,' greeted me at every threshold. The extended right hand was often grasped in both hands by the host, followed by a deep bow. The language of a smile is understood and returned by a smile by these children of Europe. They have crossed the unknown seas to try their luck on Canadian soil. God grant them peace and prosperity in their new home!

QUESTIONS:

1. List the evidence which the authors provide to prove that the Ukrainians were increasing in prosperity.
2. 'They are good settlers.' Pick out characteristics of Ukrainian settlers to support this statement.

SOME LATER EVENTS IN UKRAINIAN-CANADIAN HISTORY

There were three waves of Ukrainian immigration to Canada.

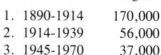

1.	1890-1914	170,000
2.	1914-1939	56,000
3.	1945-1970	37,000

As we have seen, the immigrants who arrived in the first wave were sturdy peasants in sheepskin coats. They settled mostly on farms in the Canadian West.

The Second Wave: Between the two World Wars, there was a second group of immigrants who arrived. The reasons for their coming to Canada were much the same as those of the first settlers. However, they had the advantage of more schooling and many had high school or university training. This second wave of Ukrainians tended to move into cities, and only a small number settled on farms. Many opened businesses of their own, or used their trades and skills in industry. This group had another advantage — they were not plunged into the unknown to build from nothing. The first immigrants had already established schools, churches, and a Ukrainian life style. That made their settlement into Canada easier.

The Third Wave: After the Second World War ended in 1945, a third wave of Ukrainians came to Canada. They came to us as the victims of war. Many had lost their homes, relatives, and everything they owned during the war. Others fled from the Russian Communists who were taking over the Ukraine. They came to Canada searching for freedom.

Many of the third wave of immigrants were very well educated. About 300 were doctors and dentists, 300 were university professors, and about 600 were clergymen. Others were engineers, teachers, skilled craftsmen, artists, musicians, and singers. Almost all of the immigrants settled in Canadian cities such as Winnipeg, Edmonton, and Oshawa.

Ukrainian church at Vegreville, Alberta.

QUESTIONS:

1. Prepare a bar graph to illustrate the three main waves of Ukrainian immigration to Canada.
2. How did each of the waves of Ukrainian immigrants differ from the others?

ACTIVITIES

1. Compare the qualities looked for in immigrants in the 1890s with the qualities desired in immigrants to Canada in the 1980s.
2. Collect pictures about life in your home community in the 1880s. Compare and contrast the various activities in your present-day community with activities found in early pioneer settlements.
3. Interview a social worker about the problems of new immigrants coming to Canada today. Find out the problems these people might have in adjusting to Canadian life, finding jobs, and fitting into schools.
4. Debate: 'Immigration is good for Canada.'

30
Fall of the Conservatives— Rise of the Liberals

Louis Riel, though dead, continued to influence Canadian politics. The first election after Riel's execution was held in 1887. In that election, Sir John A. Macdonald and his Conservatives began to lose seats. Since Confederation, Quebec had voted solidly for the Conservative Party. Now the Conservatives were blamed in Quebec for the hanging of Riel, and Quebec began to swing away from the party which had hung the French Roman Catholic hero. People in Quebec started to vote for the Liberal Party, and from 1887 onwards the Conservatives continued steadily to lose support in Quebec.

Macdonald faced other problems too. An economic depression had hit the western world. Canada, United States, Britain, France, Germany, and Italy were all having a hard time. Jobs were scarce because many factories had closed. Unemployment was causing poverty. Trade between the provinces and with other countries had almost died out. Canada had come to a standstill.

Many people thought that the National Policy of Macdonald and the Conservatives was no longer working. The Prairies were not filling up with settlers because of the world-wide depression. Instead, many Canadians were moving to the United States where they hoped to find work. More people were moving out of Canada than were moving in.

The second plank of the National Policy was the building of the railway. The economic depression made it difficult to raise money for such a large building project, and almost prevented the completion of the CPR.

Macdonald's third idea of protective tariffs did not appear to be working either. Taxes had been put on foreign goods coming into Canada. The plan had been to protect Canadian manufacturers from competition and to keep Canadian factories busy. But the higher tariffs did not seem to be bringing the prosperity that Macdonald had hoped for.

Many people began to question the whole idea of high tariffs. The Liberal party had a brilliant, new, French-Canadian leader, Wilfrid Laurier. He and his party thought that reciprocity was the answer to Canada's problems. If Canada had free trade with the United States, the Liberals said, this would end the depression. The Liberal party promised that if they were elected, they would bring in reciprocity with the United States.

THE ELECTION OF 1891

The election of 1891 was one of the most important elections ever held in Canada. Sir John A. was now seventy-five years old. Still, he travelled up and down the country in bitter winter weather making two or three speeches a day. Macdonald warned people that the Liberal policy of reciprocity would be a disaster for Canada. He predicted that the United States would take over Canada's trade and eventually take over Canada itself. The Conservatives were against any closer ties with the United States. They favoured stronger ties with Britain. 'A British subject I was born, a British subject I will die,' said Sir John A. to cheering crowds. He urged people to vote for his party with the slogan 'The Old Leader (Macdonald), the Old Flag (Union Jack), the Old Policy (National Policy)'.

It was a very hard-fought election, but when the votes were counted, Macdonald and the Conservatives had been returned to power. However, the election campaign had seriously weakened Sir John A. During the following spring he suffered a mild stroke, but was making a good recovery. Then in the late afternoon of Friday, 29 May 1891, he suffered a second stroke. His entire right side was paralyzed, and he lost all power of speech. The news sped by wire to every province of Canada. When the front pages of newspapers just reported 'He Is Dying', everyone in Canada knew whom they meant. On the evening

THE OLD FLAG,
THE OLD POLICY,
THE OLD LEADER.

Macdonald's funeral procession.

of 6 June 1891, Sir John A. Macdonald died. With his death an era of Canadian history had come to a close.

Two days after Macdonald's death, Wilfrid Laurier, Sir John A.'s political opponent, rose in the House of Commons to say: 'The place of Sir John A. Macdonald in this country was so large and absorbing that it is almost impossible to imagine that the politics of this country — the fate of this country — will continue without him. His loss overwhelms us. . . The career of Sir John A. Macdonald, which has just been closed, is one of the most remarkable careers of this century.'

THE MANITOBA SCHOOLS QUESTION

The Conservative party had won the election of 1891. However, it was their last session in power for some time. With Sir John A. gone, no one was able to hold the Conservatives together. Four different leaders in the next five years tried unsuccessfully to fill Macdonald's shoes. The Conservative party was divided and further weakened by the issue that arose over Manitoba schools.

When the Red River settlement became the province of Manitoba in 1870, most of the people living there were French-speaking and Roman Catholic. They had been promised that they could have Roman Catholic schools kept up by money raised from public taxes. Over the next twenty years, large numbers of English-speaking Protestants, many from Ontario, had moved into Manitoba. The French Canadians in Manitoba gradually became a minority. By 1890, most of the members of the Manitoba Provincial Parliament were English-speaking Protestants. They passed an act to set up a single school system that would not be connected with any church. All citizens of the province, whatever their religion, would pay for the school system through their taxes. The government would no longer support separate, Roman Catholic schools. Roman Catholics themselves would have to pay for separate schools if they wanted to have them.

The Roman Catholic school supporters in Manitoba complained to the Dominion government in Ottawa. They also took their case before the Canadian courts. The courts ruled that the British North America

Prairie schoolhouse.

Act stated that each province had the right to manage its own education. Education was not the business of the Dominion government. The election of 1896 was fought over the question of what should be done about the Manitoba schools.

THE ELECTION OF 1896

The Conservative party was deeply divided over what should be done with Manitoba. Some said Ottawa had no right to interfere in the province's schools. Others wanted to assist Roman Catholics in Manitoba in their struggle against their provincial government.

Laurier, leader of the Liberals, was a French Canadian and a faithful Roman Catholic. However, he believed that Manitoba did have the right to manage its own educational system. It was a case of provincial rights. Laurier said he would try to work out a compromise, an agreement acceptable to both sides. All Laurier would promise to do was to try and persuade Manitoba to pay for separate schools out of public funds.

The election of 1896 was an unusual affair. Many French Canadians did not vote for Laurier even though he was a French Canadian. They thought that he was not supporting his fellow Roman Catholics in Manitoba. On the other hand, many Protestants in Ontario did vote for Laurier even though he was a Roman Catholic. They thought, as Laurier did, that schools in Manitoba were a provincial matter. When the election was over, the Conservatives had been defeated. For the first time since the days of Alexander Mackenzie, Canada had a Liberal government in power again.

ACTIVITIES

1. Why did the Conservative party use the slogan 'The Old Leader, the Old Flag, the Old Policy' in the election of 1891?
2. Summarize the life of Canada's first Prime Minister by making a timeline of the major events of his life.
3. Pretend you are writing a letter to a friend in England just after the death of Macdonald. You are trying to express a number of opinions about Macdonald's leadership. Your letter should contain opinions about the following: his character, faults, qualities of leadership, and accomplishments.
4. Here is what Sir W. Laurier said about Macdonald: 'His actions always displayed great originality, a high level of intellect, a far-reaching vision beyond the event of the day, and a great devotion to

Canada's welfare, Canada's advancement, and Canada's glory.' What accomplishments did Laurier attribute to Macdonald? Do you agree or disagree? Do you think Macdonald was a nation-builder? How did he contribute to the growth of Canada?

5. Make a list of the qualities that you feel a Prime Minister of Canada should possess. What qualities did Macdonald exhibit that made him well-suited to be Prime Minister?

VALUES EXERCISE

Suppose you have been saving up your money for more than a year to buy a stereo of your own. The one you have chosen costs $399. One night while you are watching TV you see the same stereo advertised in the United States for $300. The next day you go down to the store and ask to purchase the same stereo but one made in the United States rather than in Canada. The clerk shows you a picture of it in a catalogue priced at $450. This is impossible since you saw it on TV for $300. But the clerk explains that the increase is due to the tariff on all products coming into Canada. In the end you buy the Canadian stereo for $399. Still, you have the feeling that you have been cheated out of $99. How fair is this situation to you as a buyer? How important is the tariff to Canada as a nation?

Was the tariff a good thing for Canada and Canadians during the 1880s and 1890s? Should Macdonald have included tariff policy as part of his National Policy? Explain your answer. Who benefited most from the tariff? Why? Who suffered most from the tariff? Why? Should Canada continue to have tariffs?

31
The Golden Age of Laurier

In 1896 Wilfrid Laurier entered the House of Commons to the sound of many cheers. He made his way to the seat that Sir John A. Macdonald had occupied for nineteen years. Now Laurier was the Prime Minister of Canada, and the next fifteen years were known as the 'Golden Age of Laurier'.

Laurier had once said that the 19th century belonged to the United States, but that the 20th century would belong to Canada. As the 19th century drew to a close, it looked as if Laurier might be right. The world depression began to clear, and prosperity started to return to Canada. Factories began to hum again, people had jobs, and there were markets for Canadian goods. Good times returned, and for the next fifteen years, things went well for Canada. It certainly was a golden age for most citizens of Canada and the Liberal party.

Laurier was Canada's first French-Canadian Prime Minister. He brought to the office his great gifts as a person and as a politician. Laurier's character was shaped by his rather unusual background. He was born near the village of St. Lin in the province of Quebec in 1841. He was a sixth-generation Canadian who could trace his ancestors back to a member of the Carignan-Salières Regiment who had settled in Quebec in the 17th century. Laurier, a French-speaking boy, was brought up as a faithful Roman Catholic. When he was eleven, his father did a surprising thing. He decided to send young Wilfrid to school in the English-speaking settlement at New Glasgow. There the boy learned and studied English, and became fluently bilingual. He lived with a family of Scottish Protestants. In this way Laurier learned

Sir Wilfrid Laurier, 1882.

a great deal about the ways and religion of English-speaking Protestants. He also learned to be tolerant of people different from himself.
In later years, as Prime Minister of a largely English-speaking Canada,
this knowledge was extremely useful. Often Laurier told students that
they owed it to themselves to be able to read and speak both languages
of Canada. He was grateful to his own father for giving him the chance
to do so.

    After High School, Laurier went to McGill University, and like
Macdonald, became a lawyer. Following his graduation, he opened
a law practice at Arthabaskaville, Quebec, a small town on the south
side of the St. Lawrence River. Here he impressed the townspeople
with his honesty, his courage, and his fair play. Eventually they chose
him to represent them at the provincial government at Quebec City in
1871. Three years later he was elected to the federal government in

Ottawa, and in 1887 he became leader of the Liberal party. In Parliament Laurier impressed everyone as an excellent speech-maker. Macdonald admired his political opponent and recognized him as a most promising politician.

Probably Laurier's greatest gift to Canada was his ability to see both the English and French points of view. His main aim was to keep both language groups together and to be sure that each treated the other fairly. Laurier's sense of fair play helped him to work out compromises that would be acceptable to both French and English Canadians.

Laurier used all his skills of compromise to solve the Manitoba Schools Question. He tried to find an answer that would satisfy both sides. He said that Manitoba had the right to decide on its own education and schools. This pleased the majority in Manitoba and Protestants in the rest of Canada. But he also persuaded the Manitoba government to allow religious instruction to be given in the last half-hour of the school day. Also, in schools where there were more than ten children speaking French or another European language, a teacher of that other language must be hired. This part of the compromise satisfied the French Roman Catholic people in Manitoba and Quebec. It also pleased the other minority groups who were moving into Manitoba from Europe.

In 1897, Laurier and his wife journeyed to London, England. They went to take part in the celebration of Queen Victoria's Diamond Jubilee. Queen Victoria had ruled for sixty years, and a great celebration was planned to honour the event. Dignitaries from all parts of the British Empire had come to honour the Queen.

The greatest parade that London had ever seen moved through the streets towards St. Paul's Cathedral. The day before the parade, the Queen had knighted Laurier. During the parade, some of the loudest cheers were reserved for Sir Wilfrid Laurier and the North-West Mounted Police.

Wherever Laurier went in Britain, he impressed people with his charm, appearance, dignity, and eloquence. He won the respect and admiration of the British for himself and for Canada. At the same time, this great pageant in London made an important impression on Laurier. He was full of admiration for the Queen and the Empire, and proud of Canada's place in it.

Before he returned to Canada, Laurier wanted to visit France. It was the country of his forefathers, and he had never been there be-

Sir Wilfrid Laurier in Queen Victoria's Diamond Jubilee procession, 22 June 1897.

fore. In two brilliant speeches in Paris, Laurier won over the French as he had the British. He explained to them how he could be loyal to his native land of Canada, which was tied to England, and still cherish his French heritage. He said, 'French-Canadians have not forgotten France. . . Here in France people are surprised at the attachment French Canadians feel for the Queen of England. We are faithful to the great nation which gave us life [France], and we are faithful to the great nation which has given us liberty [Britain].'

Sir Wilfrid Laurier returned in triumph to Canada. Canadians had never received more respect from other nations of the world. Much of the credit for this belonged to Laurier himself. Now the Prime Minister had to turn to tasks at home. He had to build up and strengthen Confederation. His most pressing tasks were to fill the West with settlers and to guide Canada into the 20th century.

Sir Wilfrid and Lady Laurier at their home in Arthabaskerville.

1. What qualities and characteristics did Laurier possess that prepared him for the position of Prime Minister?
2. Compare the characteristics and background of Prime Minister Laurier and another French-Canadian Prime Minister (Louis St. Laurent or Pierre E. Trudeau).
3. What effects did the Manitoba Schools Question have on French-English relations in Canada?

CANADA IN THE BRITISH EMPIRE

A great celebration marked the Diamond Jubilee of Queen Victoria in 1897. People from all over the British Empire travelled to London to honour Queen Victoria's sixty years on the throne. Sir Wilfrid Laurier and a detachment of North-West Mounted Policemen represented Canada.

1. Why do you think the North-West Mounted Police were enthusiastically received by the crowd in London?
2. What were the advantages of Canada belonging to the British Empire?

32
At the Turn of the Century

When Canada entered the 20th century, the young Dominion was only thirty-three years old. Already Canada had undergone tremendous changes and growth. Study the materials below to identify and account for some of these changes.

GENERAL POPULATION OF CANADA BY CENSUS DATES 1861-1911

Year	Population
1911	7 206 643
1901	5 371 315
1891	4 833 239
1881	4 324 810
1871	3 689 257
1861	3 229 633

1. What has happened to the population of Canada from 1861 to 1911?
2. Which decade (10-year period) shows the greatest increase in the total population of Canada?

POPULATION OF THE FOUR
WESTERN PROVINCES 1871-1911

	Manitoba	Saskatchewan	Alberta	British Columbia
1911	461 394	492 432	374 295	392 480
1901	255 211	91 279	73 022	178 657
1891	152 506			98 173
1881	62 260			49 459
1871	25 228			36 247

1. What was happening in western Canada between 1871-1901?
2. Which decade shows the smallest growth in population in British Columbia? Try to suggest some possible reasons for this.
3. Which decade shows the greatest growth in population in Manitoba?
4. What was the total population growth in the four provinces between 1901 and 1911? What were the reasons for this?

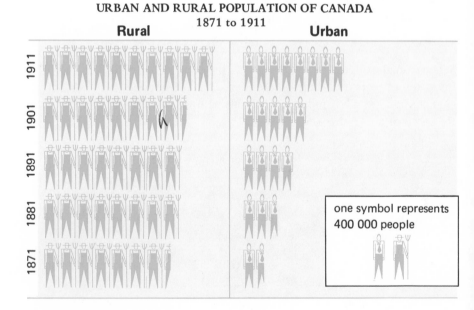

URBAN AND RURAL POPULATION OF CANADA
1871 to 1911
Rural   **Urban**

one symbol represents
400 000 people

Study the chart above. Decide whether these statements are true or false. If false, re-write the statements to make them true.

a) In 1871, most Canadians were farmers.
b) In 1901, most Canadians lived in cities.
c) Rural means city-dwellers.
d) In the decade 1891-1901, there was a greater increase of urban-dwellers than farmers.
e) This chart tells you why people moved to the cities.
f) One reason that may account for the increase in the rural population 1891-1911 was the wheat boom.
g) Canadian cities grew larger as more and more immigrants came to Canada.

ORIGINS OF POPULATION 1871-1911

ORIGIN	1871	1881	1901	1911
Austrian			10 947	44 036
Belgian			2 994	9 664
Chinese		4 383	17 312	27 831
English	706 369	881 301	1 260 899	1 871 268
Finnish			2 502	15 500
French	1 082 940	1 298 929	1 649 371	2 061 719
German	202 991	254 319	310 501	403 417
Greek	39		291	3 614
Hungarian			1 549	11 648
Italian	1 035	1 849	10 834	45 963
Irish	846 414	957 403	988 721	1 074 738
Japanese			4 738	9 067
Jewish	125	667	16 131	76 199
Native Peoples	23 037	108 547	127 941	105 611
Negro	21 496	21 394	17 437	16 994
Netherlander	29 662	30 412	33 845	55 961
Polish			6 285	33 652
Russians	607	1 227	19 825	44 376
Scandinavian	1 623	5 223	31 042	112 682
Scottish	549 946	699 863	800 154	1 027 015
Ukrainian			5 682	75 432
Others	19 477	59 293	52 314	80 256
TOTALS	3 485 761	4 324 810	5 371 315	7 206 643

WHERE IMMIGRANTS TO CANADA CAME FROM

Study the chart above. Decide whether these statements are true or false. If false, re-write the statements to make them true.

a) There were many Asians in Canada before 1871.

b) The dramatic rise in Chinese in Canada between 1871 and 1881 was probably due to the building of the railroad.

c) About two million people came to Canada between 1881 and 1901.

d) The years between 1901 and 1911 were the years of heaviest immigration to Canada.

e) After 1900, the French population in Canada declined.

f) This graph tells why immigrants came to Canada.

g) The rise in native peoples between 1871 and 1881 is probably owing to new provinces entering Canada.

h) Between 1881 and 1901, immigrants from countries in northern and western Europe outnumbered immigrants from countries in southern and eastern Europe.

j) The largest immigrant group in Canada was always made up of English, Irish, and the Scots.

j) The combination of English, Irish, and Scottish were always the largest immigrant group in Canada.

HOW DID CANADIANS EARN THEIR LIVING AT THE TURN OF THE 20TH CENTURY?

The following photographs and material show some of the many ways Canadians were earning a living in 1900. No pictures are included of the Prairies since you have just studied that region in detail. However, there are pictures representing the other regions of Canada in 1900.

Prepare a list of all the different ways in which Canadians earned their living in 1900.

THE MARITIMES

What evidence is there that the methods of fishing, lumbering and shipbuilding in the Maritimes had changed very little since Confederation? What similarities and differences exist between lumbering in the Maritimes and in British Columbia?

Blast furnaces at Sydney, Nova Scotia in 1900 produced a large proportion of Canada's steel and iron. What effects will steel, iron and

Drying cod near Caraquet, N.B.

The *Bluenose* under full sail.

the development of steam power have on the ship-building industry of the Atlantic provinces?

Experiments connected with two of the most important advances of the early 20th century took place in the Maritimes. In 1901 at St. John's, Newfoundland, Guglielmo Marconi received the first trans-

Logging crew in woods along the Miramichi River, N.B.

Log jam on the Miramichi River.

The *Silver Dart* in flight, 1909.

Atlantic wireless signal from a station in Cornwall, England. In 1907 at Baddeck, Nova Scotia, Alexander Graham Bell founded the Aerial Experiment Association. (One of its members, J.A.D. McCurdry, made the first airplane flight in the British Empire in the *Silver Dart* in 1909.) Until his death in 1922, Bell spent most of his life in Baddeck experimenting with airplanes and hydrofoils. Research the lives and inventions of Marconi and Bell, who are pictured below (l. Marconi, r. Bell).

Guglielmo Marconi.   Alexander Graham Bell.

ONTARIO AND QUEBEC

By 1895, annual production of oil at Petrolia reached 800 000 barrels. What effect would the introduction of the automobile soon have on the oil industry of Ontario?

Whose invention of the light bulb in 1879 brought new demands for electricity?

How is hydro-electricity produced?

For what purposes would electricity be used in Canadian cities in 1900?

Imperial Oil refinery stills, Petrolina, Ontario.

Electric streetcars in Montreal, 1895.

Shawinigan Falls, Quebec.

How would the power be transmitted from Shawinigan to distant cities?

What effect will electric street cars have on the growth of Canadian cities?

What advantages will electric street cars provide for the increasing number of factory workers in the cities?

Why would Toronto be a rapidly developing city in Ontario at the beginning of the 20th century?

Toronto.

Loggers in British Columbia.

BRITISH COLUMBIA

What tools are used in the logging industry shown in this picture?
What inventions have since taken place to make the work of the logger
easier?

How safe do you think this type of work was in 1900? Why?

Suggest possible uses for the Douglas Fir being cut in the picture.

How are the salmon boats propelled? Why would the beginning and
end of the fishing season be marked with the booming of a cannon?

How will most of the salmon caught by these fishermen be processed
for market? What processes are used today?

MINING PRODUCTION IN BRITISH COLUMBIA

	1891	1901
GOLD	$400 000	$5 320 000
SILVER	$3300	$3 306 000
LEAD	0	$2 235 000
COPPER	0	$4 500 000

Which materials were mined in British Columbia in 1901? In the 1850s and 1860s?

What happened to mining production in British Columbia from 1891 to 1901? Suggest reasons why this took place.

In 1897 the last great Gold Rush in North America began in the Klondike region. Thousands of men and a considerable number of women from around the world flooded into the area. During the winter of 1897, 22 000 persons were checked through the Chilkoot Pass by the North-West Mounted Police. Each person was required by the police to carry in a year's supply of food, tents, equipment, and clothing. The goods weighed about a tonne in all.

Why would the North West Mounted Police require the prospectors to carry in so many supplies? Make a list of the supplies you think the prospectors would require for their first year in the Yukon.

Salmon fleet on the Fraser River, B.C.

Chilkoot Pass, B.C.

Front Street, Dawson City, 1899.

Snake-Hips Lulu, Klondike dance-hall girl, 1898.

THE NORTH

Few of the miners returned from the Klondike with great wealth. What was there for the miner to spend his money on in Dawson City?

Not all the women in Dawson City were dance-hall girls. Some wives helped their husbands pack supplies across the Chilkoot Pass. Four Victorian Order nurses were sent to the gold fields by Lady Aberdeen, wife of the Governor-General. Lady Aberdeen had organized the public health nursing service in 1897.

What functions could the Victorian Order of Nurses provide in Dawson City? How would the presence of the four nurses in Dawson City bring favourable publicity to their newly formed organization?

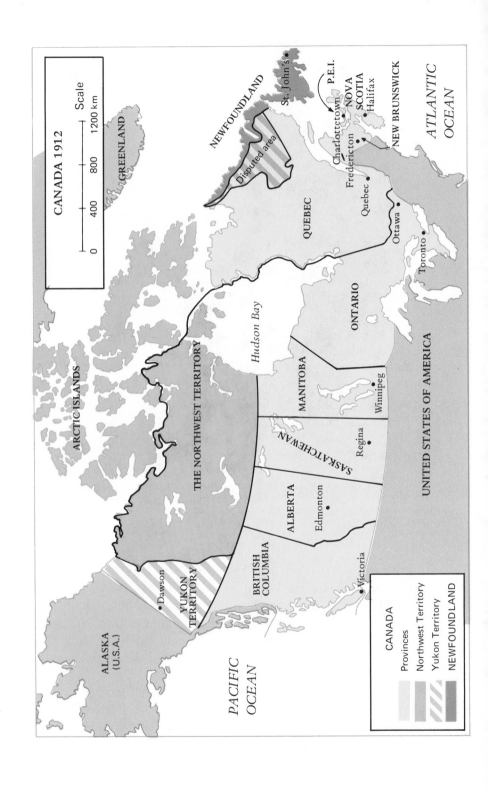

HISTORY GAME
A MOCK AUCTION AT THE TURN OF THE CENTURY

As a class, or in groups, hold a mock auction of articles from your great-grandparents' day. One student will act as auctioneer. Here are the rules of the game:

First, what you are going to sell at your auction are items from an old Eaton's catalogue. The auctioneer's job is to show the audience a picture of the item and read the description from the catalogue. The auctioneer gives a real sales pitch.

Then, when everyone has had a chance to look at the article, start the bidding. The object is to buy the item at the original price, the price at which it was offered for sale in the catalogue.

You can write everybody's name on the blackboard with their bid after their name. The bidder who came closest to the actual price in 1901 has 'bought' the article. The player who 'buys' the most items wins.

ACTIVITIES

1. What clues do the catalogue prices give you about life in 1900?
2. Compare prices in 1901 with newspaper advertisements for the same or similar articles today. What might account for the rise in prices?
3. What did people do for entertainment in 1900?
4. Make a list of the similarities and differences of life in 1900 and life today.
5. What inventions changed household chores (a) between 1800 and 1900? (b) between 1900 and today?
6. Debate: It would be more fun to be growing up in 1900 than in the 1980s.
7. Research project: Make a scrapbook to show changes in fashion over the last 80 years.
8. The materials in this section will give you an idea of what life was like at the turn of the century. A better way to find out would be to interview men and women who were children in the early years of the century. You could invite them to speak to your class. Prepare a list of questions you would like to ask these people who lived at that time.
9. Make a time-capsule to record what Canada is like today. Choose your materials carefully. You may include pictures, records, objects, filmstrips, etc.

33
Women get the Vote

On 27 January 1914, Nellie McClung and a delegation of several hundred supporters petitioned the Manitoba government to grant women the right to vote. Nellie was chief spokesperson and she confronted the Premier, Sir Rodmond Roblin, with the words: 'We are not here to ask for a gift or a favour but for a right — not for mercy but for justice!'

Premier Roblin received the women in a gentlemanly manner but dismissed their arguments by saying, 'Now you forget all this nonsense about women voting. Nice women don't want to vote!'

Nellie McClung and her supporters were angry with the Premier but decided that humour and laughter might be a better way to get action from the government. The next night, at the Walker Theatre in Winnipeg, the women staged a mock Parliament. In this Parliament all members were women and Nellie McClung was the Premier. The roles were reversed and it was the men who were asking for the right to vote. Nellie cleverly poked fun by using the same arguments Premier Roblin had used as reasons why men could never be given the vote. 'If men are given the vote,' the female Premier said, 'they will vote too much. Politics unsettles men, and unsettled men mean unsettled bills — broken furniture, broken vows and divorce.' 'Men can not be trusted with the ballot. Men's place is on the farm.'

The play was a roaring success. The audience howled with laughter and the Premier and his government were embarrassed. Requests to repeat the performance came from all over the province. Money earned was used to finance the women's campaign to win the right to vote in Manitoba. Nellie McClung and her friends were gradually winning social reform. Social reform means bringing about changes in the way

Nellie McClung.

people live. Nellie and her followers were determined to gain for women the same rights and opportunities that men enjoyed.

It may surprise many young Canadians to find out that women in this country did not receive the right to vote in federal elections until 1918. It may also surprise you to find out the position of women was very different at the turn of the 20th century.

PICTURE STUDY

Look at these pictures carefully to find out about the position held by women in Canada at the beginning of this century. Answer the following questions:

   a)   What was the chief task of women at this time?
   b)   What sort of jobs did women do in the home?
   c)   What sort of jobs did women do outside the home?
   d)   Under what kind of conditions did women have to work?

Immigrants arriving in Quebec for domestic service, 1911.

Wealthy women enjoying afternoon tea, 1906.

Women sawing on a prairie farm, 1914.

e) What were the home conditions like?
f) What were the differences between rich and poor women?
g) How did the jobs held by women and those held by men differ?
h) What problems did women face?

Clothing factory in Edmonton, 1918.

Women working in munitions factory during World War I.

Woman nursing children.

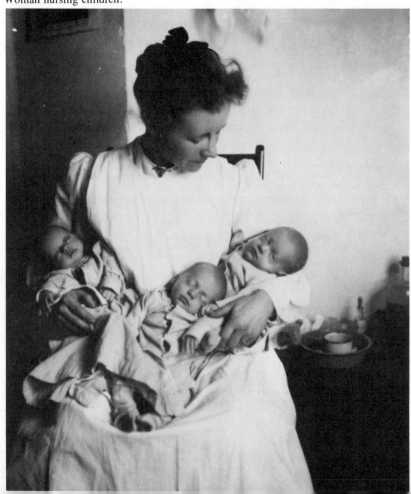

Now consider these facts about the political, legal, and educational position of women in Canada at the turn of the century:

1.   No woman had the right to vote. The Election Act of the Dominion of Canada stated 'no woman, idiot, lunatic, or criminal shall vote'.
2.   No woman could be elected to federal or provincial offices in government.
3.   A man had a great deal of control over his wife and children. At that time the father had complete control over his children. He could collect their income. Without even consulting the mother, he could put his children up for adoption!
4.   It was commonly accepted that a woman's chief function was to keep house for her husband and to bear his children. One out of every five women in Canada died in childbirth at this time.
5.   Wives had to obey their husbands and could legally be beaten.
6.   In the West, wives or single women could not claim homesteads. Only if she was the head of a household could a woman take up a homestead.
7.   Married women had the right to financial support from their husbands. However, wives and children of alcoholic men found it very difficult in practice to collect any support money.
8.   Girls could attend elementary and secondary schools but very few women in Canada went on to gain a post-secondary school education. The University of Toronto did not admit women until the 1880s. Most professions were still closed to women. People would not accept the idea that women could perform the jobs of doctors or lawyers or clergy as well as men. The first woman doctor in Canada was Dr. James Barry, who spent her whole life disguised as a man. She was born in Scotland and as a young girl longed to be a doctor. Since women were not admitted to medical school at the University of Edinburgh, she disguised herself as a man. Dr. Barry graduated and became an outstanding doctor. She was sent to Canada as Inspector-General of Hospitals. Not until her death in 1865 at the age of 71 was her secret discovered!

By 1900 ideas about women were slowly beginning to change. No longer did a girl have to disguise herself as a man in order to enter the medical profession. But it would be some time before women were granted all the same privileges of higher education that men enjoyed.

THE MOVEMENT FOR WOMEN'S SUFFRAGE

At the beginning of the twentieth century, women in many countries began to organize themselves to obtain votes for women. Members of this movement were called suffragettes in England, and suffragists in Canada. Their purpose, however, was the same: to win the rights and opportunities that men enjoyed. Getting the vote was just the first step.

In Britain the suffragettes fought a violent campaign to win their rights. They chained themselves to the gates of Buckingham Palace, smashed the windows of the Prime Minister's residence, and scuffled with the police. Time and time again they went to jail to draw attention to their cause. At the famous horse race, the Derby, one suffragette leaped in front of a race horse owned by King George V. She died before the eyes of the King and thousands of shocked spectators. Another suffragette said to the King, 'For God's sake, stop torturing women.' The King replied, 'I really don't know what the world is coming to!' What the world was coming to was a new recognition of the rights of women.

In Canada the suffragists were much more peaceful. Unlike their British sisters, the Canadian women used arguments, humour, petitions, and organized demonstrations to win what they wanted.

The Women's Suffrage Movement started in Ontario, though it was in the prairie provinces that women first got the right to vote. In 1876 Dr. Emily Stowe formed the Toronto Women's Literary Club. This name was deceiving. The purpose of the club was to teach women their rights, and to help them to secure those rights. Dr. Stowe, herself, had been denied the right to attend a Canadian medical school, and had been forced to go to the United States to get her training. This club worked not only to win the vote, but to establish a medical college for women in Ontario. Such a college was founded in 1883. The club also persuaded the University of Toronto to admit women in 1886. It struggled for laws to improve the wages and working conditions for women in industry as well.

About the same time, in 1889, a woman named Adelaide Hoodless had a great tragedy in her own life. Her eighteen-month-old son died from drinking contaminated milk. In those days of inadequate refrigeration, contaminated food was common. But Adelaide Hoodless blamed herself. She felt her ignorance had caused the death of her child.

She set out to persuade the public schools to teach domestic science to girls. She wanted girls to study sewing, sanitation, nutrition, and housekeeping skills. At first the Ontario education officials rejected the idea. However, with the support of the Young Women's Christian Association (YWCA), Adelaide Hoodless and her supporters persisted. Gradually school boards across the province introduced classes for girls in home economics.

Her most famous accomplishment was the founding of the world's first Women's Institute in 1897. This was a group of farm women who organized themselves to study nutrition, child care, household management, and sanitation. Eventually the idea of Women's Institutes spread throughout Canada and Britain. Adelaide Hoodless was not really trying to change the nature of women's work. What she was trying to do was to train girls and women in the roles of motherhood and homemaking.

Another important institution formed in the late 1800s was the Women's Christian Temperance Union. It was an organization of women whose aim was to combat the problems created by alcohol. They were very concerned about the number of wives and children who were being beaten, abused, or neglected by drunken husbands and fathers. They dedicated themselves to fighting the evils of alcohol. Through programs in schools they hoped to make the younger generation aware of the danger of drinking. The WCTU also worked hard to limit the number of stores and bars licensed to sell liquor. Their ultimate goal was to prohibit the sale of alcohol altogether.

In their crusade against liquor, many women began to realize that until they had the right to vote no government would listen to them. If they wished to force the government to pass laws forbidding the sale of alcohol, they would first have to win the vote. In that way women could defeat politicians and governments who ignored their demands. It was not surprising then that many leaders of the WCTU also became active in the movement for women's suffrage.

Nellie McClung, Canada's great social reformer, got her start in the WCTU. Born in Ontario in 1873, Nellie moved west as a small girl, living in both Winnipeg and Edmonton. She had great ability as a speaker and a writer. Through her books and articles Nellie McClung became known far beyond the borders of Manitoba. She was opposed to alcohol and held strong opinions about social reform. 'Certainly', she said, 'women belong in the home, but not for twenty-four hours a day! They should have exactly the same freedoms as men.' Because she had such strong beliefs, Nellie continued to work hard in the fight for women's rights.

When World War I broke out in Europe in 1914, it helped to prove that Nellie McClung was right. Britain and Germany were at war for four years. During that time many Canadian soldiers went to fight with British troops. With so many men away in Europe fighting the war there was a serious shortage of workers in many vital industries. Women were called upon to do the jobs formerly performed only by men. Women made bombs and shells in munitions factories for the war effort, drove street cars, worked in banks, offices, and stores. They did the same jobs as men and did them just as well as men. They proved that women were every bit as capable of working as men. Therefore, women should have exactly the same freedoms as men.

Those women who were unable to work did their bit for the war effort in volunteer labour. Throughout Canada groups of women met to roll bandages, pack parcels for the troops, and knit socks for 'the boys overseas.' In this way, the war brought women together and once together they began to talk and dream of political equality with men.

In 1915, the government of Premier Roblin of Manitoba was defeated. The new premier, Liberal T.C. Norris, came to power with the promise that Manitoba women would be given the power to vote. On 27 January 1916 — two years to the day after Nellie McClung and her army of women marched on the Manitoba Legislature — the bill was passed. At that moment the women sitting in the galleries of the Parliament Buildings stood up and sang 'O Canada'. Thus, the women of Manitoba were the first in Canada to gain the right to vote. About two months later, a similar bill was passed in Saskatchewan, and a few weeks later, in Alberta.

The day the women's suffrage bill was passed in Alberta, Alice Jamieson was in Edmonton. When the news came through that the women in Alberta had been granted the right to vote, she rushed to the telephone and called two of her friends. They were both prominent women in Canada and tireless workers for women's suffrage — Emily Murphy and Nellie McClung. The trio met and decided they must celebrate in some way. 'Being women,' said Mrs. Jamieson, 'we couldn't very well express our joy and satisfaction by going out and getting a bottle, so we walked down Jasper Avenue with our arms interlocked. Mrs. Murphy suggested that the most reckless thing we could do would be to have our pictures taken.' This picture has become one of Alberta's historical treasures, for it shows three of Canada's outstanding women taken on the most memorable day in the history of women in Alberta.

The big breakthrough for women's suffrage came during World War I. The Canadian government passed the Wartime Elections Act. This Act gave the vote to the wives, widows, mothers, sisters and daughters of Canadian soldiers serving overseas. It was only a matter of time until all Canadian women would be allowed to vote in federal elections. On 24 May 1918 women's suffrage was finally won in Canada!

A fighter for women's rights, Agnes Macphail, was the first woman to be elected to the House of Commons in 1921. She was re-elected four times. In the same year, Nellie McClung was elected to the Alberta legislature.

Nellie McClung, Alice Jamieson, and Emily Murphy on the day the women's suffrage bill was passed.

A TIMETABLE FOR WOMEN'S POLITICAL EQUALITY

Province	Suffrage (The Vote)	Eligible to Hold Of
Manitoba	28 January 1916	27 January 1916
Saskatchewan	14 March 1916	14 March 1916
Alberta	19 April 1916	19 April 1916
British Columbia	5 April 1917	5 April 1917
Ontario	12 April 1917	24 April 1919
Nova Scotia	26 April 1918	26 April 1918
Dominion of Canada	Close relatives of members of armed forces — 20 September 1917; all women — 24 May 1918	7 July 1919; Reaffirmed and ma permanent by the Dominion Election Act, 1920
New Brunswick	17 April 1919	9 March 1934
Prince Edward Island	3 May 1922	3 May 1922
Newfoundland	13 April 1925	13 April 1925
Quebec	25 April 1940	25 April 1940

Dates when women got the right to vote in other parts of the world:

DATES OF ENFRANCHISEMENT OF WOMEN

New Zealand	1893
Australia	1902
Finland	1906
Norway	1913
Denmark	1915
Canada	1917
Britain	1918
Netherlands	1919
Germany	1919
United States	1920
Sweden	1921
Turkey	1934
Brazil	1946
France	1946
Switzerland	1971

ACTIVITY

Read aloud and discuss the following questions. Do you think they were written by a man or woman? Do any of these quotations sound familiar? Are they the sort of things Canadians say today? Have you heard anyone say these things before?

1. The world has never been partial to the thinking woman — the wise ones have always foreseen danger. Long years ago, when women asked for an education, the world cried out that it would never do. If women learned to read there seemed to be a possibility that some day some good man might come home and find his wife reading and the dinner not ready — and nothing could be imagined more horrible than that! That seems to be the haunting fear of mankind — that the advancement of women will sometime, someway, someplace, interfere with some man's comfort!

2. Children do not need their mother's care always, and the mother who has given up every hope and ambition in the care of her children will find herself left all alone when her children no longer need her — a woman without a job. . . . The stationary female and the wide-ranging male is the world's accepted arrangement, but the belief that a woman must cherish no hope or ambition of her own is both cruel and unjust.

3. These tender-hearted gentlemen who tell you of their adoration for women cannot bear to think of women occupying public position. Their tender hearts shrink from the idea of women lawyers or women policemen, or even women preachers; these positions would 'rub the bloom off the peach' to use their own eloquent words. They cannot bear, they say, to see women leaving the sacred precincts of home — and yet their offices are scrubbed by women who do their work while other people sleep . . . is there any pity for them? Not that we have heard of. The tender-hearted ones can bear this with equanimity. It is the thought of women getting into comfortable and well-paid positions which wrings their manly hearts.

4. At the present time there is much discontent among women and many people are seriously alarmed about it. They say women are no longer contented with woman's sphere and woman's work. . . We may as well admit that discontent is not necessarily wicked. . . . Discontent may mean the stirring of ambition, the desire to spread out, to improve and grow. Discontent is a sign of life, corresponding to growing pains in a healthy child.

5. The time will come, we hope, when women will be economically free, and mentally and spiritually independent enough to refuse to have their food paid for by men; when women will receive equal pay for equal work and have all avenues of activity open to them; and will be free to choose their own mates, without shame, or indelicacy; when men will not be afraid of marrying because of the financial burden, but free men and free women will marry for love and together work for the sustenance of their families. It is not too ideal a thought. It is coming and the new movement among women who are crying out for a larger humanity, is going to bring it about.

All of the quotations came from a book called *In Times Like These* by Nellie McClung. It was published in 1915! Do you think that most of them could appear in a newspaper today? What do they tell us about the Women's Liberation movement? What do they tell us about the suffragists? Why is it that women have been saying these things for such a long time and the conditions still exist?

ACTIVITIES

1. Make a timeline of the major events in the Women's Suffrage Movement.
2. Describe the different methods used by women in attempting to get the vote. How effective were each of these methods?
3. Organize and present a Mock Parliament like that put on by Nellie McClung at the Walker Theatre. You might video-tape or tape record the event for replaying to the class and for discussion.
4. Not all women supported the idea of Women's Suffrage. What reasons do you think they would give for keeping things as they were? Do all women today support the Women's Liberation Movement? Why or why not?
5. Prepare on-the-spot television coverage of a women's suffrage march. Students play the roles of
   a) T.V. interviewer
   b) Nellie McClung and other suffragists
   c) Male hecklers
   d) Women opposed to suffrage.
Let students research the arguments offered for or against suffrage. Placards could be made to heighten the drama.
6. Interview your mother, grandmother, aunt, or some other female relative to find out what changes have occurred in the position of

Members of the Political Equality League for the Enfranchisement of Women, 1915.

women throughout her lifetime. Use the following questionnaire, or make up one of your own. Share with the class what you discover through your interviews.

Some Suggestions for Conducting Good Interviews:
1.   Know what information you are after — have a definite reason for the interview.
2.   Prepare well in advance by researching the topic to be talked about.
3.   Write out your questions beforehand. The right question is the only way to get the right information.
4.   Think of secondary or follow-up questions to get deeper explanations.
5.   Write down as much of the information as you can in notes or take along a tape recorder.
6.   Expand your notes as soon as possible after the interview.

Interviewer's Name _____
Date _____

DATA ON PERSON INTERVIEWED

Name _____
Relationship to me _____

1. Do you think women and men today have equal civil rights?

2. Do you think women can do most jobs as well as men?

3. What are some jobs (if any) you think only men should have?

4. What are some jobs (if any) you think only women should have?

5. How has the position of women changed in your lifetime?

6. When men and women hold the same jobs do you think they should be paid the exact same salaries?

7. In households where both the husband and wife are employed outside the home, do you think the household chores should be shared 50-50?

8. If not, how should they be shared?

9. Can you remember when women in Canada could not vote?

10. Do you think women should be encouraged to run for political office?

11. Would you vote for a woman for Prime Minister of Canada?

34
Only the Beginning

Women in Canada had won the right to vote. But they still did not enjoy all the privileges that men had.

In 1916, an event took place which pointed out this lack of equality. Emily Murphy was the first woman judge appointed in Edmonton to a court to hear cases involving women. A lawyer in her courtroom challenged her right to judge any case because she was a woman. He said that no woman was a 'person' in the eyes of the law. Emily Murphy was supported by the Supreme Court of Alberta which said that a woman had every right to be a judge. That should have settled the matter, but it did not.

During the 1920s women's groups asked the Prime Minister of Canada to appoint a woman to the Senate. The British North America Act outlined the qualifications required for an appointment to the Senate. It said that qualified 'persons' could be appointed to the Senate. Again, the old question of 'persons' was showing its ugly head. Was a woman a 'person' in the eyes of the law?

In August 1927, Emily Murphy and four of her friends decided to petition the Prime Minister. The group of women included Nellie McClung, Louise McKinney, Henrietta Edwards, Irene Parlby, and Judge Murphy. They asked, 'Does the word ''persons'' in Section 24 of the British North America Act include *female* ''persons''?' In April 1928, the Supreme Court of Canada decided that women were *not* 'persons' qualified for appointment to the Senate in Canada.

Judge Emily Murphy presiding in juvenile court, 1918.

Judge Murphy and her supporters, nicknamed the Famous Five, were discouraged but not defeated. They decided that they would appeal their case to the Privy Council in Britain. The Privy Council was the highest court of appeal in the British Empire.

After three months of consideration and four days of debate, the judges of the Privy Council announced their decision. They declared that the word 'persons' included members of the male and female sex. Women were indeed qualified to sit in the Senate of Canada. Emily Murphy had won her fight.

Since that time, several important events have taken place which affected women in Canada. In 1954, the Women's Bureau was set up by the federal government to study problems relating to women in the labour force throughout Canada. In 1960, the Canadian Bill of Rights made it illegal to treat women unfairly because of their sex. In 1967, a Royal Commission was appointed to examine the position of women in Canada. Its purpose was to make recommendations to the government concerning the equality of men and women.

ARE WOMEN REALLY EQUAL?

Examine the following case studies:

CASE 1

A hotel in northwestern Ontario employed two categories of cocktail waiters with different pay scales for each category. Those classified as Waiter I made $2.65 an hour. Those classified as Waiter II received $2.30 an hour. Everyone classified as Waiter I was male and everyone classified as Waiter II was female. Both men and women were members of the same union.

a)   What reasons could persons in category II offer to prove that they were being treated unfairly?

b)   What reasons could the management give to justify paying more to category I?

c)   There are laws to protect women from such situations. Why might women in category II be unwilling to complain to the Ontario Ministry of Labour?

CASE 2

Joanne S. lives in a small town in northern Ontario. The biggest and best paying employer in the area is an open pit iron ore mine. Joanne applied at the mine for a job. She heard that there was a shortage of truck drivers.

Several weeks passed after she filled out an application, but she heard nothing. Joanne made repeated attempts to find out what had happened to her application. She was told that the Mining Act forbade the employment of women at a mine. The company also claimed that women could not be hired because there were no lockers, showers, or toilet facilities for them.

a)   What do you think was the real reason why Joanne's application was ignored?

b)   Do you think there are any jobs that women cannot do? should not be allowed to do?

c)   Do you think there are any jobs that men cannot do? should not be allowed to do?

d)   Debate: Joanne should/should not be hired.

CASE 3

Irene Murdoch's marriage to an Alberta rancher broke down after 25 years. Mrs. Murdoch claimed that she had a right to a share in the ranch property that they had acquired and worked on together. The farm was in Mr. Murdoch's name. Mrs. Murdoch said she did haying, raking, mowing, driving trucks and tractors, branding cattle and any other jobs that had to be done on the ranch. She had never received a pay check for carrying out any of her normal wifely duties. The highest court in Canada ruled that Mrs. Murdoch had no claim to a share of the property.

a) Why would the Supreme Court's ruling in the Murdoch case shock women across Canada?

b) What changes could be made in the law to give more protection to married women's property rights?

c) In 1975, a Gallup Poll found that 49% of those surveyed, male and female, favoured a salary for housewives. Do you think husbands should pay a salary to their wives who stay at home?

CHART STUDY

PROPORTION OF WOMEN IN MAJOR OCCUPATIONAL GROUPS

	1951	1961	1971
	percentage of total employment in group		
Managerial	11.1	11.1	9.3
Professional and technical	35.3	42.0	41.1
Clerical	56.2	62.4	72.2
Service	44.6	48.7	60.1
Transportation and communication	7.7	9.0	9.7
Farmers and farm workers	7.6	8.3	12.9
Logging, hunting and fishing	—	—	—
Mining, quarrying, etc.	—	—	—
Crafts and production process	14.6	14.6	14.1
Labourers	—	—	8.0
All Occupations	22.0	27.7	33.3

From *Perspective Canada: A Compendium of Social Statistics* by Statistics Canada.

Women have often worked as secretaries. Real estate office in Alberta, 1914.

1. In which categories of the work force do you find more than 50% of the workers are women? What sort of jobs would be done by workers in these categories?

2. Which categories would be the highest paying jobs? Which categories would be the lowest paying jobs? In which category are most women?

Government departments have been set up in Canada to receive complaints of women who are treated unfairly because of their sex. Another purpose they have is to make people more aware of women's rights. It is hoped that some day soon all Canadians will recognize that women have the same abilities and make the same contributions to society as men. When that happens it will at last be truly said that in Canada women and men are treated as equals.

CANADIAN WOMEN TO BE PROUD OF

1769   The first novel concerning Canada, *The History of Emily Montague*, is written by Frances Brooke. She lived in Canada while her husband was chaplain of the British troops at Quebec.

1836   Catherine Parr Traill records her journey to and early experiences in Canada in *The Backwoods of Canada*.

1852   Susanna Moodie's *Roughing It in the Bush*, about pioneer life in Canada, is published.

1861   Pauline Johnson, the first woman poet of note in Canada, is born. She is the daughter of an Englishwoman and a Mohawk leader.

1882   Cora Hind is turned down for a job with the Winnipeg *Free Press* in 1882 because she is a woman. She rents a typewriter, learns to type, and sets up business as the first woman stenographer in the Canadian West. Eventually she is hired by the *Free Press* and becomes agricultural editor and world-wide authority on grain.

1883   Augusta Stowe-Gullen, daughter of Dr. Emily Stowe, is the first woman to study and graduate in medicine from a Canadian university.

1893   The National Council of Women is founded by Lady Aberdeen, wife of the Governor-General.

1897   Adelaide Hoodless founds the first Women's Institute.

1911   Elizabeth Simcoe's *Diary* is published. It records what life was like in Upper Canada more than a century earlier.

1913   Alys McKey Bryant is the first woman to pilot an airplane in Canada.

1916   Emily Murphy is appointed a Police Magistrate in Edmonton. She is the first woman in the British Empire to hold such a post.

1917   Louise McKinney and Roberta McAdams are elected to the Alberta legislature. They are the first female members of any Parliament in Canada or the British Empire.

1921   Agnes Campbell Macphail is the first woman elected to Parliament in Canada. She serves for 19 years in the House of Commons.

1927   Emily Carr is the first Canadian woman to achieve world-wide recognition as a painter. The National Gallery of Canada exhibits some of her best work. Her favourite themes are west coast Indians and the forests of British Columbia.

1928   Ethel Catherwood (high jump), Bobbie Rosenfeld, Ethel

Forest Landscape (1) by Emily Carr.

Smith, Myrtle Cook, and Florence Bell (one hundred metre relay), are the first Canadian women to win Olympic Gold Medals in Amsterdam.

1929   Thérèse Casgrain becomes leader of the League of Women's Rights in the province of Quebec until the vote was won in Quebec in 1940.

1931   Cairine MacKay Wilson becomes Canada's first woman senator.

1935   Nellie McClung's autobiography, *Clearing in the West: My Own Story*, is published. This book tells how Nellie became a champion of women's rights in Canada.

1937   Laura Goodman Salverson wins the Governor General's Award for literature for her novel *The Dark Weaver*. The novel is set in Manitoba and deals with her observations of the life of an Icelandic immigrant. Two years later she wins this award again. This time she writes the story of her life in *Confessions of an Immigrant's Daughter*.

1940   The Edmonton Grads, a women's basketball team, is disbanded. From 1915 to 1940 their record was 502 wins and only 20 losses. The Grads were acknowledged as world champions at tournaments in 1924, 1928, 1932, and 1936.

1945   Nellie McClung publishes the second volume of her autobiography, *The Stream Runs Fast*. It deals with her married life and her role as a political force in Manitoba and Alberta.

1948   Barbara Ann Scott wins the Olympic, World, and European figure-skating titles.

1951   Charlotte Whitton becomes the first woman Mayor of Ottawa. She is later re-elected in 1952 and 1954.

1954   Sixteen-year old Marilyn Bell successfully swims lake Ontario.

1956   Barbara Wagner (pairs figure skating) and Anne Heggtveit (alpine skiing) win gold medals in the Olympic Games.

1957   Ellen Fairclough is the first woman appointed a Cabinet Minister.

1961   Claire Kirkland-Casgrain is the first woman elected to the Quebec Legislature.

1967   The Royal Commission on the Status of Women is set up to inquire into and report on the status of women in Canada. Its purpose is to recommend steps that might be taken to ensure for women equal opportunities with men in all aspects of Canadian society.

1968   Nancy Greene wins a gold medal for skiing at the Olympic Games.

1973   Karen Magnussen wins the World Championship in figure-skating.

1975   Flora Macdonald campaigns for the leadership of the Progressive Conservative Party of Canada.
        International Women's Year.
        Grace Hartman is elected president of CUPE (Canadian Union

of Public Employees), one of the most important unions in Canada.

1976   Jean Sutherland Boggs is Director of the National Gallery in Ottawa until 1976 — the first woman in the world to head a major art institution.

Her successor, another woman, is Shih Hsio-Yen.

Kathy Kreiner wins the Olympic slalom skiing gold medal.

1977   Sylvia Burka is the World sprint speedskating champion.

Cindy Nicholas crosses the English Channel in over-and-back swims in record-breaking time.

1978   Sylvia Ostry is named Chairperson of the Economic Council of Canada.

ACTIVITY

Let each member of the class 'skim' a chapter in a Canadian history book. List the people mentioned by name in the chapter. Share your list with the class and make a master list on the blackboard. Group the persons listed on the master list according to their sex.

1. Why is the list of men much longer than the list of women?
2. What kind of things do people do who are 'remembered' in history?
3. Can you think of historically important women who might have been included but were not?
4. Who do you think writes most of the history books, men or women?

Why are few women, compared with men, mentioned in Canadian history books? Check out possible reasons for this. Groups may discuss and investigate the following hypotheses or others:

1. Only a few women did anything important back then. If a woman had done something important, she would be in the book the same as a man.
2. Women were kept busy at home with their children and so they couldn't be explorers, pioneers, and politicians. What women did was important but they didn't do the kind of things that get written in history books.
3. Men have usually written the history books and they chose to write about what men do. There were just as many important women explorers and pioneers and adventurers and politicians but they were left out of the books on purpose by the men historians.

Make a list of your general conclusions about why relatively few women are mentioned in Canadian history books.

Make a collection of the pictures of Canadian women who have made an important contribution to the life and growth of Canada.

1. How many of these famous Canadian women can you identify? Tell why each is famous.
2. Find out something about those you don't already know.
3. Classify these famous Canadian women by occupation.
4. What makes a person a 'great' Canadian? Make a list of the factors which you think are important.
5. Do some further research on one of these Canadian women who interest you.
6. Name other Canadian women, living or dead, whom you would add to the list of famous Canadian women. Why would you add these names?

The Report of the Royal Commission on the Status of Women said, 'As of January 1970, there were only four women Senators in a Senate with 102 seats. Such a situation cannot be explained by a lack of women competent to hold office. The main function of the Senate is to provide regional representation on a non-elected basis and to assist in the law-making of Canada by providing a "sober-second thought" to the decisions made by the House of Commons. We cannot believe that it is not possible to find 50 women in the ten provinces who could fulfill the duties of a Senator.'

a) Why do you think there have been so few women appointed to the Senate?

b) Name some Canadian women of today that you would recommend for appointment to the Senate. Give your reasons.

35 Workers and the Winnipeg General Strike

World War I ended in November 1917. War-time industries, such as munitions factories, had closed down. Women, who had played such an important role in the wartime factories, now found they were under pressure to return to household duties so that men could have jobs. Thousands of soldiers were returning home to Canada and looking for work. But jobs were hard to find and many war veterans were unemployed and bitter. They also resented the fact that while they were in Europe fighting, many businessmen at home had become enormously rich by producing goods for the war. They had made huge profits while the soldiers had been risking their lives. Now veterans felt that the country owed them something — at least a job and a chance to make an honest living.

Those who did have jobs in Canada in 1919 were not much better off. The problem was the rapid rise in inflation. This meant that the prices of basic things like food and clothing had increased greatly, while wages had not.

The growing unrest and discontent in Canada can be seen in the increase of strikes and lockouts. In 1917 there had been 160; in 1918 the number rose to 230; and in 1919 to 326. Most Canadian labour leaders began to feel that the only way to improve conditions for workers would be to join together to form one big union.

In March 1919, leaders from the western provinces met in Calgary and formed the One Big Union (OBU). They believed that together they

Riot during the Winnipeg General Strike.

could force employers to give them higher wages and shorter working hours. For the OBU the ultimate weapon was the general strike. In a general strike all industries and key services would be shut down.

The strike in Winnipeg began on 1 May when the Building and Metal Trades Councils voted to go on strike. The basic things they wanted were decent wages (85¢ per hour), an eight-hour day, and the right to bargain collectively for better working conditions. The Building and Trade Councils asked for the support of all fellow-workers in Winnipeg. All the craft unions of the city were represented in the Winnipeg Trades and Labour Council. When a vote was taken it was found that there was a great deal of sympathy among other workers for the Building and Metal Trades craftsmen. On 15 May 1919, 30 000 workers in Winnipeg walked off the job. At least 12 000 of these people were not even members of unions, but they gave their support to the Building and Metal Trades workers. 'Sympathy strikes' were also held in Vancouver, Toronto, and Montreal. A 'sympathy strike' is a strike by workers not directly involved in the labour dispute. The most successful of these was in Vancouver where 12 000 workers left their jobs for thirty days to support the Winnipeg strike.

In Winnipeg, the strike spread from industry to industry. Only the railway operators did not join the strikers. Almost all other necessary services were withdrawn. Stores and factories closed down. Milkmen and bakers refused to make deliveries. Street car operators, garbagemen, postal workers, telephone operators, butchers, firemen, and hydro workers refused to work. Even the police expressed their support for the strike but agreed to remain on duty when the strike leaders asked them to do so. Winnipeg was slowly being crippled and split into two hostile camps.

On one side were the strikers, their families and supporters, including several thousand war veterans. The strike was under the control and direction of a Strike Committee. In the interests of public health and safety, the Strike Committee allowed some bakers, milkmen, and electric power operators to resume their work. But these workers were required to carry signs stating:

PERMITTED BY
AUTHORITY OF
STRIKE COMMITTEE

PLACARD CARRIED BY THE MILK AND BREAD WAGGONS

These signs were issued so that the authorized workers could not be accused of strike-breaking. A strike breaker is a person who goes against the idea of a strike, and works throughout the strike.

On the other side were the owners, the employers, professional people, many church leaders, war veterans, and leading citizens of Winnipeg. They called themselves The Committee of One Thousand and were strongly opposed to the unions and the strike. Many of them were convinced that this was no ordinary strike.

Citizens of Winnipeg were afraid that violence would break out. Some factory owners even feared for their lives and slept in churches in case striking employees tried to murder them at night. The Strike Committee, however, was determined to avoid any violence. Workers were urged by the Strike Committee to stay at home or go fishing. They understood that if the workers held mass meetings or marches this would provide city officials with an excuse to call in the army to put down the strike. For several weeks the Strike Committee was able to control the workers and prevent any outbreak of violence. However, in June events took a turn for the worse.

The Canadian government became increasingly alarmed by the news of the crippling strike in Winnipeg. Ottawa sent Senator G.D. Robertson (the Minister of Labour) and Arthur Meighen (Acting Minister of Justice) to investigate the strike. They met with the city officials of Winnipeg, factory owners, and the Committee of 1000. However, they did not meet with the strikers or with the Strike Committee.

The federal government, Winnipeg city officials, and the Committee of 1000 appeared determined to crush the strike. They ordered the striking postal workers to come back to work or lose their jobs. However, only about 75 of the 400 striking postal workers obeyed the order. Newspapers in Winnipeg and across the country were generally hostile towards the strikers. The Winnipeg *Citizen* favoured the employers against the strikers. It accused the strikers of trying to bring about a revolution. These reports added fuel to the fire and created even more tension among the Winnipeg citizens. Then Mayor Gray banned all parades and mass demonstrations in the city. On the same day the federal government made changes to the Criminal Code law. Now any foreign-born person who was even suspected of trying to bring about a revolution could be arrested and sent out of the country without a hearing or trial. Meanwhile Ottawa was sending troops and machine guns to Winnipeg. Policemen who had been sympathetic to the strikers were fired by the Police Commission. They were replaced by 'specials' who could be counted on to be against the strike.

As the strike dragged on into June the families of many strikers were experiencing real hardship. There were no funds to provide strike pay. Some strikers were becoming discouraged, giving up the struggle, and drifting back to their old jobs. In spite of the growing tension and frustration being felt by the strikers, there had been very few outbreaks of violence. On one occasion an angry crowd overturned a street car when citizen volunteers began to get the streetcars back into operation. Then in the early morning hours of 17 June the Royal North-West Mounted Police raided the homes of the Union leaders and labour headquarters. Documents were seized and ten of the strike leaders were arrested and hustled off to Stoney Mountain Penitentiary.

By now the general strike had lasted thirty-seven days. Thousands of men were idle and tempers were strained to the breaking point. On 21 June, a day that became known as 'Bloody Saturday', violence erupted in Winnipeg.

From eyewitness accounts, D.C. Masters has put together an account of 'Bloody Saturday.'

The crowd in front of the City Hall became more and more dense. There were soldiers in uniform and civilians in working clothes and holiday attire. Some had come to parade and others to see the excitement. People were moving up and down Main Street in large groups. Soldiers had begun to line up the silent parade in the square. . . .

Before long the Mounties, immaculate in red or khaki coats, clattered along Portage and wheeled down Main. Armed with baseball bats they galloped into the crowd. Soon they were slowed to a walk in the seething mass of people, but still they

Winnipeg General Strike.

pressed on, vigorously flailing out with their bats. They passed the City Hall, turned south and fought their way towards Portage amid a shower of tin cans, stones, bricks, and lumps of concrete. At length they reached McDermot Avenue, a sadly dishevelled group. Two of the horses were riderless.

Amid wild confusion the Mayor emerged on the front platform of the City Hall and read the Riot Act. His voice was drowned in bedlam. Again the Mounties came north and, as they did so, each transferred his club to the left hand and drew "an ugly-looking black revolver." They swung left on William Avenue and fired a volley into the crowd. They rounded the City Hall and slowed to a walk at the corner of Market and Main Streets. Again they drove into the crowd which was surging around a street car beleaguered and on fire in front of the City Hall. This the crowd was attempting to upset. The Mounties fired their second volley and Mike Sokolowiski, who stood in front of the Manitoba Hotel, was shot in the heart and killed instantly. Other prostrate figures lay on the street and road. The Mounties continued southward. Opposite the Confederation Life Building they encountered another shower of missiles and fired a third volley. They reached McDermot Avenue and stopped for a few minutes to re-form.

At 11:00 p.m., troops and police were withdrawn from the streets. The 'riot' of 21 June was over.

From *The Winnipeg General Strike* by D.C. Masters

THE RIOT ACT

His Majesty the King charges and commands all persons being assembled immediately to disperse and peaceably to depart to their habitation or their lawful business upon pain of being guilty of an offence for which upon conviction they may be sentenced to imprisonment for life.

Later, both sides accused the other of firing the first shot. Mayor Gray testified that he heard the first shots coming from the direction of the crowd. An RNWMP officer reported he picked up several 22 calibre cartridges, whereas the police were using 45s. This suggested that some of the people were armed and may have provoked the Mounties to fire in self-defence. On the other hand, the *Western Labour News* supported the strikers. Their reporters on the scene claimed that the police had opened fire on a crowd which was armed with nothing more than bricks and pieces of concrete.

WAS THE STRIKE A SUCCESS OR A FAILURE?

'Bloody Saturday' convinced the Strike Committee that the General Strike had collapsed. The combined forces of governments, factory owners and police had defeated the strikers. Now there was nothing to do but order workers to return to their jobs. That order was given 25 June 1919, exactly six weeks less a day after the strike began.

To many it looked as if the Winnipeg General Strike had been a complete failure. The strike leaders had been arrested, and later would be sentenced to jail terms. Many of the strikers and their families were on the brink of poverty. Having received no income for six weeks, most were heavily in debt. Their savings were gone, and many would never recover from their financial losses.

Those who were lucky enough still to have their jobs returned to work. Some employers got their revenge by forcing returning employees to sign 'yellow-dog contracts' in order to get their jobs back. In a 'yellow-dog' contract the worker gave a solemn promise not to become a union member or to take part in union activities. Others were not so fortunate. They found they had no jobs to go back to. Four hundred and three postal workers, 119 telephone operators, and 53 firemen were fired, and strike leaders were not re-employed because employers branded them as troublemakers.

Business in Winnipeg had also suffered on account of the strike. Summer construction projects and markets for farm products were especially hard hit. Industries saw customers and sales going to other cities not crippled by strikes. The city of Winnipeg was left with enormous debts which the taxpayers would have to shoulder. The cost of the special police force alone was $210 000.

The hatred built up by the strike could not be forgotten quickly in Winnipeg. Bitterness between employers and employees, and between strikers and non-strikers would last for a long time. Many citizens believed that the time had come for more strict laws to prevent similar events from happening again. In July 1919, Section 98 of the Criminal Code was changed by the government. Now, anyone who proposed using violence to bring about political or economic changes could be searched without search warrants, his property seized, and he himself put into jail for up to twenty years. A person attending a strike meeting or handing out strike literature could be charged with being a member of an illegal organization and imprisoned for up to twenty years. This unfair legislation was not changed until 1936.

On the positive side, certain good things came out of the Winnipeg General Strike. Thinking citizens began to appreciate how important the worker was to the community. The superintendent of nurses of a Winnipeg hospital wrote, 'I still cling stubbornly to the belief that the Winnipeg General Strike served a useful purpose. It made the people of Winnipeg realize that no modern community can function without the workers to carry on the humble and monotonous tasks which make a city safe and healthy to live in.'

The strike drew attention to the social and economic problems faced by many working people. A Royal Commission was appointed by the government to investigate the causes and the conduct of the strike. H.A. Robson, who headed the Royal Commission, showed great sympathy for the suffering of the workers. He concluded that the strike was owing to the high cost of living, and the low wages paid to workers, while factory owners kept huge profits. Robson also decided that the Winnipeg strike was not an attempt to start a violent revolution. In fact, in all the police raids on the properties of the strikers, no firearms were ever discovered.

In spite of the collapse of the strike, it did show that workers could achieve solidarity by standing together. The OBU continued to grow and expand, especially in western Canada.

ACTIVITIES

NECESSARY SERVICES

Many people think the government should not allow strikes to take place in 'essential services'. Which of the services listed below are essential?

Group the services into the following categories:

    a)   absolutely essential (should not be allowed to strike any time)
    b)   important, but can do without for awhile
    c)   could do without for a period of time.

Pilots	Gas Station Attendants
Traffic Controllers	Grave Diggers
Ambulance Drivers	Lawyers
Auto Assembly Line Workers	Newspaper Printers
Bank Tellers	Nurses

Bus Drivers	Pharmacists
Butchers	Plumbers
Construction Workers	Police Officers
Day Care Workers	Postal Workers
Dock Workers	Railway Workers
Doctors	Snowplough Drivers
Farmers	Teachers
Fire Fighters	Telephone Operators
Food Store Cashiers	Television Announcers
Garbage Collectors	Veterinarians

Are any of these groups of workers forbidden to strike in your province? Who are they? Should any of the workers listed above be forbidden to strike? Why?

ROLE-PLAY

A Royal Commission was set up to investigate the Winnipeg General Strike. More than half the class should play the role of strikers. Others may play the role of owners and a few students take the role of judges. The role cards and questions for each group to work on are below:

STRIKERS

You are the workers and you have gone on strike to force the owners to meet your demands. The cost of living has gone up, food prices have risen, but your wages have remained the same. The bosses have refused to recognize your union. Your fellow-workers in other Canadian cities have gone on 'sympathy strikes' to support you. You are fighting for your right to organize a union which will help you get higher wages and better working conditions.

With these things in mind answer the following questions and try to develop the attitudes and opinions of the strikers:

1. As a worker, why do you think you went on strike?
2. Are your reasons justified? Why?
3. Who are your leaders?
4. Why does management oppose you?
5. Do you consider yourself a radical?
6. What are the demands of the workers?

OWNERS

You are the bosses, the management and the owners of the factories in Winnipeg. A bunch of workers have gone on strike in Winnipeg, shut down the city, and caused you to lose money and profits. The strike has spread to Hamilton, Vancouver, Toronto, and Regina.

With these things in mind answer the following questions and try to develop the opinions which you think bosses and owners would have:

1. As an owner, why do you think the workers went on strike?
2. Do you think that the workers were justified in doing this?
3. In your opinion, who are the leaders of the workers? What are your reasons for saying this?
4. Why do you oppose the strike?
5. Should men have the right to strike and join unions? Why or why not?
6. If these men give up the strike will you allow them back to work without punishing them?

JUDGES

You are the judges in this court case. You are trying to find out exactly what happened and to make a decision about who is right — the management or the strikers. You may decide that both groups are partly right or partly wrong. The decision is up to you.

In the strike there has been violence, death and property loss. Cities have shut down, factories have closed. Two groups in society with different attitudes and opinions are in conflict. Listen to both sides with their stories and then ask questions of both sides. You must keep order so that all sides of the controversy may be heard in court. Do not hesitate to tell people to let someone else speak, if necessary. If workers or bosses are merely sitting there, try to get their opinions. You may ask direct questions to individuals if you wish. You should make up some questions in advance that you wish to ask both sides.

36
Alternatives
to the Strike

The Winnipeg General Strike was a bitter experience for both workers and owners. However, both sides learned a lesson. From this time on, labourers and owners were more tolerant of each other. Each side now saw how disastrous a general strike could be. In the future both sides would be less likely to push the other to the point where a similar struggle might occur. An important result of the strike was that a general strike was seldom used again as a weapon in Canada.

The most important result of the strike was that labour leaders began to get involved in politics. They decided that the best way to solve unemployment and economic problems facing workers was to have a say in government. Many of the strike leaders went on to play an important role in government. The attention they had won during the strike, and their trials and imprisonment, turned them into martyrs or heroes in many people's minds. In the provincial election of 1920, strike leaders Ivens, Queen, Armstrong, and Dickson were elected to the Manitoba government while still in prison. In that election, the year after the strike, more labour representatives were sent into the provincial government than ever before. Other strike leaders came to prominence in city government as aldermen or school trustees. Queen was elected mayor of Winnipeg seven times.

In the federal election of 1921, J.S. Woodsworth became Member of Parliament for Winnipeg North Centre, a post he held until his death in 1941. Though Woodsworth had played only a minor part in the Winnipeg General Strike, his ability and his concern for people were now recognized. He went on to become the first leader of the Co-operative Commonwealth Federation (CCF) party which was a pro-worker political party in Canada.

A.A. Heaps, who had played a vital part in the Strike Committee, was elected to Parliament as a member for Winnipeg North in 1925. He held that seat until 1940. Both Woodsworth and Heaps rose to a place of national prominence as a result of the Winnipeg General Strike. In the years to come they were tireless champions of labour and social reform.

ABRAHAM ALBERT HEAPS (1889-1954)

Heaps was born in England, the eldest of seven children of Polish immigrants. Though he was a very bright schoolboy, his family was so poor that he could not take up a scholarship that he had won. Instead, he had to go out to work to help support his poverty-stricken family. He learned the trade of an upholsterer and became an expert workman. Years later, when he was a Member of Parliament, he re-upholstered the old office chair of Sir Wilfrid Laurier for Prime Minister Mackenzie King.

In 1911, Heaps emigrated to Winnipeg and within two years was elected to an office in the Trades and Labour Council. In 1917, he was elected to the Winnipeg City Council. Heaps was arrested during the Winnipeg General Strike but defended himself in a long and eloquent speech. At his trial he was found 'not guilty' by the jury on all counts. In 1925 he was elected as a Member of Parliament, and later joined the CCF party. He dedicated his whole life to improving conditions for the Canadian workingman.

THE GREAT DEPRESSION

In October 1929, a world-wide depression struck. It began with the stock market crash. The prices of stocks fell sharply, and people who owned large amounts of stock lost a great deal of money. The worst depression in our history began. Factories closed and hundreds of thousands of workers lost their jobs. Many families could not afford the things they needed in order to live. Conditions got worse instead of better. By 1932, 600 000 people were out of work. The hungry and the unemployed marched towards Ottawa in 1935 to protest conditions. This march was called the On-to-Ottawa Trek. People in the cities feared they would lose their homes, farmers were afraid they would lose their farms, and businesses could not stay open because most people had no money to buy their goods. Especially hard hit were the prairie provinces where long periods of drought made it impossible to raise crops.

Demonstration during the Winnipeg General Strike.

M.J. Coldwell, a former national leader of the CCF, described conditions:

There was bitterness everywhere. There were young men roaming all over Canada riding in railway boxcars looking for work. We lived in Regina and quite frequently young fellows would come to our door and ask for food.

I shall never forget either, going among some of the people and seeing the children. I remember addressing a meeting in a hall and seeing children in the late fall or early winter with no shoes or stockings but with their feet bound with strips of sacking.

You would find children going to school dressed in clothes made of flour bags. All across Saskatchewan there were farm children who were so poor that they had never seen an apple. If they were shown one, they would ask what it was and if it was good to eat.

I am quite sure that most of the young people today can't realize the conditions that then existed.

From *Years of Hard Labour* by Morden Lazarus.

In order to do something about these horrible conditions several politicians formed the Co-operative Commonwealth Federation in July 1933. The CCF was born in Saskatchewan, and was an association of farmers, labourers, and intellectuals. Its leader was J.S. Woodsworth who, since the days of the Winnipeg General Strike, had been a spokesman for the underprivileged in Canada. Woodsworth was a former clergyman. His Christian beliefs filled him with great compassion for poor and oppressed people everywhere. Tommy Douglas, one of the early leaders of the CCF, recalled an Ottawa winter day in the 1930s. The tiny figure of Woodsworth, wearing his father's old overcoat which had been cut down for him, made his way toward the Parliament Buildings. A pathetic crowd of unemployed men raised a cheer as he passed by. Douglas found Woodsworth in the entrance of the building with tears running down his cheeks. Such was the great feeling held by Woodsworth for the poor people of Canada.

The program of the CCF was adopted at the party's first National Convention in Regina in 1933. It was known as the Regina Manifesto. It suggested that the government should have control over most parts of the economy. The government should also own certain key industries, such as banks, telephone and hydro electric companies, and natural resources such as minerals and timber. In addition, the Regina Manifesto had some specific plans to bring about better living standards for all Canadians. These included unemployment insurance, old age pensions, hospital and medical services, family allowances, insurance against crop failure, and financial help for farmers so they could not lose their farms if they fell behind in paying their bills. All of these programs would be paid for by heavy taxes on wealthy individuals and businesses.

Although the CCF did not succeed in electing large numbers of candidates to the federal government, it did become a powerful force in many provincial legislatures. In 1944 the CCF became the government of Saskatchewan under T.C. (Tommy) Douglas. By the time of the 1945 federal election, the CCF was gaining in popularity with many Canadians. The Liberal government responded to the pressure and introduced the CCF idea of family allowances in 1944. Other CCF ideas, such as unemployment insurance, were promised as well. Almost every plan to improve living and working conditions put forward by the CCF has since been adopted in Canada. Frequently it was put into effect by the other political parties.

In 1961 the CCF and the Canadian Labour Congress (the CLC was the

Relief demonstrations, Vancouver, B.C., 1937.

chief labour body in Canada) organized the New Democratic Party (NDP). The purpose of the NDP is to represent the interests of workers in federal and provincial governments. Members of the party are dedicated to trying to influence the government to make laws favourable to the working people of Canada.

ACTIVITY

There were several other famous strikes in Canada: the Asbestos Workers' Strike of 1949, Quebec; the Quebec Teachers' Strike of 1966, Quebec; the Stratford Strike of 1933, Ontario; the Ford Windsor Strike of 1945, Ontario; and the National Railway Strike of 1966. As an individual, or in groups, investigate one or all of these strikes. Answer the following questions in your report:

    a)   What were the workers striking for?

    b)   What were the major events of the strike?

    c)   What position was held by the management or factory owners?

Strike at Windsor, Ontario, 1940.

d) What was the attitude of the press and the public towards the strike?

e) What was the outcome of the strike?

f) What advances were made by the strike?

LABOUR FINDS OTHER WAYS TO BRING ABOUT CHANGE

Is the strike the only way?

Up to this point you may think that labour unions do nothing but cause strikes and disruptions to society. Actually few people realize that more than 95% of contracts worked out between workers and managers are settled peacefully, without strikes. The average loss of working time caused by strikes from 1969 to 1974 was less than two-fifths of one percent. Much more time is lost through sickness, accidents, and unemployment than is lost through strikes.

A procedure known as collective bargaining has been developed.

Collective bargaining provides an orderly means by which workers may improve their conditions without going on strike. Strikes are supposed to become the very last resort in collective bargaining. The collective bargaining process usually follows these steps.

STEPS IN COLLECTIVE BARGAINING

STEP 1

a) Union officials bargain with the employer about such items as wages, vacations, hours of work, working conditions, and pension plans.

b) The union outlines the terms it would like to see in the collective bargaining agreement.

c) The employer outlines the terms he is willing to accept.

d) Together they work out an acceptable agreement.

e) The union officials may ask the union members (employees) to vote on the collective bargaining offer — if union members accept the offer from management, the contract is signed.

STEP 2

a) When employers and union officials cannot agree, they may ask the government to appoint a mediator or a conciliator.

b) A mediator is a private individual; a conciliator is a government official.

c) The mediator listens to both sides and makes recommendations on how to solve the dispute.

d) Sometimes he recommends a 'cooling-off' period so that both sides can think over the recommendations carefully before they take any further action.

STEP 3

a) When both sides reject the mediator's report, the parties can ask for an arbitrator to be appointed.

b) The arbitrator is appointed by the Labour Board to hear the dispute and settle it.

c) The arbitrator draws up an agreement between the two opposing offers which he thinks is fair and realistic.

d) Usually both sides have agreed in advance that they will accept whatever the arbitrator decides.

e) If both sides do not agree in advance to accept the arbitrator's decision as final, then strike and lockout may follow.

STEP 4

LOCKOUT!

a) The ultimate weapon for the employer is the lockout.

b) The employer refuses entrance and work to all or certain employees to force a labour settlement.

STRIKE!

a) The ultimate weapon available to the union is the strike.

b) This means stopping work until the employer meets the union's demands.

Binding Arbritation

STEP 5

    a) If the government decides the strike cannot be settled, it can bring in binding arbitration.

    b) The two sides are compelled by law to accept the arbitrator's decision.

Picket line protesting discrimination against women.

ACTIVITIES

Labour disputes can sometimes be compared with family problems. The six family solutions described below are similar to approaches used in solving labour-management conflicts: bargaining, a cooling-off period, mediation and conciliation, arbitration, compulsory arbitration, and contract agreement. Decide which of these six terms can be used to describe each of the family solutions below:

Conflict

Solution

1. Rob and his father are constantly arguing over the use of the family car. Neither can count on getting it when he wants it.

Father and son make an agreement: for every hour that Rob works around the house, he gets three hours' use of the car — providing he gives his father a day's notice.

2. Rob and his sister Helen fight over the use of the family camping equipment.

Mother announces that she will listen to both sides of the story after dinner.

3. Helen loses her temper when her mother sets a midnight curfew hour for Saturday dates.

Helen's mother sends her to her room for two hours to calm down before further discussion.

4. Rob wants to watch one T.V. program and John wants to watch another. The family has one T.V. set.

Father shuts off the set. He advises the boys to discuss the matter on their own until they reach an agreement.

5. After listening to Rob and John's argument about the use of the T.V. set, their parents cannot reach a decision.

Rob and John ask that their parents call in a neighbour for advice on a decision.

6. Rob thinks that 20 minutes of homework a night is enough. His father thinks that he should spend at least 60 minutes each evening on homework.

Rob and his father agree to ask the guidance counsellor for his advice, with the understanding that both must accept it.

How many of the methods used here were used in the strikes that you read about? Are there reasons why any of these methods were not used? Which method do you think was the most effective in the strikes that you read about?

1. Were the objectives of the Winnipeg Strike achieved? If so, when?
2. Why were so many labour candidates active in provincial and federal elections following the Winnipeg General Strike?
3. How effective were strikes in solving the problems of workers in 1919? How effective are strikes today? Suggest other ways in which workers can get what they want. What are the advantages of these other ways?
4. Why do workers wish to keep the right to strike?
5. Invite an official of the union in your community to come and speak to the class. Ask him to explain how the collective bargaining process works.
6. George Meany is one of the most powerful men in North America's labour movement. He once said that 'strikes no longer make any sense and we should eliminate them.' Do you agree or disagree with Mr. Meany's statement? Give reasons for your position.
7. Attack or defend the following statement, giving the reasons for your position: 'The workers of Canada would not have gained fair treatment from their employers without violence.'
8. What should be the federal government's role in helping to settle labour disputes? Should the minister of labour have an important influence upon negotiations? Why or why not?

Today unions are concerned with much more than money and benefits for their members. For example, they are involved in researching health hazards on the job, pollution, and the effects of increased leisure time on workers. Some labour groups have become involved in setting up co-operative housing, stores where workers can buy at low prices, and community health clinics. Others have shown special interest in the needs of the aged and senior citizens, and also developed programs to combat alcoholism and drug abuse among workers. Frequent presentations are made to governments on such concerns as rising unemployment and the increasing cost of living. In this way, labour's viewpoint on these issues is sure to be heard by the government.

SOCIAL REFORM IN THE FUTURE

The age in which you are living, and the future years ahead, will be filled with many changes. You have read about the pioneer reformers who worked for social change in women's rights and trade unionism. What social changes do you think will come about in your lifetime? New problems will require new and thoughtful solutions. Social reformers will find challenges in the future just as great as those of the past!

SPECIAL ACTIVITY ON SOCIAL REFORM

Choose a topic of social reform for further research. For example:

- human rights — how groups and individuals have won new rights and responsibilities;
- capital punishment — how changes have been brought about in the law regarding the death penalty for certain crimes;
- prison reform — how the treatment of criminals and the conditions of prisons have changed.

Be sure you ask these questions:

a) What were the conditions under which people had to live and work?

b) What did individuals or groups do to try and improve conditions and bring about change?

c) How did these reforms affect the reformers' lives and ours?

Bibliography

FOR FURTHER STUDENT READING

AUTHOR, TITLE, PUBLISHER	DESCRIPTION

TOPIC: THE REBELLION OF 1837

Reaney, James, *The Boy with an ℜ in His Hands,* Macmillan Company of Canada Ltd.	Set in York in 1826, the novel shows the conditions that led to the Rebellion. Young Alec Buchanan witnesses the smashing of MacKenzie's printing press and soon has a narrow escape.
Turner, D. H., *To Hang a Rebel,* Gage Publishing Limited.	Fifteen-year-old Doug Lachlan becomes a spy for William Lyon Mackenzie.

TOPIC: CONFEDERATION

Jefferys, C. W., *The Picture Gallery of Canadian History* McGraw-Hill Ryerson Ltd.	Volume 3 covers the years 1830-1900.
Waite, P. B., *John A. Macdonald* Fitzhenry and Whiteside Ltd.	This biography shows Macdonald's strengths and weaknesses.

TOPIC: CANADIAN WORKERS

Freeman, Bill, *The Last Voyage of the Scotian,* James Lorimer & Co.	This novel is an authentic picture of conditions on a 19th-century sailing ship. It shows the captain's life-and-death power over the crew, and the horrible conditions in which they worked.

Freeman, Bill, *Shantymen of Cache Lake,*
   James Lorimer & Co.

A young brother and sister work as cook's helpers in a lumber camp in eastern Ontario in 1873. They become involved in the formation of one of Canada's first unions.

TOPIC: OPENING THE WEST

Craig, John, *No Word for Goodbye,*
   Peter Martin Associates Limited.

This is a novel about prejudice against the Indians, and two boys who try to do something about it.

Charters, Dean, *Mountie: 1873-1973,*
   Collier-Macmillan Canada Ltd.

This book is a pictorial history of the first one hundred years of the Mounties.

Dewdney, Selwyn, *They Shared to Survive,*
   Macmillan Company of Canada Ltd.

This is a thorough account of the native peoples of Canada written for young readers. There are excellent drawings and maps.

Freeman, Madeline, *A Horse for Running Buffalo,*
   Scholastic Tab Publications Ltd.

This novel, about an Indian boy, is set in Blackfoot Territory. It describes the Indian culture and the problems created by the arrival of whitemen.

McNamee, James, *My Uncle Joe,*
   Viking Press, Inc.

A twelve-year-old boy and his wily Uncle Joe journey through western Canada a few months before the defeat of Riel at Batoche.

Pfeifer, Lillian, *The Wolfers,*
   Burns & MacEachern Ltd.

A group of wolfers (whiskey traders) who sell liquor to the Indians is tracked down by a young boy trying to avenge the death of his father.

TOPIC: SETTLING THE WEST

Bruce, Jean, *The Last Best West*, Fitzhenry and Whiteside Ltd.

This is a collection of photographs and quotations about the Canadian West from 1896 to 1914.

Burke, Marguerite, *The Ukrainian Canadians*, Van Nostrand Reinhold Ltd.

The lives of three generations of Ukrainian immigrants to Canada are traced. Attractive photographs and drawings are included.

Gregor, Alexander, *Vilhjalmur Stefansson and the Arctic*, The Book Society of Canada Ltd.

The author provides an exciting account of the explorations of Stefansson.

Hoffer, Clara, *Township Twenty-Five*, Saskatchewan Department of Youth and Culture.

This book describes the trials and challenges of pioneer days on the Prairies.

Marlyn, John, *Under the Ribs of Death*, McClelland and Stewart Ltd.

The problems of new immigrants to Canada around the year 1900 are told in this novel. Sandor, son of Hungarian parents, struggles to be accepted as 'Canadian' in Winnipeg.

TOPIC: AT THE TURN OF THE CENTURY

Berton, Pierre, *The Golden Trail*, Macmillan Company of Canada Ltd.

A lively account of the gold rush, told especially for young readers.

Eaton's 1901 Catalogue, Musson Book Company.

This is a reproduction of the spring, fall, and winter catalogues of 1901.

Stanton, James, *Ho for the Klondike*,
   Hancock House Publishers Ltd.

The gold rush days are remembered in pictures and stories.

Women's Costume in Ontario, 1867-1907
   Royal Ontario Museum Publication Services.

This book traces the changes in style in the dress of women after Confederation.

TOPIC: SOCIAL REFORM

Benham, Mary, *Nellie McClung*,
   Fitzhenry and Whiteside Ltd.

The author provides an account of the life of the well-known Canadian suffrage leader.

Davis, Bob, and Burron, Bruce, *Singin' About Us*,
   James Lorimer & Co.

This volume contains songs about Canada. Some are about work and the problems of work, women's liberation, unemployment, and the selling of Canadian resources.

Gray, Jack, *Striker Schneiderman*,
   University of Toronto Press.

This play is set in Winnipeg during the General Strike of 1919.

MacEwan, Grant, *And Mighty Women Too: Stories of Notable Western-Canadian Women*,
   Western Producer Prairie Books.

The lives of Cora Hind, Irene Parlby, Emily Carr, and others are sketched in this collection.

Nostbaaken, James, and Humphreys, Jack, *The Canadian Inventions Book*,
   Greey de Pencier.

Readers will be surprised to find out that Canadians invented frozen food, pablum, standard time, the telephone, the snowmobile, and hundreds of other well-known inventions.

Rasmussen, Linda, and Wheeler, Anne, *A Harvest Yet to Reap,* Canadian Women's Educational Press.

The courage, good humour, creativity, and determination of prairie women are described here. Many excellent photographs are included.

Acknowledgements

BARRY BROADFOOT. Extracts from Barry Broadfoot, *The Pioneer Years* (Toronto: Doubleday Canada). Copyright 1976 by Barry Broadfoot. Reprinted by permission of the publisher. KATE JOHNSON. Extract reprinted from 'Cameos of Pioneer Life in Western Canada' by permission of the Provincial Archives of Manitoba. VLADIMIR KAYE. Extract reprinted from *Early Ukrainian Settlements in Canada* (Toronto: The University of Toronto Press, 1964). EDRIC LLOYD. Extract reprinted by permission of the Glenbow Archives. D. B. SEALEY. Extract reprinted from *Cuthbert Grant and the Métis* (Agincourt: The Book Society of Canada Limited, 1976).

PHOTO CREDITS

Page 2, Public Archives of Canada (hereafter called PAC), C-4784; p.3 Metropolitan Toronto Central Library; p.5, Metropolitan Toronto Central Library; p.10, PAC, C-1590; p.14, PAC, C-4426; p.15, Metropolitan Toronto Central Library; p.18, Metropolitan Toronto Central Library; p.22, PAC, C-4785; p.28, PAC, C-396; p.29, PAC, C-3653; p.32, PAC, C-9725; p.38, PAC, C-16467; p.40, PAC; p.41, PAC; p.43, PAC, p.47, PAC, C-6998; p.49, PAC, C-6165; p.55, PAC, C-18737; p.57, PAC, C-28864; p.64, PAC, PA-54069; p.66, Pac, C-57; p.68, Notman Photographic Archives, McCord Museum, No. 48,435-I; p.70, PAC, C-8774; p.72, PAC, C-4746; p.74, Roger Boulton; p.78, PAC, C-733; p.82, PAC, C-78676; p.85, PAC, PA-103063; p.87, PAC, PA-103906; p.89, PAC, C-453; p.92, PAC, C-44982 and C-44994; p.97, Confederation Life Collection; p.98, Confederation Life Collection; p.101, PAC, C-2500; p.107, Queen's University Archives; p.108, PAC, PA-31177; p.110, PAC, C-20028; p.115, PAC, C-918; p.117, PAC, p.118, PAC, PA-13466; p.123, PAC, PA-16141; p.125, PAC, C-8199; p.131, PAC, C-30953; p.135, PAC, C-30945; p.139, PAC, C-31012; p.143, PAC, C-30952; p.147, PAC, C-38601; p.148, PAC, C-4228; p.151, PAC, C-81787; p.153, PAC, C-79643; p.154, PAC, C-1517; p.159, PAC, C-6692; p.162, Metropolitan Toronto Central Library; p.163, Provincial Archives of Manitoba; p.165, PAC, C-20658; p.169, Royal Canadian Mounted Police; p.170, PAC, C-1315, p.173, Royal Canadian Mounted Police, 797-2; p.174, Royal Canadian Mounted Police, 266; p.177, PAC, C-21815; p.179, Glenbow-Alberta Institute, NA-2310-1; p.181, Royal Canadian Mounted Police, 756 1; p.185, PAC, C-8214; p.186, Canadian Pacific, 6679; p.189, PAC, C-56472; p.193, Pac, C-33340; p.199, Imperial Oil Limited; p.203, Provincial Archives of Alberta, B-M 403; p.204, PAC, C-14128; p.207, Notman Photographic Archives, McCord Museum, No. 63,346-I; p.207, PAC, C-8549; p.208, PAC, PA-38495; p.211, Glenbow-Alberta Institute, NA-782-6; p.212, Provincial Archives of Alberta, B-2273; p.215, PAC, C-2601; p.218, Glenbow-Alberta Institute, NA-2419-1; p.221, PAC, C-2880; p.222, Canadian Pacific, 3997; p.227, PAC, C-1602; p.229, PAC, C-1602; p.229, PAC, C-14464; p.230, Canadian Pacific, 12968; p.233, PAC, A-206; p.237, Provincial Archives of Saskatchewan; A-2294; p.239, PAC, C-1876; p.240, PAC, C-2424; p.243, PAC, C-4522; p.247, PAC, C-2426; p.249, PAC, PA-28853; p.249, Glenbow-Alberta Institute. NA-1063-1; p.249, PAC, PA-12197; p.249, PAC, C-17430; p.253, Provincial Archives of Manitoba; p.255, PAC, C-1879; p.256, PAC, C-22249; p.262, PAC, C-30145; p.267, Glenbow-Alberta Institute, NA-474-4; p.269, Glenbow-Alberta Institute, NA-264-1; p.270, Provincial Archives of Saskatchewan, A-7348; p.274, PAC, C-9671; p.277, Glenbow-Alberta Institute, NA-984-2; p.281, PAC, C-52819; p.285, PAC, PA-38567; p.287, PAC, PA-11453; p.289, PAC, PA-30820; p.293, PAC, C-38706; p.297, PAC, C-15020; p.300, PAC, PA-88504; p.303, Provincial Archives of Alberta, B-2738; p.307, PAC, C-6536; p.308, PAC, C-7126; p.309, PAC, C-3862; p.313, PAC, PA-13133; p.315, PAC, C-28727; p.316, PAC, C-3775; p.321, Provincial Archives of New

Brunswick, L-588; p.321, PAC, PA-30803; p.322, Provincial Archives of New Brunswick, L-210 and L209; p.323, Glenbow-Alberta Institute, PA-372-3; p.323, PAC, PA-93113; p.323, PAC, C-8355; p.324, PAC, PA-15908; p.324, Notman Photographic Archives, McCord Museum, No. 111,371; p.325, PAC, PA-21743; p.325, Metropolitan Toronto Central Library; p.326, Vancouver Public Library; p.326, PAC, C-4677; p.328, PAC, C-4491; p.328, PAC, C-14258; p.329, PAC, C-14477; p.333, PAC, PA-30212, p.334, PAC, C-9652; p.334, Provincial Archives of Alberta, B-4737; p.335, Glenbow-Alberta Institute, NA-2083-6; p.335, Glenbow-Alberta Institute, NC-6-3269; p.336, PAC, C-18864; p.336, Provincial Archives of Alberta, B-3805; p.341, Provincial Archives of British Columbia, No. 39854; p.345, Provincial Archives of Manitoba; p.348, Glenbow-Alberta Institute, NC-6-3152; p.351, Glenbow-Alberta Institute, NA-772-8; p.353, The National Gallery of Canada, 5041; p.358, PAC, C-34020; p.361, Provincial Archives of Manitoba; p.369, PAC; p.371, PAC, C-79022; p.372, PAC, PA-93813; p.374, PAC, PA-93697.

Index

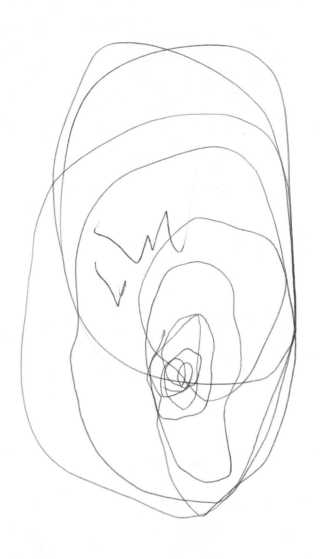